THE NAVAL SERVICE OF CANADA
1910–2010

THE CENTENNIAL STORY

The Canadian Navy gratefully acknowledges the support of the W. Garfield Weston Foundation and the Weston-Loblaw Group of Companies in making this book possible.

THE NAVAL SERVICE OF CANADA
1910–2010

THE CENTENNIAL STORY

Edited by

Richard H. Gimblett

DUNDURN PRESS

Toronto

Published by Dundurn Press Limited in co-operation with Department of National Defence and Government Services Canada.

Project Editor: Michael Carroll
Copy Editor: Nigel Heseltine
Design: Kim Monteforte, WeMakeBooks.ca
Printer: Friesens

Library and Archives Canada Cataloguing in Publication

The naval service of Canada, 1910–2010 : the centennial story / edited by Richard H. Gimblett.

Issued also in French under title: Le Service naval du Canada, 1910–2010.

Includes bibliographical references and index.

ISBN 978-1-55488-470-4

1. Canada—History, Naval. 2. Canada. Royal Canadian Navy—History. 3. Canada. Canadian Armed Forces. Maritime Command—History. I. Gimblett, Richard Howard, 1956–

VA400.N375 2009   359.00971   C2009-902462-4

1   2   3   4   5   13   12   11   10   09

Canada Council for the Arts   Conseil des Arts du Canada   Canada   ONTARIO ARTS COUNCIL   CONSEIL DES ARTS DE L'ONTARIO

We acknowledge the support of the **Canada Council for the Arts** and the **Ontario Arts Council** for our publishing program. We also acknowledge the financial support of the **Government of Canada** through the **Book Publishing Industry Development Program** and **The Association for the Export of Canadian Books**, and the **Government of Ontario** through the **Ontario Book Publishers Tax Credit program**, and the **Ontario Media Development Corporation**.

Printed and bound in Canada.
www.dundurn.com

Dundurn Press
3 Church Street, Suite 500
Toronto, Ontario, Canada
M5E 1M2

Gazelle Book Services Limited
White Cross Mills
High Town, Lancaster, England
LA1 4XS

Dundurn Press
2250 Military Road
Tonawanda, NY
U.S.A. 14150

Contents

Foreword

LA GOUVERNEURE GÉNÉRALE
THE GOVERNOR GENERAL

RIDEAU HALL
OTTAWA

It was Sir Wilfrid Laurier, in 1910, who said, "Mark my words, whoever may take over the reins of power will have to have a navy, as every nation with a seashore must have and has had in the past." Two world wars, numerous international and domestic crises and natural disasters later, subsequent governments have come to understand only too well his prediction.

Canada was still a relatively young country a century ago when it embarked upon the ambitious project of building a sea-going navy. History has recorded, time and again, that the navy has been Canada's 'first responder' to events at home and abroad; there is no reason to expect this will change in the future.

The aim of this centennial celebration, in part, is to build and strengthen in Canadians an appreciation for their navy and its contributions over the past 100 years. Events and activities being held across the country will honour the past, recognize and promote current achievements, and acknowledge the navy's commitment to the future of Canada, all beneath the banner of the centennial slogan: Commemorate, Celebrate, Commit.

This dedicatory volume is an impressive expression of that endeavour. The stirring words of its authors, accompanied by wonderful examples of marine art and photography, marvellously illustrate the important role the navy has played in the development and security of our nation. It records the immense contributions and sacrifices made in times of peace and war by the men and women who have served Canada, and captures the strength of the families who remained at home while their loved ones served at sea.

On this special occasion, it is my privilege, as Commander-in-Chief, to wish all serving and former sailors 'fair winds and following seas' into the future. Your dedication to your country will be remembered by generations of grateful Canadians.

Editor's Preface and Acknowledgements

M any volumes have been written on Canada's navy, and several more are bound to appear in the course of the Centennial of its founding. Two questions, as such, naturally arise concerning the publication of this one: First, what is its purpose? Second, why this title?

In answer to the first question, the institution that is the Canadian Navy wanted to celebrate its proud century of service to the nation by presenting a token of appreciation to the Canadian people who have supported it in their hearts and with their pocketbooks over the decades. Books are universally accessible and they convey the stuff of memory well. Having decided to produce a commemorative history, and recognizing it would be impracticable to give away a copy to each and every citizen, the director of the Canadian Naval Centennial (CNC) project, Navy Captain John Pickford, opted to publish a distinctive volume at a minimal purchase price. To this end, the Canadian Navy gratefully acknowledges the support of the W. Garfield Weston Foundation and the Weston-Loblaw Group of Companies in making this book possible.

Turning to the title, the somewhat old-fashioned phrase, "The Naval Service of Canada," admittedly is not stirring, but we thought clarity in the identifier should be the paramount consideration. A better choice would have been "Canada's Navy," but that title was already taken by a contributor to this volume, Marc Milner, whose original 1999 study is being updated for re-release this year. The alternate title, "The Canadian Navy," was discarded, as much because it could easily be confused with Milner's as for the fact that technically the phrase was not used for the three decades following unification in 1968, during which the Royal Canadian Navy was disbanded and the naval branch of the Canadian Forces was dubbed "Maritime Command." Only recently has "Canadian Navy" come back into general official usage

Department of National Defence

The Royal Canadian Navy (RCN) badge as approved by King George VI in 1944.

(without "Royal"). As will be explained below, this is not an "official" history, but as it is an institutionally sanctioned one, special care must be taken with terminology and the more generic descriptor "naval service" does not present the same difficulty. The astute reader, however, will note use of the simpler word "Navy" throughout the text itself.

Compiling a multi-author volume has many other challenges, but in this case they were greatly offset by the rewards reaped along the way. One of the first concerns was deciding who should do what. The assignment of different chapters to various individuals was made in close collaboration with my colleague Michael Whitby, the senior naval historian at the Department of National Defence's (DND's) Directorate of History and Heritage (DHH), our idea being to expose readers to the range of scholarship on the Canadian Navy. This assemblage includes many giants of the Canadian naval historical community, each with special knowledge of their allotted period. In the interest of space, I refer you to their respective biographies in the "Contributors" section at the back of the book, recognizing that these abbreviated citations cannot do justice to their records of accomplishment.

The Maritime Command (MARCOM) badge as approved by Queen Elizabeth II in 1968.

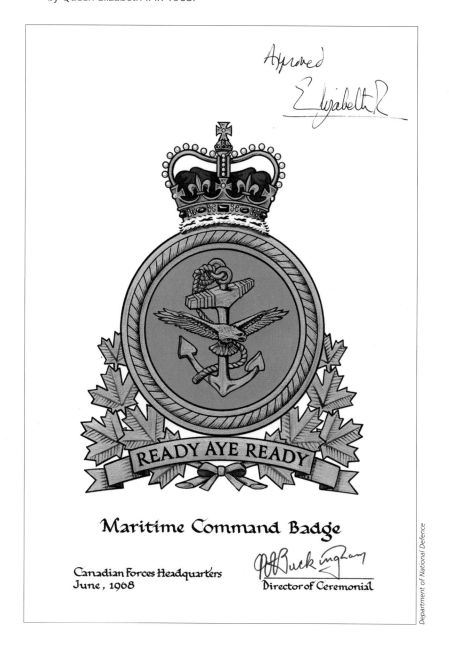

Maritime Command Badge

Canadian Forces Headquarters
June, 1968

Director of Ceremonial

Department of National Defence

Although many of the chapter authors have contributed in some fashion at some point in their careers toward the official history project, another concern was that this volume not be considered a substitute for the magisterial work being assembled by the present naval team at DHH. Each chapter here, at a mere 5,000–7,000 words, represents but a cursory survey of the period under consideration. By way of comparison, each period would rate several full chapters of 30,000 words in the official history, or in the case of the three chapters given here that cover the Second World War, two full volumes totalling some 1,300 tightly worded pages. Indeed, it was challenging to keep the authors "down" to distilling a lifetime of work to the imposed maximum limit. Instead of words, this book makes deliberate use of illustrations to introduce a more general readership to the richness of a century's activity of an important national institution, in the hope that they — you the reader — will be encouraged to delve deeper into the official histories.

Working with these preeminent scholars has been a rewarding professional experience. At the most basic level, as a reader, myself, of this survey history, I happily admit to learning something new from each of them. At the more prosaic level of editor, I hardly found it necessary to improve upon the efforts of such masters of their craft, and I decided early on

not to attempt to impose a common overall "voice" upon the volume, other than ensuring consistent use of stylistic and grammatical conventions. Each chapter will therefore be seen to have its own character and tone, reflecting the interests and personality of its author. This should not distract most readers, and those seeking a more rigorous approach again are invited to turn to the official histories.

One other editorial note arises in the related issue of attribution of reference material. Generally, notes are employed only to identify the sources of direct quotes. It should be understood that the various chapter authors have referred to a multitude of primary archival sources and secondary volumes by other authors in the course of their writing. But including even a cursory bibliography of writing on Canadian naval history would expand this volume by too many pages better devoted to illustrations. Those interested in further reading may wish to explore a website set up for the educational purpose: *www.navy.forces.gc.ca/ centennial/11/11-c_eng.asp*.

Most prominent among the illustrations reproduced here are the paintings commissioned for the Centennial to commemorate the six major conflicts in which the naval service of Canada has been engaged; each is the centrepiece of its pertinent chapter, where they are complemented by Karl Gagnon's exquisitely detailed profile drawings of major ship and aircraft classes. These are augmented by a selection of war art from the collections of the Canadian War museum (CWM), and of John Horton, president of the Canadian Society of Marine Artists (CSMA).

Defence Research Establishment Atlantic (DREA) badge.

Some attention was given to finding photographs that have been rarely seen, although certain iconic shots proved unavoidable simply because they so finely illustrate a point or they truly are unique because nothing else exists. Many were suggested by the authors, but the bulk were chosen with the assistance of the fine team of Dean Boettger, Kevin Sirko, Carl Gagnon, and Nathalie Ménard from the Canadian Naval Centennial project, who culled the tens of thousands of images residing in the collections of the Library and Archives Canada (LAC), the Canadian Forces Joint Imagery Centre (CFJIC), and the Canadian Forces Base Esquimalt Naval and Military Museum. Archivist Valerie Casbourn at the Directorate of History and Heritage helpfully retrieved items from the DHH collections. Some shots came from the collections of the Imperial War Museum (IWM), the United States Naval Institute (USNI), and the City of Vancouver, as well as from private collections that

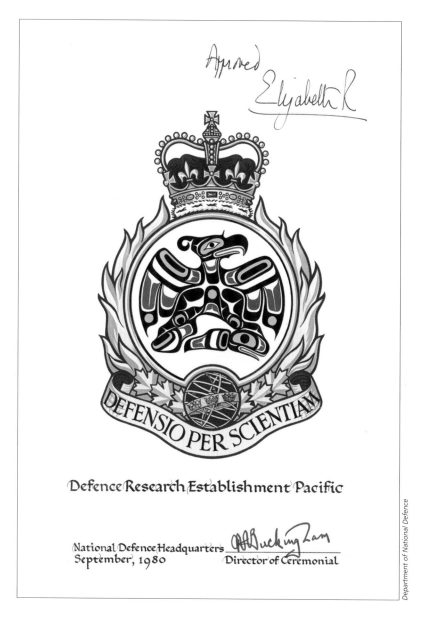

Department of National Defence

Defence Research Establishment
Pacific (DREP) badge.

are credited in the appropriate captions. To all these various people and institutions, I extend our deep appreciation.

At the beginning of this preface, I noted the critical role of Captain Pickford in providing support to the production of this volume. In addition to the members of his Canadian Naval Centennial team, I must express my gratitude also to the others who contributed in their various ways: Commodore René J. Marin, Commander Barry Houle, and Samaneh Bakhshi. Ross Graham, Bob Thwaites, and Mark Tunnicliffe facilitated the inclusion of the maritime research and development material that appears at the end of most chapters. Annie Williams produced the superb French translation of the manuscript, and Professor Serge Durflinger from l'Université d'Ottawa reviewed the text in both languages for consistency. Finally, it has been my absolute delight to be reunited in working with the fine team under Kirk Howard at Dundurn for the publication of the book — Michael Carroll, Beth Bruder, Margaret Bryant, Jennifer Scott, Nigel Heseltine, and Jennifer McKnight made it such an enjoyable affair that I am already longing for the next opportunity, knowing I will not have to await another century.

Richard H. Gimblett, CD, Ph.D.
Navy Command Historian
Ottawa, April 2009

Introduction

Alec Douglas

At the outset, Canada's peacetime navy should comprise two cruis-ers, probably two light fleet carriers, ten to twelve destroyers, and the necessary ancillary craft, all ... of the latest and most modern type, while in reserve and for training purposes, we will continue to hold a certain number of frigates.... A good workable little fleet.... It can easily be expanded if need be.
— MINISTER OF NATIONAL DEFENCE
DOUGLAS ABBOTT, HOUSE OF COMMONS
DEBATES, OCTOBER 1945

At the end of the Second World War, the principal task of Douglas Abbott — who had replaced Angus L. Macdonald as minister of national defence for naval serv-ices in April 1945, and then replaced General Andrew McNaughton as minister of national defence in August — was the demobilization of the largest army, navy and air force in Canada's history. He approached the task with the caution and perception for which he was famous. In proposing "a good, workable little fleet" he was reflecting the admittedly modest ambition the navy had been striving for since its inception, yet for various reasons had never been able to attain. Canadian naval planners in 1945 finally were able to argue convincingly for a navy that served national purposes, rather than — as circumstances had tended to dictate in pre-war days — simply being a fleet unit of the British Commonwealth. It was a natural outcome of the great national contribution to victory, and henceforth this is what would shape the form of the navy to this day.

A Canadian navy serving Canadian interests has in fact very deep roots. From the sev-enteenth to the nineteenth centuries, improvised local naval forces and privateers in North America made up for the inadequate protection of trade and territory provided by the impe-rial navies responsible for their protection, which were stretched too thin. They complemented those navies in operations against mutual foes, and sometimes, like state navies in the Amer-ican colonies during the war of the American revolution, they challenged imperial navies. In the process, they gave an outlet to seafarers wedded to local as much as, or more than, imperial interests. It was such activities in the years leading up to the First World War that led to a permanent Canadian naval service.

After the Treaty of Washington of 1871 Canada formed fisheries protection forces, when the Royal Navy declined to do so, to ensure United States adherence to the treaty. In 1903 the Royal Navy, under the command of Admiral "Jacky" Fisher, made it policy to withdraw British naval forces from distant stations in order to centralize and increase naval strength close to home. This was of course the most cost-effective answer to the threat posed by German naval expansion. But for Canadians, with their growing sense of national self-sufficiency, it created a dilemma: Should they contribute to assured British naval supremacy by direct assistance to Britain, or look to their own naval defence? Britain turned over the naval dockyards at Halifax, Nova Scotia, and Esquimalt (in Victoria, British Columbia) to Canada in 1907. Prime Minister Sir Wilfrid Laurier (who predicted in 1904 that the twentieth century would belong to Canada), and his minister of marine and fisheries, Louis-Philippe Brodeur, with their acute sense of national pride, decided to fill the vacuum with Canadian government ships. When the Prince of Wales visited Quebec in 1908 for the tercentenary celebrations there was a fleet review with ships of the Royal Navy (RN) and United States Navies, and along with them the Canadian Government Ship *Canada*, carrying a number of young men under training who would form the nucleus of the future Royal Canadian Navy (RCN).

This did not sit well with many of Laurier's political opponents, but in 1909 there was sufficient agreement in Conservative as well as Liberal ranks for a member of the Conservative opposition to table the resolution for a naval service bill. His language — repeated in the motion that came before the House on 29 March 1909 — reflected the times. Canada's "great and varied resources, … her geographical position and national environment, and … that spirit of self-help and self-respect which alone befits a strong and growing people" struck the right note for Parliament, after much subsequent discussion, to pass the Naval Service Act on 4 May 1910. To be sure, as will be seen, the very Canadian attributes described by George Foster in 1909 expressed themselves in passionate political debate, and by 19 August 1911, when the Naval Service of Canada was permitted to designate itself the "Royal Canadian Navy," Robert Borden's Conservatives had defeated the Laurier government, in part over the matter of naval policy.

Borden had promised to repeal the Naval Service Act, but after talking to the new first lord of the admiralty, Winston Churchill, he decided also to put through a Naval Aid Bill

The Canadian Government Ship *Canada* (foreground), with the Prince of Wales (future King George V) and Governor General Lord Grey embarked, receives a salute from the British, French, and American fleets anchored in the St. Lawrence River for the Quebec Tercentenary review in July 1908.

for direct assistance to the Royal Navy. When this was defeated in the Senate in 1913 he adopted a classic Canadian compromise: do nothing. By the outbreak of war in 1914 the RCN consisted principally of small ships capable of coastal defence and the protection of trade. This was more or less in line with the initial recommendations made in 1909 by the future director of the naval service (the Canadian-born Rear-Admiral, later Admiral, Sir Charles Edmund Kingsmill, RN), based particularly on his experience commanding ships on the Australian station.

It was not the fleet unit that enthusiasts had envisioned, but in four years of war it would demonstrate that Canada needed a navy capable of complementing the navies of its more powerful allies. More important, as would be the case with the short-lived Royal Canadian Naval Air Service in 1918, it had to ensure that Canada would never depend completely on its allies for its own defence. Thanks largely to the few seasoned British sailors who were available in Canada, and who understood the needs of the RCN, the infant navy not only survived the severe test of war but was effective in preventing serious shipping losses in the face of the German submarine threat off the East Coast. It must be said, however, that in comparison with the Canadian Corps, and with Canadian airmen on the Western Front, the RCN gained no great fighting reputation from its First World War record.

None of Canada's armed forces fared well between the two world wars. The navy nearly disappeared. In 1919 the naval minister, C. C. Ballantyne, told Admiral of the Fleet Lord Jellicoe (who agreed) that unless a serious start was made in establishing the peacetime navy he intended "to wipe out completely the present Canadian naval service as being a pure waste of money." In 1922 Ottawa closed the Royal Naval College of Canada, formed in 1910, which had provided an excellent grounding for the young men who would devote their lives to naval service, but whose hopes were disappointed by the dismal prospects they could now expect. In the face of post-war recession the government rejected most of the recommendations made in 1919 by Lord Jellicoe, and paid off (decommissioned) all but two destroyers. In 1932, Chief of the General Staff, Lieutenant-General Andrew McNaughton, who was pushing for expanded air defence in Canada, told Sir Maurice Hankey (Clerk of the Privy Council in London) that "The Canadian navy as presently constituted is not an answer to any problem of Canadian defence." The next year, when the depression forced severe cuts in defence expenditure, he recommended sacrificing the navy as the least necessary of the three services, leaving coastal defence to the army and air force.

In such adversity, without the kind of fighting reputation built up by the army and by Canadian airmen during the First World War, extraordinary measures were necessary to safeguard the Canadian Navy. Kingsmill's replacement, Walter Hose, refused to accept subordination to the generals, won recognition in 1928 as the chief of the naval staff rather than simply the director of the naval service, and established volunteer reserve divisions across the country. At the same time, largely because policy-makers threw the navy back on its own resources, the RCN became in some respects more British than Canadian, a close-knit family dependent on the Royal Navy for guidance and support, relying on Britain for training, and on Admiralty regulations for its governance. And that compounded the problem. Brooke Claxton, when he was minister of national defence a generation later, said of senior RCN

NAVAL ASSEMBLY
ATLANTIC
HALIFAX – NOVA SCOTIA
21-26 JUNE 1967

The naval assembly in Halifax for Canada's Centennial in 1967.

officers: "They had all joined about the year 1914, had been trained largely with the RN, and served together through every rank and course, had English accents and fixed ideas."[1]

There was some truth in this slander, but it was a superficial judgement. The British writer James Morris observed in 1973 that, "… in the era of British climax, whose last years the middle-aged can remember," the Royal Navy was " … the supreme symbol of patriotism. The Royal Navy was 'British and Best.' The Royal Navy always travelled first class.… The service itself assumed an anthropomorphic character — hard drinking but always alert, eccentric but superbly professional, breezy, naughty, posh, kindly, Nelsonically ready to disobey an order in a good cause, or blow any number of undeserving foreigners out of the water.…"[2] Those who had joined between the wars usually had this vision of a navy, and some may have hoped to use the RCN as a jumping off point to the RN. Or as Commander L.B. Jenson said, when asked in 1938 by Lieutenant-Commander E. Rollo Mainguy why he wanted to join, "My uncle is a captain in the Royal Navy and has had a very interesting life. I do not want to stay in Calgary and see the grain elevators every day. I love the water and want to see the world."[3]

"Sailors are sailors the world over," an eloquent Gunnery Instructor by the name of Chief Petty Officer Harry Catley, once observed.[4] Canadian sailors certainly would not have denied possessing the virtues listed by James Morris, virtues that cried out for emulation. Men who kept the Canadian Navy going between the wars were very much in that tradition, but no less Canadian for it. The story is told of a young officer returning to a Canadian ship after two years with the Royal Navy, hearing his captain respond to what a defaulter had to say for himself with the simple comment "bullshit," and realizing with pleasure that he was back in the RCN. It was these few sailors, all of them — officers and men of the lower deck — professional to the core, very close to their British counterparts, and still conscious of their Canadian identity, around which the wartime navy was built.

In the Second World War the Canadian Navy grew from six destroyers, three minesweepers, and less than 3,000 men to a peak in June 1944 of over 90,000 men and women, and 385 fighting ships. In six years, serving in every theatre and in virtually every type of naval operation, the RCN made itself particularly indispensable to allied victory by its greatest strategic achievement — the safe escort of tens of thousands of merchant vessels carrying vital supplies across the Atlantic to northwest Europe, through the Mediterranean to North Africa, and by way of the Arctic seas to northern Russia. As a result, from a small, tight-knit force that was so evidently an offshoot of the RN, the RCN would become a major national institution.

It was a painful transition. Post-war retrenchment and difficulties in adjusting to the changed circumstances of a peacetime navy hurt morale. Shrinkage from a force of nearly 100,000 to a mere 7,500, and the desire by a number of old school sailors to return to pre-war customs, promised prospects little better than the Navy had offered between the wars. Certain "incidents" in RCN ships led to a famous inquiry chaired by Rear-Admiral Rollo Mainguy (now vice-chief of naval staff), producing a report that emphasized the "Canadianization" of the RCN. It was in many respects the Canadian Navy's Magna Carta, but a good many of the measures recommended did not take immediate effect, whether because of foot dragging by the naval establishment, or the slow workings of the bureaucracy under considerable budget limitation. And it was not until recent decades that there was sufficient encouragement for francophones to join the navy. Those who took part in an international exercise in the Mediterranean in 1958 will recall the embarrassment of the Canadian debriefing team when — none of them being sufficiently fluent in French to understand the proceedings — a captain in the Royal Navy had to act as translator.

Nevertheless, the navy has been a useful instrument of both diplomatic and military policy, serving Canadian interests, since the Second World War. The Korean War and the Cold War again forced Canada to increase the size and capability of the RCN. A fleet review in 1960, the fiftieth anniversary of the RCN, revealed the largest peacetime naval force in its history. In the Cuban Missile Crisis of 1962 the Canadian Navy earned praise for its ability to respond rapidly and effectively to an international crisis. It was a Canadian naval icebreaker, Her Majesty's Canadian Ship (HMCS) *Labrador*, that achieved the first deep draft ship transit of the Northwest Passage (an achievement that was somewhat dampened by the subsequent transfer of *Labrador* to the Canadian Coast Guard). Since then it has had to weather more cutbacks, overcome the traumatic effects of unification of the armed forces, and suffer a severe gap between its capability and the commitments it is expected to meet, but it has demonstrated Canadian

Canadian War Museum 3309-2011-0593-035

Poster for the Canadian Navy's 75th anniversary, 1985.

scientific and engineering skill in technical developments. During the Second World War Halifax scientists invented the Canadian Anti-acoustic Torpedo (CAAT) gear. In post-war years, the RCN's championing of the first successful helicopter haul-down systems for naval ships, laying the foundation for inter-ship computer-to-computer "datalinks," and advances in active and passive sonar technology deserve special mention. Indeed, Canadian naval success in developing the ship as an integrated system was achieved in ways that the navies of Britain and United States were unable to do because of the sheer size of their design teams.

Since the end of the Cold War, following what historian Marc Milner has called a "renaissance" of a significant buildup of modern and well-equipped ships, our naval forces have distinguished themselves in their response to various international crises, particularly the so-called war on terror, as will be seen in this book. Canadians have often been slow to acknowledge how well their navy has served them — possibly because so many live so far from the sea — but that navy in all its ups and downs, in its ability to survive its first century in spite of so many obstacles to survival, has shown itself to be a remarkable expression of the Canadian spirit.

Notes

1. Brook Claxton Papers, cited by James Eayrs, *In Defence of Canada: Peacemaking and Deterrence* (Toronto: University of Toronto Press, 1972), 59.
2. James Morris, *Encounter* (1973).
3. L.B. Jenson, *Tin Hats, Oilskins and Seaboots: A Naval Journey, 1938–1945* (Toronto: Robin Brass Studio, 2000), 25.
4. Chief Petty Officer Harry Catley, Gunner's Mate, *Gate and Gaiters. A Book of Naval Humour and Anecdotes. Including a glossary of naval language for the uninformed* (Toronto: Thorn Press, 1949), 28.

CHAPTER 1

Toward a Canadian Naval Service, 1867–1914

Roger Sarty

*It has been in contemplation to organize gradually a naval force,
and we believe the time has come now ... [W]e should be prepared,
we should be anxious to relieve the mother country from the
responsibility of defending our coasts and our harbours.... [W]e
should take up seriously the question of local defence of the sea ...
we should follow it on the lines of local autonomy ...*
— SIR FREDERICK BORDEN, MINISTER OF
MILITIA AND DEFENCE, HOUSE OF COMMONS
DEBATES, 10 FEBRUARY 1910

The establishment of the Canadian Navy is remarkable, both for the lateness of that event and the meagre results. Canada, whose motto translates as "from sea unto sea," has the longest coastline of any country. Even so, the navy was not founded until 4 May 1910, nearly 43 years after the creation of the modern Canadian state on 1 July 1867. Despite growing tensions in international relations, the new service was so politically controversial that it was nearly stillborn, and Canada remained desperately unprepared when Europe descended into war in the summer of 1914.

The paradox arose from Canada's development as a part of the British Empire. The empire owed its creation and expansion to Britain's Royal Navy, the world's most powerful

The RCN's first recruiting poster.

from the late seventeenth century until the beginning of the 1940s. Britain was able to seize France's colonies in North America during the Seven Years' War because the Royal Navy's predominance in the Atlantic allowed the British to mass their forces for the assaults on the main French strongholds of Louisbourg in 1758 and Quebec in 1759, while cutting off New France from reinforcements. Britain's own American colonies were able to secure their independence in 1783 because a European alliance led by France temporarily achieved the advantage over the Royal Navy. Yet, the Royal Navy turned back an American invasion of Canada in 1775–76, and again prevented the conquest of the remaining British North American colonies when the United States repeatedly invaded in 1812–14. It was the menace the Royal Navy posed to the U.S. seaboard from bases at Halifax, Bermuda, and Jamaica that ultimately secured Canada from American Manifest Destiny during crises in the 1830s, 1840s, 1850s, and 1860s.

Military dependency upon Britain and cheap defence were foundation stones of Canada. The primary cause of the revolt of the American colonies in 1775 had been British efforts to tax the colonists to pay the enormous costs of the British forces that had conquered Canada in 1754–63 to secure the American territories against French incursions.

Thereafter, Britain did not generally attempt to recoup the costs of its forces on colonial service, particularly in the case of Canada whose French-speaking inhabitants viewed the British military as occupiers, not protectors.

At issue were land, not naval, forces. Since the American invasion of 1775, the southern border of the northern colonies had to be protected by fortifications, garrisoned by troops from Britain's small, expensive professional army, to prevent the territories being overrun while the Royal Navy conducted offensive operations against American trade and coastal cities. In the 1840s and 1850s, the British government responded to political unrest in the northern colonies by granting self-government in internal matters, but also began to cut back the garrisons sharply, linking self-government to greater responsibility for self-defence — and incidentally, relief to the British treasury. When the American Civil War of 1861–65 threatened to engulf the colonies, the British Army massively reinforced the garrisons, but the steep cost of this effort was an important reason why the British government supported confederation of the colonies to create the Dominion of Canada in 1867. Britain withdrew all of its troops from the interior of the new country in 1871, and defence of the border became the responsibility of the Canadian militia, a force of some 40,000 part-time volunteers administered and instructed by a "permanent force" of full-time professionals that numbered no more than 1,000 until the early 1900s.

The ultimate guarantee of Canadian security was still the Royal Navy. Even the most cost-conscious British politicians admitted that protection to Canada was the incidental product of Britain's need to control the North Atlantic, the heart of the seaborne trade that

was Britain's lifeblood. Britain retained its strongly fortified dockyards at Halifax and Bermuda, together with the permanent naval squadrons that operated in the western Atlantic and the eastern Pacific, including the new British dockyard at Esquimalt, British Columbia. British Army garrisons of about 2,000 troops remained at Halifax and Bermuda, and British troops later developed defences at Esquimalt. Canadian leaders of the late nineteenth century, believing that the British naval presence persuaded the United States not to attempt domination of Canada, avoided naval defence undertakings for fear these would encourage British cutbacks.

The possibility of a distinctly Canadian path to naval development emerged in the late 1880s when an Atlantic fisheries dispute with the United States brought the government to organize a fisheries protection service of six to eight small armed vessels to arrest American fishing craft that illegally entered Canadian territorial waters — waters within three nautical miles (approximately six kilometres) of shore. The vessels and their crews formed part of the Canadian Department of Marine and Fisheries, whose principal responsibilities included lighthouses and other aids to navigation and the regulation of civilian shipping. Ex–Royal Navy officers who the Canadian government hired to run the service and British officials in Canada saw the possibilities for developing the fisheries protection service into a naval force. The Admiralty was not interested. Rapid progress in technology saw the development by the late 1880s of large, fast, long-ranged steel-built warships, renewing confidence that the Royal Navy's main fleets, centrally controlled from London in their global deployments, could, just as in the days of sail, intercept any but the smallest enemy forces. In 1887 the Australian colonies and New Zealand began to make annual payments to the Admiralty to subsidize the assignment of additional Royal Navy cruisers to their waters.

By the late 1890s the idea that the empire should become a more tightly organized military alliance to meet sharply increasing competition among the great powers won widespread support in Britain and all the self-governing colonies. When in 1899 Britain went to war with the Boer republics in South Africa, the Liberal government of Wilfrid Laurier, Canada's first French-Canadian prime minister, was caught between demands for participation from English Canadians and strong resistance from French Canadians. Laurier's compromise, to send contingents comprised solely of young men and women who volunteered to serve, by no means healed the rift in opinion. The brilliant Liberal member of parliament (MP) and journalist Henri Bourassa broke with the prime minister to campaign against military cooperation with Britain; he especially warned against naval initiatives because of the Admiralty's doctrine of centralized control of the empire's naval defences. Even Bourassa admitted, however, that there was a need for fisheries protection.

Laurier tried to square the political circle by casting military reforms as national defence measures that enhanced Canadian status, but also strengthened the empire by relieving Britain's over-stretched armed forces of commitments in North America. He was prepared to undertake naval development of the fisheries protection service, and in 1903–04 the government procured the CGS *Canada*, a 910-tonne steamer built to naval specifications. Further naval initiatives, however, were put on hold in December 1904, when Britain, as part of its efforts to concentrate its armed forces closer to home to meet growing dangers in Europe, closed the dockyards at Halifax and Esquimalt, and announced that the Royal

Flying Squadron. Esquimault. 1870

The Royal Navy's Pacific Flying Squadron anchored in Esquimalt Harbour, 1870, including (bottom left) then-HMS *Charybdis*.

Navy squadrons that had operated on the Atlantic and Pacific coasts of North America would be withdrawn. The defences at Halifax and Esquimalt would still be needed to provide secure operating bases for the British fleet, so Laurier seized the opportunity for a nationalist initiative warmly endorsed by both French and English Canadians, by offering to take full responsibility for the permanent garrisons and fortifications at both Halifax and Esquimalt. This gesture, which the British gratefully accepted, entailed tripling the size of the 1,000-man permanent land force, and was the main reason why the land militia's annual budget doubled to some $6 million a year.

Laurier still maintained that the fisheries protection service was the "nucleus" of a navy, but any grander schemes were effectively scuttled. Further development came as the result of scandal. Early in 1908 a royal commission reported that the Department of Marine and Fisheries was hopelessly inefficient. Laurier and the minister, Louis-Philippe Brodeur, a lawyer whose early career in Quebec nationalist politics gave him credibility in that province, cleaned house immediately. Georges Desbarats, an engineer in the department with a reputation as a talented administrator, became deputy minister. Laurier had already met, and been impressed by, Charles E. Kingsmill, a Canadian who had entered the Royal Navy in 1869 at the age of 14 and risen to the rank of captain. Kingsmill accepted the invitation to take charge of the government's marine services. Promoted rear-admiral on his retirement from the Royal Navy, his professional credentials were on an entirely different plane than those of his predecessors, who typically had left the British service as very junior lieutenants.

The Conservatives, led by Robert Borden since 1900, were no more anxious than the Liberals to confront the contentious naval issue. They contented themselves with periodically tweaking the government to get on with naval development of the fisheries protection service. In January 1909 Sir George Foster, one of Borden's senior colleagues and a former minister of marine and fisheries in the Macdonald era, placed on the order paper for the new session of Parliament a resolution that "Canada should no longer delay in assuming her proper share of the responsibility and financial burden incident to the suitable protection of her exposed coast line and great seaports." The resolution had been inspired by an Australian initiative to end the annual subsidies to the Royal Navy, and instead revive their own naval organization. The Admiralty, holding firm on the need for British control of seagoing warships, allowed that any colonial service could acquire the improved coastal torpedo craft, including destroyers and submarines, that had been developed since the late 1880s. The torpedo craft would make local ports more secure to support strategic deployments of the British fleet.

Before the Foster resolution came up for debate, the politics of the naval issue were transformed by developments overseas. On 16 March, Reginald McKenna, First Lord of the Admiralty in Britain's Liberal government, requested additional funds for battleship construction, citing evidence of acceleration in Germany's building program. In 1905–06 the Royal Navy had stolen a march on competitors by building the revolutionary His Majesty's Ship (HMS) *Dreadnought*, the first large (16,270-tonne) modern battleship to carry a uniform battery of 10 of the heaviest guns — 12-inch — in place of the mix of a few heavy and

The future CGS *Canada* fitting out in the Vickers yard at Barrow-in-Furness, 1904, lying outboard of HMS *Dominion*, also still under construction and whose first captain in 1906 would be Captain C.E. Kingsmill, Royal Navy (RN).

Directorate of History and Heritage 0-233

other lighter guns in existing 9,100-tonne designs. Now, intelligence suggested, Germany might be able to match Britain in numbers of its own "dreadnoughts" as early as 1912.

The news that Britain's maritime supremacy was so seriously challenged by a single power exploded like a "bomb shell," in the words of one contemporary Canadian commentator. New Zealand quickly offered to make a special, one time payment to the British government sufficient to build one or, if necessary, two dreadnoughts. There were widespread demands among English Canadians in both the Liberal and Conservative parties that Canada do the same, creating a nearly identical problem for Laurier and Borden, both of whose French Canadian supporters had grave doubts about any form of naval initiative. In the face of these common problems the parties worked out a compromise in a single day of debate of Foster's resolution, on 29 March 1909. In a new resolution supported by both parties, Laurier promised the "speedy" organization of a coastal defence force in consultation with the Admiralty on the model of the Australian scheme (that, of course, he had always insisted was built on the example of Canadian local defence by forces under Canadian control). Laurier's draft ruled out any cash contributions to the British government, but at Borden's insistence the final version rejected only regular contributions and thus did not specifically rule out a future one-time "emergency" payment.

A few weeks later, in fulfilment of the joint resolution's commitment to cooperation with British authorities, Laurier announced in Parliament in April that Brodeur and the militia minister, Sir Frederick Borden (the Conservative leader's cousin) would soon visit the Admiralty to consult on Canadian naval development. Admiral Kingsmill prepared a discussion paper proposing the initial acquisition of three small (3,100-tonne) cruisers, two large ocean-going destroyers, and six small destroyers or large torpedo boats.

The British government, surprised at the interest and commitment to action in the dominions, moved quickly to take advantage by calling a special imperial defence conference, which met in London in August. It now dawned on the Admiralty that encouragement of the dominions' desire for their own armed forces was the only hope for a substantial, long-term commitment that would ease pressure on British defence spending. There was particular scope for action by the dominions on the Pacific, which had been denuded of battleships in the concentration of the British fleet in European waters since 1904. So instead of organizing only the supporting elements of a naval organization, as in the Australian and Canadian coastal defence schemes, the Admiralty presented a new scheme for full-blown imperial cooperation: the dominions should each raise an ocean going "fleet unit" consisting of a single dreadnought battlecruiser (a vessel with less heavy armour plating than a dreadnought battleship, but faster still, and with a similar all big-gun armament), and three large Bristol class cruisers of 4,370 tonnes, together with six destroyers and three submarines. New Zealand's cash contribution would be used for a third dreadnought battlecruiser that would be stationed in the Far East. The Canadian fleet unit would be stationed on the Pacific coast, ready in an emergency to combine with the Australian and New Zealand ships.

Laurier was appalled at the idea because of the potential opposition in Quebec to "imperial" schemes. Brodeur and Sir Frederick Borden made it clear that any action would have to be based on the Canadian parliamentary resolution. Beyond Quebec, Canadian

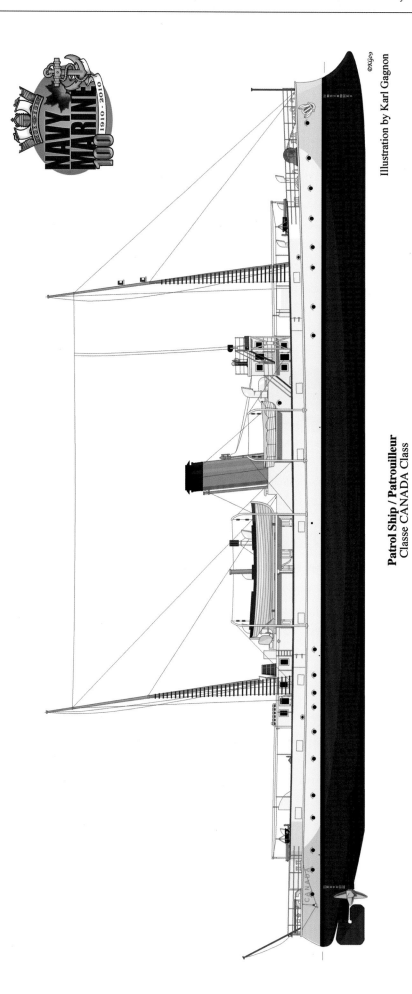

Illustration by Karl Gagnon

Patrol Ship / Patrouilleur
Classe CANADA Class

0 m   5 m   10 m

C.G.S. CANADA
1904

Launched in 1904. Built by Vickers-Armstrong, Barrow.

Dimensions: 62.8 m x 7.6 m x 3.9 m
Displacement: 557 tons   Speed: 22 knots   Crew: 60
Armament: 4 x I - 3-pound guns.

N.G.C. CANADA
1904

Lancé en 1904. Construit par Vickers-Armstrong, Barrow.

Dimensions: 62,8 m x 7,6 m x 3,9 m
Déplacement: 557 tonnes   Vitesse: 22 noeuds   Equipage: 60
Armement: 4 x I - canons de 3 livres.

political realities were that the main centres of population (and voters) were in the eastern part of the country, so any scheme would have to give as much weight to the Atlantic as the Pacific coast, not least because the largest seafaring population and pool of potential recruits was on the Atlantic. The dreadnought battlecruiser was also unacceptable, Borden explained, because "it must be remembered that Canada was only beginning to establish a navy, and that it was desirable to proceed gradually, by gaining experience with vessels of a smaller type in the first instance."[1]

Brodeur asked the Admiralty to put forward two schemes, one that would cost £400,000 (approximately $2 million) and the other £600,000 (approximately $3 million). The significant figure was £600,000, which showed Laurier's commitment to political consensus. Robert Borden had indicated that a suitable Canadian naval effort should involve the commitment of funds at about half of the level of spending on the land militia, then approximately $6 millions a year. The request for the smaller, £400,000, scheme signalled Canada's determination not to be nudged toward the full-fleet unit.

To its credit, the Admiralty provided reasonable responses for the two schemes. The larger one, for an annual expenditure of about £600,000, reached quick mutual agreement. It included six ocean-going destroyers, a flotilla leader (a small cruiser that could act as the command ship for the destroyer force) and four improved Bristol-class cruisers; the whole destroyer force and two Bristols would be stationed on the Atlantic coast and two Bristols on the Pacific. The Admiralty also deferred to the strong Canadian desire that the warships should be built in Canada. Both the Liberals and Conservatives had prominently cited this benefit to industry in the debate on 29 March 1909. The estimated time required to build the destroyers and cruisers in Canada was six years, and the Admiralty agreed to assist the Canadians in building toward this force by supporting the scheme that Kingsmill had drafted in April. Kingsmill, who accompanied Brodeur and Borden, initially asked for two Apollo-class cruisers of 3,100 tonnes and two destroyers: one cruiser for the Pacific coast, and the rest to receive the larger number of recruits anticipated on the Atlantic coast. In November 1909 the Canadian government bought one Apollo, HMS *Rainbow*, for the West Coast. The Admiralty offered a second Apollo, but no destroyers were available, so Kingsmill arranged for the purchase, in January 1910, of a much larger Diadem-class cruiser, HMS *Niobe*, to accommodate East Coast trainees. *Niobe* displaced 10,000 tonnes and had a complement of 705 personnel, as compared to 273 for the smaller Apollos. *Niobe* was also a more modern ship, having been completed in 1899; *Rainbow* had been completed in 1893. The funds for *Niobe*, £215,000, were found by dropping the flotilla leader from the list of modern ships to be acquired.

On 12 January 1910, Laurier introduced the Naval Service Bill in the House of Commons. It was ultimately carried by the Liberal majority, and received royal assent on 4 May 1910, thereby creating the new Naval Service of Canada, and the Department of the Naval Service to administer it. True to its distinctly Canadian roots, the new organization grew out of the Department of Marine and Fisheries. There was no separate minister, Brodeur continuing to head Marine and Fisheries while also taking responsibility for the new department. Canadian politicians had long responded to criticisms of inaction in naval defence by noting that Marine and Fisheries had carried out important functions that in

Britain were a naval responsibility. Following passage of the Naval Service Act these "naval" components of Marine and Fisheries — the Fisheries Protection Service, the Hydrographic Survey, Tidal and Current Survey, and the Wireless Radiotelegraph organization of coastal radio stations for ship to shore communications — were transferred to the new department. Desbarats transferred as deputy minister, and Admiral Kingsmill became "director of the naval service," the department's professional head. National control was enshrined by the provision that the Canadian Naval Service, or any part of it, could be transferred for service with the Royal Navy under British command only by the explicit action of the Canadian government, which in turn had immediately to seek the approval of Parliament.

What is striking about Laurier's naval policy is the extent to which it focused on building a political consensus, how closely he constructed that policy on the same nationalist principles as his most dramatic militia reforms, and how quickly and confidently he acted, a direct result of the political success of his militia reforms.

The crew of CGS *Canada* performing naval militia drills on their winter 1905 cruise to Bermuda.

Library and Archives Canada PA-123952

The Admiralty, in consultation with Kingsmill, arranged to loan Canada some 50 officers and over 500 enlisted personnel for secondments of two to five years to operate the cruisers and instruct Canadian recruits. The symbolic inauguration of the Canadian Navy came on 21 October 1910 when *Niobe* arrived at Halifax and was escorted up the harbour by CGS *Canada*, the fisheries protection vessel that the Laurier government had touted as the "nucleus" of the Canadian Navy. *Rainbow*, after a passage of some 15,000 nautical miles (28,000 kilometres) and nearly 12 weeks from England around South America by way of the Straits of Magellan, arrived at Esquimalt on 7 November 1910.

The first members of the Canadian Navy to join the new ships were six officer cadets from CGS *Canada* who transferred to *Niobe* the day after it reached Halifax. Two of the cadets had started training in *Canada* in 1908, and the other four in 1909, as part of the efforts begun with the arrival of Admiral Kingsmill to improve the Fisheries Protection Service. The two cadets from the original 1908 entry included Percy W. Nelles, the son of an officer in the Royal Canadian Dragoons, the cavalry regiment of Canada's small regular army. Percy, according to a newspaper interview much later in his career, had been raised at Brantford, Ontario, and been fascinated by the shipping on the Grand River. When, as he turned 16, his father asked him what career he would like to prepare for, Percy surprised him by saying he would like to join the navy. Nelles would become chief of naval staff in 1933, and in that position lead the service through its enormous expansion during the Second World War.

Among the 1909 group of entries was Brodeur's own son, Victor Gabriel. As the latter recounted, he was at home in bed recovering from appendicitis early in October 1909, when his father:

> *came into my room ... and he said: "Victor, how would you like to join the*
> *Navy?" Well, previously I had been around the Gulf of St. Lawrence several times*
> *in ships and I was very fond of the sea. I just jumped at the suggestion because I*
> *had to go back to [Mont-St-Louis] college and give a lecture, and there is one thing*
> *that I hated and that was to lecture or make a speech. So he said, "alright ... next*
> *month I'll take you out and we'll take you down to Halifax." And that was that.[2]*

Victor Gabriel Brodeur, who reached the rank of rear-admiral during the Second World War, during which time he commanded the Canadian Navy on the West Coast and also served for several years as Canada's naval representative in Washington, was known to at least some in the Canadian service as "the gift."

This promising start did not last long. What Louis-Philippe Brodeur clearly understood was that the essential element in creating a truly Canadian navy was not ships or dockyards, or guns or state-of-the-art radio equipment, but Canada's own naval professionals. Despite offers from the Admiralty to admit Canadian officer cadets to the Royal Navy's colleges, the Naval Service Act included provision for Canada's own naval college, which had a precedent in the land forces' Royal Military College of Canada in Kingston, established in 1876. The Royal Naval College of Canada opened its doors in the former naval hospital in the Halifax dockyard, with a staff of officers and instructors on loan from the Admiralty,

A November 1909 Toronto *Globe* political cartoon shows Prime Minister Wilfrid Laurier at the helm of the future navy, navigating the conflicting nationalist and imperialist sentiments generated by the issue.

in January 1911 on the entry of the first class of 21 cadets. To man the two cruisers, a national campaign began with posters and notices in newspapers in February 1911. Postmasters were empowered to enter recruits, and local doctors undertook the required medical examinations.

Brodeur's intention for *Niobe* to make an extended training cruise to the West Indies in the early months of 1911 was stymied when British legal authorities maintained that the dominions did not have legal powers beyond the three-mile limit of territorial waters. Brodeur complained furiously to a sympathetic Governor General Lord Grey, but to no avail:

> *I do not see why they would not trust Canada…. Do they fear some illegal acts … ? We have for years and years a Fisheries Protection Service which has come constantly into contact with foreign vessels … but we never did anything which brought the Imperial Authorities into serious difficulties.[3]*

Negotiations at an imperial conference held in May-June 1911 resulted in a workable compromise. The British government designated adjacent ocean areas of the northwestern Atlantic and eastern Pacific, including the waters off the seaboards of the United States, as "Canadian" naval stations, where Canadian warships could operate without consulting the Admiralty. Laurier and Brodeur were delighted, for the British had in effect endorsed their argument that the new Canadian Navy was primarily a regional force for the protection of waters adjacent to Canada. In August 1911, the Naval Service of Canada also acquired a new name, when word arrived from London that the king had approved the government's application to use the term "Royal Canadian Navy." He also sanctioned the style already adopted by the dominion for its new cruisers, "His Majesty's Canadian Ships."

Niobe, as it turned out, did not go anywhere else. On the night of 31 July 1911, while returning from a port visit to Yarmouth, Nova Scotia, it ran onto the rocks off Cape Sable. Had it not been for the coolness of the Royal Navy crew and the young Canadian recruits on board, it might well have been lost. It was later towed free and into Halifax, but repairs

Library and Archives Canada C-002082

Prime Minister Robert Borden leaving the Admiralty with First Lord Winston Churchill, July 1912.

were not completed until December 1912. By that time the new navy was as badly stranded as the cruiser had been off Cape Sable.

Laurier's naval policy, much as he had tailored it to win political consensus, proved to be a political disaster. The difficulties had started in the fall of 1909, in response to the Laurier government's position at the London conference. Leading English Canadian Conservatives were appalled that Laurier had refused to procure a dreadnought battle-cruiser, the type that the Admiralty said was most urgently needed. At the same time, F.D. Monk, the leading French Canadian Conservative, denounced the results of the conference for exactly opposite reasons. He charged Laurier with "Imperial drunkenness" for having been goaded by the Admiralty into a naval scheme that was more ambitious than the coastal defence and improved fisheries protection force envisaged in the parliamentary resolution.

From the beginning of the debate on the naval service in the House of Commons in 1910, Conservative leader Robert Borden endeavoured to unite his divided party by going on the attack. Borden now called for an immediate emergency contribution of cash to the Admiralty. At the same time, in a gesture that strongly appealed to both the pro-empire and French-Canadian wings of the party, he flatly rejected Laurier's Naval Service Act. He particularly denounced the nationalist provision in the legislation that Canadian warships would be transferred to British control only with the explicit agreement of the Canadian government, and he drew a humiliating picture of British ships coming under enemy fire as Canadian warships stood helpless to intervene, awaiting orders from Ottawa. The bill, he concluded, was nothing less than a declaration of Canada's separation from the empire.

The danger that the political controversy posed to the government became clear on 3 November 1910. A by-election in Drummond-Arthabaska, the former riding of Laurier himself and a long-time Liberal stronghold, was lost to a little known nationalist candidate who presented himself as an opponent of Laurier's "imperial" naval policy. Laurier's grip on Quebec had been shaken. In the following months the government virtually ceased action for naval development, and did not place contracts for the construction of modern warships even though the complex process of tendering was completed. The Canadian Navy had in fact been overtaken by other events. Laurier's government had succeeded in negotiating a "reciprocity" free trade agreement with the United States, and the prime minister called an election on the issue for 21 September 1911. Robert Borden's Conservatives won that election by playing on fears of American economic dominance.

When the new Parliament met in March 1912, Robert Borden had reassessed the European situation and decided there was in fact no pressing need for the emergency contribution. He would, however, get rid of the hated Laurier legislation, and immediately cut the naval estimates from $3 million to $1.6 million. This was intended, as Desbarats noted in his diary, to keep the existing organization going on a "mark time" basis until the government could cooperate much more closely with the Admiralty than Laurier had done in framing a new Canadian naval organization.

On the very day Borden promised caution and due process in Ottawa, however, the First Lord of the Admiralty, now Winston Churchill, rose in the British House to reveal

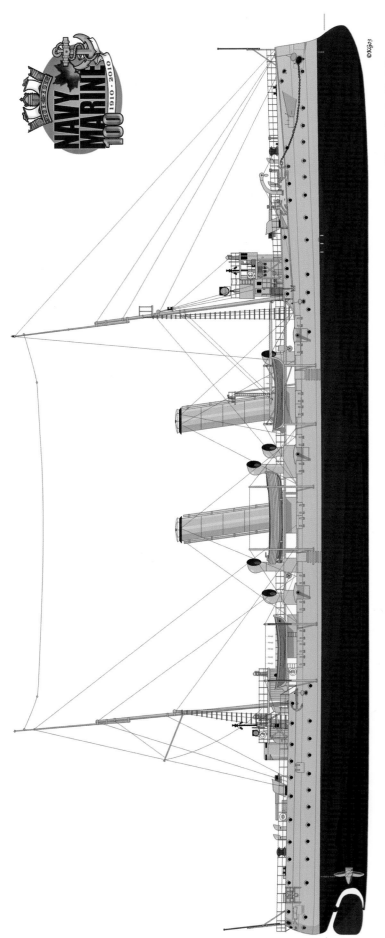

Illustration by Karl Gagnon

Cruiser / Croiseur
Classe APOLLO Class

0 m   5 m   10 m

N.C.S.M. RAINBOW (I)
1910
(ex H.M.S. RAINBOW)
Lancé le 25 mars 1891. Construit par Palmers, Hebburn-on-Tyne.

04 août 1910 - 01 juin 1920

Dimensions: 95,9 m x 13,2 m x 5 m   Équipage: 273
Déplacement: 3 600 tonnes   Vitesse: 18 noeuds
Armement: 2 x I - 152 mm; 6 x I - 102 mm; 8 x I - 6 livres; 2 x II - TLT de 356 mm.

H.M.C.S. RAINBOW (I)
1910
(ex H.M.S. RAINBOW)
Launched 25 March 1891. Built by Palmers, Hebburn-on-Tyne.

04 August 1910 - 01 June 1920

Dimensions: 95.9 m x 13.2 m x 5 m   Crew: 273
Displacement: 3,600 tons   Speed: 18 knots
Armament: 2 x I - 152-mm; 6 x I - 102-mm; 8 x I - 6 pound; 2 x II - 356 mm TT.

another, more ominous, expansion of the German dreadnought program. Britain had to make extraordinary efforts to maintain its margin against Germany. When Borden went to London in July 1912 to consult with Churchill on a "permanent policy," Churchill asked the Canadian leader to make good on his earlier commitments to an emergency contribution. Borden agreed to provide $35 million to Britain, enough to build three of the latest "super dreadnoughts," and in December 1912 introduced the Naval Aid Bill. The Liberals resisted furiously, and the government introduced closure for the first time in Canadian history to shut down debate. The Conservative majority in the Commons carried the bill on 15 May 1913. The Liberals, however, still had a majority in the unelected Senate, where two weeks later they defeated the bill.

Leading members of both parties had already been trying to achieve a compromise, and would continue to do so into the early months of 1914. Among the English Canadian politicians there was strong agreement that Canada must develop its own navy, and the deals discussed included such measures as the expenditure of part of the Naval Aid funds on expansion of the Canadian service, and the assignment of Canadian personnel to crew the dreadnoughts purchased for Britain with a view to Canada ultimately taking over the big ships. All of these proposals foundered on the Naval Service Act, on which neither party leader believed he could give way: Laurier had staked his party's unity on that act, and Borden had staked his party's unity on his promise to revoke it. This intransigence was not mere political posturing, but grew from fundamentally different visions of Canada and its future. Laurier most valued the country's autonomy and freedom of action: to him, Canada might or might not participate in Britain's wars depending upon circumstances. Borden by contrast looked to Canada assuming a more prominent role within the empire: in exchange for the automatic availability of Canadian naval forces to the Admiralty and such assistance as the emergency cash contribution, the British government must allow regular and continuous participation by a high-level Canadian representative in the decision-making bodies of the British government. Canada, in other words, although bound to participate in British wars, would have a key say in the policy that led to the British decision for war.

The fiasco of the Naval Aid Bill left the Canadian Navy in a state of limbo. The new government authorized no special efforts to obtain recruits, did not pursue the many deserters, and did not replace any of the borrowed Royal Navy personnel who departed on the completion of their two-year engagements. The strength of the RCN shrank from a peak of over 700 personnel (the borrowed British personnel and Canadian recruits) in the spring of 1911 to 330 by the spring of 1914. The first class of cadets at the college completed their course in December 1912, and did credit to the new service by all passing examinations set by the Admiralty, and achieving an average "higher than usual." For lack of crew the Canadian cruisers could no longer sail to provide the sea training intended to follow the initial college program, so the Royal Navy stepped into the breach and accepted the cadets in the cruiser HMS *Berwick*. Already the cadets who entered in 1908 and 1909 and joined *Niobe* on its arrival had gone to England for further professional experience in HMS *Dreadnought*, the namesake of the new class of battleship. Even so the numbers of young men applying to the college fell, and there were only four students in the class that started in 1914.

Why maintain the two cruisers at all? The government asked that question of Kingsmill in October 1912. Even if the government decided not to acquire modern warships, he responded, there would still be a need for trained personnel, at the least to carry out basic coastal defence measures, such as the operation of coastal communications facilities, the establishment of "examination" services (small vessels that stopped merchant ships arriving at defended ports such as Halifax to ensure they were not disguised enemy vessels), and to operate armed civilian vessels for such functions as minesweeping and coastal patrols. The cruisers, even if permanently alongside, were good training facilities in peacetime, and, if properly maintained, in war could go to sea to help protect shipping leaving and arriving in Canadian waters.

In fact, one of the main activities of the Canadian Navy in 1912–14 was assisting preparations for coastal defence. The ships and crews of the fisheries protection service, the chain of coastal wireless stations, and resources of other departments, such as customs agents, were vital for these efforts. Starting in 1912, CGS *Canada* and other fisheries protection vessels began to carry out minesweeping and examination service exercises at Halifax, in conjunction with militia mobilization exercises at the forts, duties these same vessels and militia garrisons would begin to carry out in earnest starting in August 1914.

Commander Walter Hose, captain of *Rainbow*, was one of a group of seconded British-born RN officers who, despite the poor prospects of the Canadian service, chose to transfer to the RCN and played a crucial role in its survival. He later recalled this period in the Canadian Navy's history as its "heartbreaking starvation time":

> *In the spring of 1912 the Director of Naval Service visited Esquimalt.... The old man seemed very depressed and was much afraid that the new Government would carry out the pre-election statement by Mr. Borden that he would repeal the Naval Service Act.*
>
> *... I told him I thought, from all I had read, that it would be difficult to get popular support for a navy across this continental country, and I suggested taking a leaf out of the militia hand-book and creating a citizen navy — a naval volunteer reserve with units across the country. The reply I got from him was "My dear Hose, you don't understand — it can't be done."*[4]

Hose nevertheless gave every encouragement to a group of young men who wanted to establish a naval volunteer unit in Victoria. In a well-orchestrated lobbying effort, the unit won support from Sir Richard McBride, the Conservative premier of British Columbia, and groups of supporters for a volunteer force in other cities, including, notably, Vancouver where another unit was forming, and Toronto. The lobbying convinced Borden, who ignored protests from his French-Canadian members, and avoided the political pitfall of implementing Laurier's legislation by establishing the Royal Naval Canadian Volunteer Reserves (RNCVR) by a separate order-in-council in May 1914, even though its terms, for three years' service, were identical to provisions for a "Naval Volunteer Force" in the Naval Service Act.

The volunteers saw active service almost the moment they received recognition. Early in 1914 the Borden government agreed that Canada should take its turn in enforcing a ban

Vancouver City Archives LGN 1031.1, W.J. Moore, photographer

HMCS *Rainbow* watches over the SS *Komagata Maru* in Vancouver, July 1914.

on sealing in the Bering Sea that resulted from an agreement between Britain and the United States in which Canada had a strong interest. *Rainbow* was the only suitable Canadian or British ship available on the Pacific coast, and to augment the cruiser's depleted crew, a detachment of Royal Navy sailors came from England, another from *Niobe*, and another from the volunteers in Victoria and Vancouver. *Rainbow* never reached the Bering Sea. On 20 July Hose received instructions from Ottawa to sail to Vancouver, where the Japanese steamer *Komagata Maru* had been immobilized for over two months. Aboard were 400 Indian Sikh passengers, who, as British subjects, demanded entry into Canada as immigrants, and refused to accept their ineligibility under Canadian regulations. Police who had attempted to board the vessel had recently been driven back by a hail of coal used by the passengers as projectiles. With the appearance of the cruiser, however, the Indians agreed to depart; the vessel sailed from Vancouver on 23 July, with *Rainbow* escorting it out of Canadian waters.

The cruiser returned to Esquimalt to complete preparations for the sealing patrol, but less than a week later, on 29 July 1914, Britain dispatched a "precautionary" telegram warning of apprehended war with Germany and the Austro-Hungarian empire. The frantic preparations that followed in response to reports, mostly false, that fast German cruisers were making for Canadian waters on both coasts had elements of a contemporary music-hall slapstick comedy. There was also courage and the potential for tragedy when, on 2 August, *Rainbow* rushed south in response to a request from the Admiralty to protect the small British sloop HMS *Shearwater*, then on passage north from Mexican waters where a German cruiser was known to be operating. *Rainbow* would have had no chance against the faster, better-armed German warship.

The larger point is that the Canadian Navy was able quickly to undertake basic measures for security of the coasts, particularly at Halifax and Esquimalt, thus providing the defended bases required for the British and other allied warships that soon arrived to protect shipping off shore. *Rainbow* on the West Coast and, after only a few weeks of recruiting, *Niobe* on the East Coast were able to take their place in these vital trade defence efforts. These were remarkable achievements for a new service that had effectively been abandoned by the government within a few months of its establishment.

Notes

1. LAC, MG 26, G, Laurier Papers, Vol. 773, Notes of the Proceedings of Conference at the Admiralty on Monday, 9 August 1909, between representatives of the Admiralty and of the Dominion of Canada.
2. DHH, BIOG file, Rear-Admiral V-G Brodeur interview transcript.
3. LAC, MG 27, II, C4, Brodeur Papers, Brodeur to Lord Grey, 16 March 1911.
4. DHH, BIOG file, Rear-Admiral Walter Hose, "The Early Years of the Royal Canadian Navy," 19 February 1960.

Maritime Research and Development to the End of the First World War

Harold Merklinger

Before the First World War there were relatively few organizations in Canada conducting scientific research or development. For that reason, the many significant early Canadian contributions to marine and naval science were made in either commercial or other national employ. These included Simon Newcomb (1835–1909), born in Canada but who died as a rear-admiral of the U.S. Navy. Perhaps the best known American scientist of his day, he simplified the nautical almanac astronomical tables that were essential to marine navigation calculations until the dawn of the computer age.

Better known to Canadians was Alexander Graham Bell (1847–1922), who among other things formed the Aerial Experiment Association in Baddeck, Nova Scotia, with Frederick W. "Casey" Baldwin and J.A.D. McCurdy. Their efforts with fluid dynamics resulted not only in the first heavier than air flight in the British Empire (on 23 February 1909), but also in the development of marine hydrofoil craft, which they proposed (unsuccessfully) for use as submarine-chasers during the war.

Another early aeronautical worker was Wallace R. Turnbull (1870–1954) of Rothesay, New Brunswick, who in 1902 built Canada's first wind tunnel; his later (1927) invention of the controllable-pitch propeller was adopted for use in ships as well as aircraft. Reginald Fessenden (1866–1932) of East Bolton, Quebec, did early work on voice modulation of single-frequency radio waves that permitted multiple simultaneous communication channels, representing radio as we know it today, and on Christmas Eve 1906 he gave the first public radio broadcast. In 1914 he demonstrated the first practical use of what would become known as "active sonar." Intending to find icebergs, he mainly detected the ocean bottom. The invention found immediate application as a fathometer. His wartime developments included an acoustic system to locate artillery fire, and further work on sonar for British submarines.

With the passage of the Naval Service Act in 1910, the Canadian Navy assumed responsibility for hydrographic work. Acquisition of the CGS *Acadia* in 1913 made surveys in ice-infested waters possible and it was immediately deployed to the Hudson Strait. The RCN also co-sponsored the expedition of Vilhjalmur Stefansson to the western arctic in 1913 in the CGS *Karluk*. Over a period of five years he would complete the map of Canada's Far North. In 1915 the department undertook the first major oceanographic survey of the East Coast, under the direction of Dr. Johan Hjort and the officer commanding *Acadia*, Captain F. Anderson. The resulting naval service report characterizing the East Coast water structure became the benchmark study of Canadian marine biology and oceanography.

Still, there remained no organized structure in Canada for bringing scientific and technical information into the defence plan. During the war, the British government recommended that scientific research committees be established in Canada to monitor and focus technical resources on industrial and defence issues. Eventually, in 1916 the Canadian government established a body later known as the National Research Council (NRC). While the NRC would not begin actual research until 1925, its establishment was critical

Bell's "hydrodome" HD-4 at speed on Bras d'Or Lake, Cape Breton.

for providing the nation with the science, engineering and industrial implementation capacity that would be sorely needed in the future.

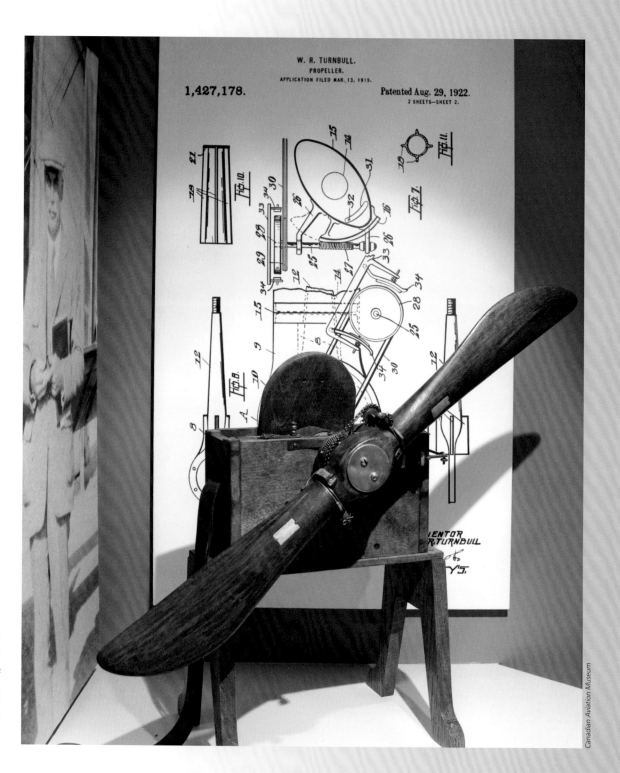

The variable-pitch propeller was among the inventions of Wallace R. Turnbull that had naval applications.

Canadian Aviation Museum

CHAPTER 2

The Royal Canadian Navy and the First World War

William Johnston

> *Regarding co-operation [of] Canada [in] naval defence during the war, Admiralty inform me [they] don't think anything effectual can now be done as [war]ships take too long to build and advise Canadian assistance be concentrated on Army.*
> — SIR GEORGE PERLEY, ACTING HIGH COMMISSIONER TO GREAT BRITAIN, TO PRIME MINISTER SIR ROBERT BORDEN, 10 OCTOBER 1914, *DOCUMENTS ON CANADIAN EXTERNAL RELATIONS, 1909–1918*

By the time the Canadian high commissioner communicated the British government's view that the Royal Canadian Navy was irrelevant to the empire's war effort, the First World War was already two months old. As disappointing as London's response may have been to the officers at Naval Service Headquarters (NSHQ) in Ottawa, it reflected the pre-war naval policy — or lack of naval policy — of the Borden administration. Perley's telegram was also a strong indication that many of the basic decisions about Canada's naval defence during the war would be made by the Admiralty and not by Ottawa. Although London's naval advice during the war was often inconsistent and its promises of assistance would usually prove empty, the Borden government was never willing to go against it or adopt

Department of National Defence SU2007-0281-05-A

Peter Rindlisbacher, *HMCS Niobe at Daybreak*, depicting the ship proceeding out to sea.

a course of action put forward by its own, more informed naval professionals at NSHQ. In keeping with British wishes, Canada recruited and maintained a four-division corps of the Canadian Expeditionary Force (CEF) on the battlefields of France and Belgium — one that would gain a well-deserved reputation as one of the shock formations of the British Empire — but the Borden government was never willing to provide Canada's navy with resources adequate to meet its wartime responsibilities. As a result, the remnants of Laurier's fledgling naval service would have to safeguard Canada's maritime interests with a rather motley collection of seconded civilian vessels, war-built trawlers, and drifters and, at war's end, with a handful of American-manned motorboats and seaplanes on loan from south of the border.

In anticipation of the British declaration of war on 4 August 1914, the RCN's largest warship, the cruiser *Niobe*, was in dockyard hands at Halifax being fitted for duty (it would not emerge from drydock to begin its power trials until early September), while the navy's other warship, *Rainbow*, based in the Pacific at Esquimalt, had already proceeded to sea. Under the terms of the Naval Service Act, both cruisers, despite their obsolescence, were placed at the disposal of the British Admiralty "for general service in the Royal Navy" once war was declared. The navy's remaining duties were largely supervisory ones at the nation's various ports, since the civilian crews of government vessels carried out most of the actual work. At Halifax, for instance, the navy's wartime responsibilities consisted variously of: blocking the eastern passage into the harbour past MacNab Island; placing net defences, making minesweeping arrangements, and buoying the war channel; establishing an examination service; assuming control of the wireless station at Camperdown, and transporting censorship staff and militia detachments to other coastal wireless stations; and controlling traffic in the harbour. On 12 August, the captain-in-charge of the port informed the director of the naval service, Rear-Admiral Charles E. Kingsmill, that "everything has been completed in revised defence scheme except buoying the channel for war," while the progress in preparing *Niobe* for sea was reported as "satisfactory."[1]

With the RCN's largest warship alongside at Halifax, the first operational cruise of the war was made on the West Coast. *Rainbow's* commanding officer, Commander Walter Hose, had been ordered on 1 August to prepare his cruiser for active service, because Admiral Maximilian von Spee's China Squadron, which included the heavy cruisers *Scharnhorst* and *Gneisenau*, had departed the Far East for the eastern Pacific. Indeed, on 2 August, the Admiralty reported that the German cruiser *Leipzig* had left the Mexican port of Mazatlan on the morning of 30 July, and *Rainbow* was instructed to proceed south at once to guard the trade routes north of the equator. Despite concerns about the obsolete gunpowder shells *Rainbow* carried for its two six-inch guns and the large number of Royal Naval Canadian Volunteer Reservists in its scratch crew, Hose shaped course south on 5 August after receiving further instructions from Ottawa to protect the British sloops *Algerine* and *Shearwater* as they made their way north from San Diego, California.

The Canadian cruiser arrived at San Francisco on the morning of 7 August intending to coal at the port. American officials strictly enforced U.S. President Woodrow Wilson's neutrality proclamation, however, and *Rainbow* was only allowed to embark some 50 tonnes. With his ship's radius of action curtailed, Hose decided to patrol off San Francisco:

> It appeared to me that it was my duty, being apparently so close to the enemy, to try and get in touch with him at once, consequently I got under way at midnight and proceeded in misty weather to a point on the three mile limit fifteen miles to the southward of San Francisco, from there I steamed slowly to the southward all that forenoon, the weather being foggy and clear alternately.[2]

Rainbow continued to patrol off the California port without sighting the enemy until the morning of 10 August when fuel concerns forced Hose to return to Esquimalt. The timing proved fortunate as *Leipzig* — whose 10 higher velocity 4.1-inch guns easily outranged *Rainbow's* obsolete six-inch armament — appeared off San Francisco on 11 August and remained in northern California waters until sailing south on 18 August. It was the closest the Canadian cruiser would come to intercepting its German adversary.

In the meantime, fears of the havoc enemy raiders might have on the relatively undefended West Coast had prompted the provincial government of British Columbia to purchase two submarines clandestinely from a Seattle, Washington shipyard. Commissioned as *CC1* and *CC2*, the two boats were manned at Esquimalt by Canadian reservists together with a handful of experienced professionals. By the time the RCN submarines were operational, however, the German threat to the West Coast had largely passed. Concentrating his two

HMCS *Rainbow* returns to Esquimalt with the captured German schooner, *Leonor*, May 1916.

heavy and three light cruisers off western South America by mid-October, von Spee easily defeated the first British naval force sent to engage him, Rear-Admiral Sir Christopher Craddock's squadron of two older armoured cruisers, a light cruiser, and an armed merchant cruiser. The Battle of Coronel, fought off the coast of Chile on the evening of 1 November 1914, ended with the sinking of both British armoured cruisers, but was most notable from a Canadian perspective because four RCN midshipmen, all recently assigned to Craddock's flagship and killed along with the rest of the RN crew, were the first RCN casualties of the war. The victorious German squadron was subsequently intercepted and sunk by a powerful British force, which included the battlecruisers *Invincible* and *Inflexible*, off the Falkland Islands on 8 December. Following the British victory in the South Atlantic, the only real concern on the West Coast lay in the potential danger posed by German merchantmen in neutral ports should they be fitted out as armed commerce raiders. In that case, however, although it was over 20 years old, *Rainbow* was still faster than all but a few commercial vessels and adequately armed to subdue them.

The potential threat of German merchantmen lying in America's eastern ports was the RCN's chief concern on the Atlantic coast. As mentioned, *Niobe* was already being fitted for sea when war was declared on 4 August. The obsolescent cruiser was scheduled to join the RN squadron on the North America and West Indies (NA and WI) Station to keep watch over the western North Atlantic shipping lanes, particularly their main focal point off New York, against a number of German ocean liners that had been fitted out as auxiliary cruisers. After emerging from drydock, *Niobe* was ready for a full power trial on 1 September, and it remained only to crew it. The decision to pay off *Algerine* and *Shearwater* at Esquimalt freed their crews for service with the Canadian cruiser, including Captain Robert Corbett, the commanding officer of *Algerine*, who now assumed the same position in *Niobe*. Altogether some 16 RN officers and 194 ratings joined the cruiser's crew. These were supplemented by 28 RCN and RNCVR officers, and 360 ratings. The crew was brought up to full strength when the government of Newfoundland agreed to assign one officer and 106 ratings from the Newfoundland Division of the Royal Naval Reserve to the ship. Very quickly, therefore, from October 1914 to July 1915, *Niobe* took its place in the regular rotation of British cruisers patrolling the American coast. Writing in 1944, its executive officer, Commander C.E. Aglionby, RCN, recalled that *Niobe* was part of "the blockading squadron of the Royal Navy off New York harbour, inside which there were thirty-eight German ships including some fast liners, which could act as commerce destroyers if they could escape":

> *We boarded and searched all vessels leaving the harbour, and in the early days took off many German reservists who were trying to get back to Germany in neutral ships.... We had to pass many things in neutral ships which we knew were destined for Germany, to be used against our men. One particular example I remember was a large sailing ship carrying a cargo of cotton bound for Hamburg, but this was not contraband at that time and we had to allow it to go on. It was very monotonous work, especially after the first few weeks when, owing to reports of possible submarine attacks, we had to keep steaming up and down, zig-zagging the whole time. After the first few weeks, owing to complaints in the American press by German sympathizers to the effect that we were sitting on Uncle Sam's doorstep preventing people coming in and out, we had to keep our patrol almost out of sight of land. The American Navy were very friendly to us, and when their ships passed us they used to cheer ship and play British tunes.[3]*

By September 1915, however, the cruiser's deteriorating condition meant that it had to be removed from operations, and was recommissioned as a depot ship at Halifax for the remainder of the war. It also served as a parent ship for vessels employed on patrol work and provided office space for the various Canadian naval staff officers employed at Halifax. *Niobe*'s new duties also reflected the changing nature of Germany's *guerre de course* against merchant shipping as the enemy shifted its focus from surface raiders to U-boats. The annihilation of von Spee's Pacific squadron at the Falkland Islands and the general ineffectiveness of other surface raiders in disrupting Allied trade during the war's opening months led the German *Admiralstab* to launch an unrestricted submarine campaign against merchant shipping on 1 February 1915.

Despite a shortage of U-boats that could operate in British waters at any one time — an average of four in early 1915, only two of which were likely to be on station to the west of the British Isles — the results achieved by the German submariners more than made up

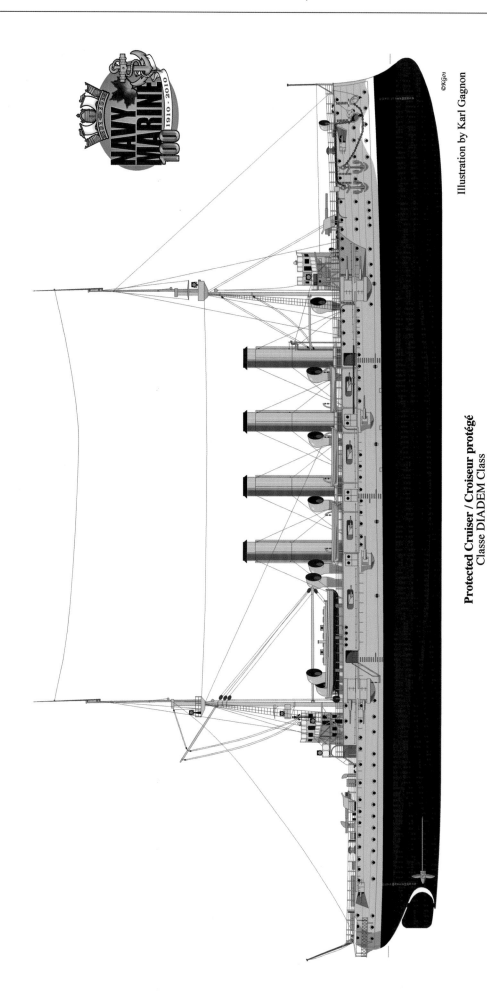

©XGjo1

Illustration by Karl Gagnon

Protected Cruiser / Croiseur protégé
Classe DIADEM Class

H.M.C.S. NIOBE (I)
1915
(ex H.M.S. NIOBE)
Launched 20 February 1897. Built by Vickers, Barrow.

06 September 1910 - 06 September 1915

Dimensions: 141 m x 21 m x 7,8 m
Displacement: 11,000 tons   Speed: 21 knots   Crew: 677
Armement: 16 x 1 - 152-mm; 12 x 1 - 12-pound; 5 x 1 - 3-pound; 2 - 458-mm TT.

N.C.S.M. NIOBE (I)
1915
(ex H.M.S. NIOBE)
Lancé le 20 février 1897. Construit par Vickers, Barrow.

06 septembre 1910 - 06 septembre 1915

Dimensions: 141 m x 21 m x 7,8 m
Déplacement: 11 000 tonnes   Vitesse: 21 noeuds   Équipage: 677
Armement: 16 x 1 - 152 mm; 12 x 1 - 12 livres; 5 x 1 - 3 livres; 2 - TLT de 458 mm.

0   5   10 m

for their small numbers. During the first seven months of the campaign, U-boats sank 470 ships totalling some 715,500 tonnes, including the large British passenger liner *Lusitania* on 7 May 1915. Against this background of sinkings in British waters, Admiralty intelligence alerted Naval Service Headquarters that German agents south of the border might attempt to establish supply bases for submarines along remote stretches of the Newfoundland and Canadian coasts. By late June the Canadian Navy's chief of staff, Commander R.M. Stephens, proposed a scheme for 10 patrol vessels to watch the waters of the Gulf and the coast of Nova Scotia between Halifax, Cape Race and the Strait of Belle Isle. The five auxiliary patrol vessels already available — HMC Ships *Canada*, *Margaret*, *Sable I*, *Premier*, and *Tuna* — were typical of the warships the RCN was to employ during the war. The first two were fisheries patrol vessels that had at least been built along naval lines, while *Premier* and *Sable I* were civilian vessels chartered by the navy. *Tuna*, on the other hand, was a small, turbine-powered American yacht that was purchased by a wealthy Montreal playboy, J.K.L. Ross, and presented to the RCN as a gift. Ross later arranged the purchase of a second, larger turbine-yacht from the United States that was commissioned into Canadian service as HMCS *Grilse*. Armed with two 12-pounder guns and a torpedo tube, NSHQ recognized *Grilse's* operational possibilities from the outset and the vessel was intended for employment near the Gulf's shipping lanes as the RCN's primary offensive unit. Two other large American yachts, albeit ones with reciprocating engines, were also purchased and commissioned in mid-August as HMC Ships *Stadacona* and *Hochelaga*.

In organizing the Gulf patrol, Kingsmill wisely decided to set it up as a command separate from Halifax. Undoubtedly concerned that the British might try to exercise *de facto* control of Gulf operations with little reference to Canadian needs or priorities, the Canadian naval director wanted to ensure that the patrol remained exclusively in NSHQ's hands by placing in command an officer with his headquarters at Sydney acting under Ottawa's direct orders. The work of the Gulf flotilla began in mid-July with *Margaret* and *Sable* keeping watch on the Cabot Strait, while the Canadian Navy hired civilian motorboats to patrol the shoreline. Command of the patrol was given to Captain F.F.C. Pasco, an officer who had been serving with the Royal Navy in Australia. After being rejected by the Australian army on the grounds of age, Pasco readily accepted Canada's offer to command the Gulf patrol flotilla and arrived at Sydney on 5 September 1915. According to a junior RCN officer who served under him, Pasco "was a gruff old fellow who's [sic] specialty was 'finding fault.' ... For us this meant having every button on duty with no deviation from rules contained in the so-called Naval Bible, 'King's Rules and Regulations' [sic]."[4]

The small force that Pasco found waiting for him in Sydney could not have inspired much confidence. The additional hiring of civilian motorboats to keep an eye on the many bays and inlets along the Gulf of St Lawrence coast at least gave the RCN a reason to maintain a presence in the area and investigate the numerous rumours and false sightings being reported by the anxious civilian population. A mix of Royal Navy and Royal Naval Reserve (RNR) officers and senior ratings gave the flotilla's largely RNCVR crews a measure of naval experience and provided on-the-job instruction during patrols. As *ad hoc* a grouping of vessels as the Gulf patrol was, the quality of its warships would not be improved upon — despite NSHQ's best efforts to do so — for the remainder of the war.

Although German U-boats had not crossed the Atlantic in 1915, the increasing volume of Canadian war supplies being transported to Europe suggested that enemy submarines would eventually operate in North American waters. In early March 1916, therefore, NSHQ asked the Admiralty what measures they would recommend with regard to naval patrols in 1916, and also what, if any, assistance the Admiralty could provide. London's reply did not recommend any significant changes to the 1915 arrangements and indicated that no assistance should be expected from Britain in any event. Kingsmill believed that if the British were "unable to supply any additional vessels at present, it is very unlikely that they will ever be able to do so,"[5] and suggested building destroyers for the RCN at the Canadian Vickers shipyard in Montreal. Both politicians and bureaucrats in Ottawa were well aware that the Montreal yard had assembled "H"-class submarines for the British government in 1915 and was currently constructing motor launches for the Royal Navy. Letting contracts in the spring of 1916 would allow Vickers to complete the destroyers by the fall of 1917.

Although the Canadian destroyer proposal was viewed favourably as it made its way through the corridors of the Admiralty in April 1916, a sceptical First Sea Lord suggested that Canadian shipbuilding capacity might be better employed in constructing merchant ships, a view that was endorsed by the first lord, Sir Arthur Balfour. Without the Admiralty's endorsement, Kingsmill's destroyer plans were dead in the water. Having been elected with a naval policy that called for the scrapping of Laurier's planned navy and replacing it with financial support for the Royal Navy, the Borden government would have needed a strong directive from London for it to have considered building sizable warships, even though the proposed destroyers would have given the RCN a far more effective naval force with which to combat the U-boat campaign that developed in Canadian waters in the summer of 1918.

Although the Canadian Navy was primarily occupied in deploying its makeshift patrol force to protect the East Coast shipping lanes in 1916, the RCN continued to maintain a naval presence in the Pacific where *Rainbow*, despite its obsolescence, performed useful reconnaissance work against German shipping activity along the coasts of Mexico and Central America. The Canadian cruiser, still under the command of Walter Hose, was earmarked for the operation because no other British ship was available. It spent the spring of 1916 patrolling the West Coast of Mexico and Central America, eventually capturing two German-owned schooners. The U.S.-flagged *Oregon* was boarded and seized on 23 April while the *Leonor* was taken on 2 May, and *Rainbow* arrived at Esquimalt with its prize in tow on the morning of the 21st.

Despite Canada's war effort being concentrated on its expeditionary force, there were a number of young Canadians who wished to serve in the navy instead of the army. Early in the war, NSHQ had arranged transportation for any RNR officers and men resident in Canada who wished to return to Britain, and had also assisted the Admiralty in enrolling men directly into British

HMCS *Niobe* in the Halifax drydock being readied for war, August 1914.

Department of National Defence CN-6593

service. With the RCN preoccupied throughout 1915 with keeping the crews of its two cruisers up to strength and then with organizing and manning a patrol service in the Gulf of St Lawrence, it was not until early 1916 that the question of sending sailors overseas was raised once again. The Admiralty responded favourably to a February proposal put forward by the naval minister, suggesting that Canadians should be enrolled at British rates of pay for service in the RN's auxiliary patrol. But British recruiters quickly discovered that Canadians were uninterested in joining the RN whose pay for an able-bodied seaman was only 40 cents a day, while the RCN paid 70 cents and the CEF $1.10 for similarly qualified men. Ottawa then offered to recruit an overseas division of the RNCVR and place the sailors at

R. W. CROMWELL

ROLL OF HONOR, CANADIAN NAVAL SERVICE—Passed with H.M.S. Good Hope in Southern Seas, while fighting for the Empire. (No. 1) Midshipman Silver, Halifax, N.S. ; (No. 2) Midshipman Palmer, Halifax, N.S. ; (No. 3) Midshipman Cann, Yarmouth, N.S. ; (No. 4) Midshipman Hatheway, Fredericton, N.B.

Canada's first naval casualties: the four midshipmen embarked in HMS *Good Hope* who were lost with the ship at the Battle of Coronel, 1 November 1914.

the disposal of the Admiralty. The personnel needs of the RCN's expanded patrol forces during the final two years of the war, however, meant that a far greater proportion of RNCVR recruits remained in Canada than were sent overseas. As a result, while Ottawa's original proposal had been to send up to 5,000 Canadians to the Royal Navy as part of the Overseas Division, only some 1,700 RNCVRs were sent across the Atlantic, while the majority, 6,300 volunteer sailors, served in Canadian waters during the war.

Even as NSHQ was looking to assist the Royal Navy in European waters, North America's vulnerability to submarine attack was dramatically brought home to both British and Canadian naval authorities by the sudden arrival of an unarmed German submarine freighter, *U-Deutschland*, off the coast of the United States in July 1916. The potential threat was reinforced when the combat submarine *U-53* appeared off the Nantucket lightship on 8 October and proceeded to sink four merchant ships, totalling 15,355 tonnes, and the British-registered passenger ship *Stephano* bound from Halifax to New York with 146 passengers. In each case, the Germans adhered to accepted laws of war: they stopped the ship, examined its papers, and allowed the crew and passengers to take to lifeboats before sinking the vessel with either gunfire, scuttling charges, or torpedoes. With the USN destroyers on scene unable to intervene, aside from rescuing survivors, *U-53* was free to conduct its attacks before setting course for Germany late that night.

The vulnerability of the North American shipping lanes was reinforced three weeks later when *U-Deutschland* undertook another commercial voyage. This third successful trans-Atlantic voyage by a German submarine finally convinced the Admiralty of the need to revise its advice regarding the RCN's defence arrangements. On 11 November 1916, the British government informed the Canadian of its sudden reversal of policy. But other than noting that the present 12 vessels were insufficient and suggesting an expansion to 36 patrol vessels, the only actual British assistance was an offer "to lend an officer experienced in patrol work to advise the Newfoundland and Canadian governments as regards procuring and organizing vessels."[6]

The 36-vessel auxiliary patrol now being advocated by the British government offered some protection to merchant ships in the immediate approaches to Saint John or Halifax during the winter shipping season, but did not provide for any effective escorts along the heavily-travelled Gulf of St. Lawrence route during the remainder of the year when Montreal resumed its place as Canada's main Atlantic port. Moreover, the RCN was only able to make limited progress in acquiring additional auxiliary patrol vessels from the supply of suitable civilian vessels. Of the two government ships transferred from the department's hydrographic survey, *Cartier* could manage a useful 12 knots, but the larger *Acadia* could make only eight. To these the Canadian Navy was only able to add the 320-tonne, 11-knot steamer *Laurentian* purchased from Canada Steamship Lines, and the 440-tonne, nine-knot *Lady Evelyn* transferred from the postmaster-general's department later that spring. Looking to the United States, the RCN was able to purchase seven New England-built fishing trawlers, commissioned as *PV I* to *PV VII*, even though their eight-knot speed was best suited to minesweeping duties.

Since the 11 additional vessels still left the RCN well short of the 36 suggested by the Admiralty, the naval department approached Canadian shipyards to see if they could build auxiliary vessels for the patrol service. In mid-February 1917, contracts were let to construct a dozen 40-metre, 320-tonne Battle-class steam trawlers, six each at the Polson Iron Works shipyard in Toronto and the Vickers yard in Montreal — marking these inauspicious vessels as the first class purpose-built for the RCN. At the same time, the Admiralty decided to place orders for 36 trawlers and 100 wooden drifters with various Canadian shipyards, both classes to be capable of nine or 10 knots, with the former being armed with a single 12-pounder and the latter with a single six-pounder. In the event, shortages of labour and material delayed construction and the RCN did not begin to receive the vessels until late 1917.

In February 1917 the German high command had decided to gamble on victory by launching an unrestricted submarine campaign even though it risked bringing the United States into the war on the Allied side. Some 500 ships representing over 910,000 tonnes were sent to the bottom by the end of March, and in April the Allies lost 395 ships sunk totalling 800,933 tonnes, the highest shipping losses sustained in a single month during the war. It was a rate of loss that simply could not be sustained by the Allied merchant fleets. While successful in sinking ships, Germany's gamble also produced the result it had feared the most when the United States declared war on 6 April 1917 as an "associate" power on the Allied side. As shipping losses mounted, a desperate Admiralty turned to a tactic it had previously resisted adopting — convoy. After several successful trial convoys, a comprehensive system was put in place over the summer. The first of the regular North American convoys, the "HH" series (Homeward from Hampton Roads) were started at four-day intervals on 2 July. "HN" convoys (homeward from New York) began sailing at eight-day intervals

By late 1917, trawlers and drifters purpose-built in Canada were ready to join the East Coast Patrols.

on 14 July. On 22 June the commander-in-chief, North America and West Indies station was informed that the Admiralty had decided to extend the convoy system to Canadian ports as well. The first of the "HS" convoys (homeward from Sydney), a total of 17 merchant ships, sailed from the Cape Breton port on 10 July commencing a regular eight-day cycle. A troopship "HX" convoy (homeward from Halifax) sailed for the first time on 21 August and included any merchant ships from New York or Montreal that were capable of maintaining 12.5 knots or more.

As successful as the introduction of convoy was in curtailing losses, its adoption also contributed to one of the country's most devastating catastrophes. On the morning of 6 December 1917, a Belgian Relief Committee ship, SS *Imo*, was proceeding out of Bedford Basin on its way to New York just as a French merchant ship, *Mont Blanc*, was entering the harbour to await the next HX convoy. New York shipping agents had loaded the 2,840-tonne *Mont Blanc* with over 2,360 tonnes of wet and dry picric acid, TNT, and gun cotton. In addition, drums of flammable benzol were stacked three or four high on its fore and after decks. Running behind its scheduled departure, *Imo* was steaming south at high speed down the wrong side of the shipping channel when it collided with the slow-moving French steamer, a kilometre north of the naval dockyard. With some of the benzol drums rupturing and bursting into flame from the force of the collision, the French sailors quickly abandoned their burning ship to drift aground on the Halifax shore. Twenty minutes after the initial collision, as RCN sailors from *Niobe* raced to fight the fire, the munitions ship exploded in the largest detonation of manufactured explosives to that time.

The massive blast killed some 1,600 people, most of them instantaneously, and injured another 9,000, many of whom were cut by flying glass as they stood at windows looking out at the burning ship. It also left some 6,000 Haligonians homeless in the heavily damaged northeastern section of the city. About 700 metres to the south, the naval dockyard suffered extensive damage as well. For the RCN, however, the Halifax explosion's greatest impact resulted from the public's desire to assign blame to someone in authority. Although NSHQ was well aware that the main cause of the disaster had been the dangerous loading of *Mont Blanc* at New York and its subsequent routing to Halifax for convoy, it was determined that the Canadian government did not have jurisdiction to investigate the Admiralty. As a result, the public enquiry chaired by Judge Arthur Drysdale was unable to investigate the circumstances of the French ship until after its arrival at Halifax, a decision that excluded the Admiralty's culpability from the proceedings while placing the actions of RCN officers under the public's microscope. In the face of the understandably intense anger residents of Halifax felt because the disaster happened, and ignoring the actual circumstances of the collision, the inquiry placed the full blame on the captain and pilot of the *Mont Blanc*, but also found the RCN's chief examination officer to be guilty of neglect in not keeping himself fully acquainted with the movements of vessels in the harbour.

Despite the black eye the Canadian Navy received as a result of Drysdale's findings, NSHQ's biggest problem in early 1918 was the need to plan for the upcoming shipping season without having a single effective anti-submarine vessel in its patrol force. In January, the Admiralty had provided Ottawa with a candid assessment of the likely scale of attack and the forces the RCN would need to meet it. Anticipating one or two long-range submarines to be operating off the Canadian coast at any one time, London stated that six destroyers, six four-inch-gunned fast trawlers, 36 additional trawlers, and 36 drifters would be required to supplement the RCN's existing patrol force and meet the threat. The Admiralty telegram also assured Ottawa that the most important warships in the scheme, the six destroyers and the six fast trawlers, would be supplied either from the RN or the USN. Based on London's promise of assistance, a relieved NSHQ set about planning its first adequate defence scheme of the war — only to have the rug pulled out from under them a few weeks later. In mid-March the Admiralty tersely informed Ottawa that the promised fast trawlers would not be sent, while the question of the six destroyers "should the necessity for them arise, is being discussed by [the British] C-in-C [NA&WI] with United States naval authorities."[7]

As a result, the navy once again had to contemplate defending Canada's shipping lanes with only slow, inadequately-armed auxiliary vessels, trawlers, and drifters. The arrival of the Canadian-built trawlers and drifters at Halifax and Sydney in June and July 1918 finally allowed the captain of patrols to expand his defence schemes for the approaches to the two convoy assembly ports. As a result, Captain Hose, who had been in charge of the East Coast patrol force since the previous August, had to draw up yet another defence scheme in early June. Although the navy would not have the 12 destroyers and fast trawlers that had been central to the scheme devised by Hose and Kingsmill in March, limited reinforcements had arrived from the United States Navy in the form of six submarine chasers — motorboats armed with depth charges — and two very old torpedo boats. The threat to Canada's East Coast shipping lanes was emphasized when the first enemy submarine, *U-151*, began sinking merchant vessels off the coast of the United States in late May and into June. By mid-July a second U-cruiser, *U-156*, was also reported heading for New York where it laid mines in the port's approaches. On 19 July the 12,440-tonne American armoured cruiser USS *San Diego* sank after hitting one of the U-boat's mines off Long Island with the loss of six sailors. It was the largest American warship lost during the war.

On 22 July, *U-156* made a bold daylight attack on a tug and four barges only five kilometres off Cape Cod in front of thousands of stunned, sunbathing onlookers. Any doubts that the German submarine was moving into Canadian waters rather than returning to the busier shipping lanes off New York were removed on 2 August when the U-boat sank the Canadian four-masted schooner *Dornfontein* 40 kilometres south-southwest of Grand Manan Island at the mouth of the Bay of Fundy. The U-boat continued east across the south coast of Nova Scotia where it sank four American and three Canadian fishing vessels between 3 and 5 August before turning north and heading for the approaches to Halifax. Late on the morning of the 5 August, *U-156* torpedoed the tanker *Luz Blanca* 58 kilometres south-southwest of the Sambro lightship.

While the Halifax command made a creditable effort in flooding the area of the attack with every trawler, drifter, and submarine chaser it had available (and *U-156* spent the next two weeks cruising in U.S. waters), the *Luz Blanca*'s sinking convinced the naval authorities to shift the convoy assembly port to Quebec City for the remainder of the war. With the Halifax shipping lanes virtually devoid of traffic following the shift of convoys to the St. Lawrence, the only ships left in the area when *U-156* returned to the Nova Scotia coast on 18 August were the many fishing vessels plying their trade on the Canadian and

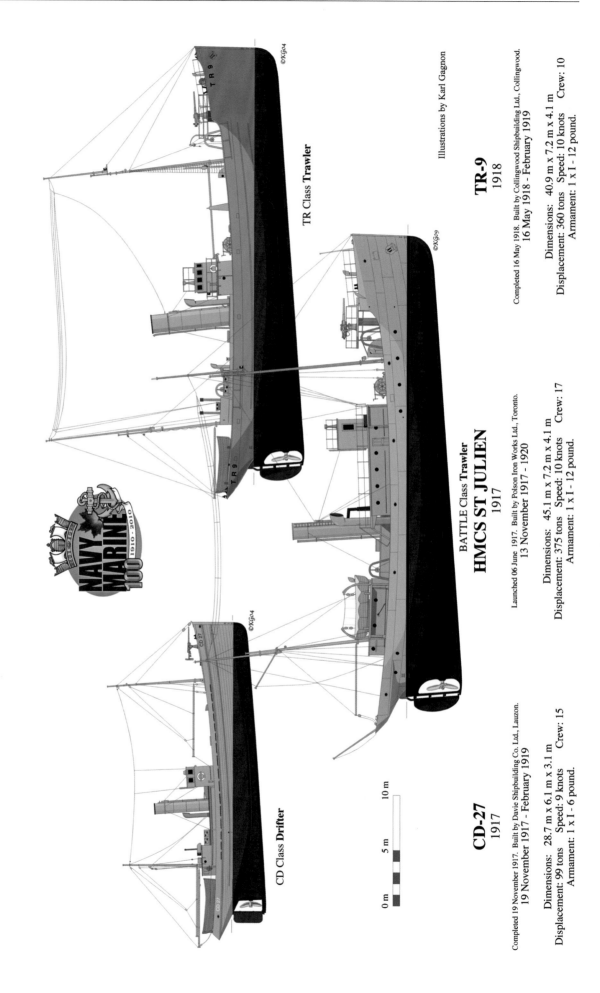

TR Class **Trawler**

Illustrations by Karl Gagnon

TR-9
1918

Completed 16 May 1918. Built by Collingwood Shipbuilding Ltd., Collingwood.
16 May 1918 - February 1919

Dimensions: 40.9 m x 7.2 m x 4.1 m
Displacement: 360 tons Speed: 10 knots Crew: 10
Armament: 1 x 1 - 12 pound.

BATTLE Class **Trawler**
HMCS ST JULIEN
1917

Launched 06 June 1917. Built by Polson Iron Works Ltd., Toronto.
13 November 1917 - 1920

Dimensions: 45.1 m x 7.2 m x 4.1 m
Displacement: 375 tons Speed: 10 knots Crew: 17
Armament: 1 x 1 - 12 pound.

CD Class **Drifter**

CD-27
1917

Completed 19 November 1917. Built by Davie Shipbuilding Co. Ltd., Lauzon.
19 November 1917 - February 1919

Dimensions: 28.7 m x 6.1 m x 3.1 m
Displacement: 99 tons Speed: 9 knots Crew: 15
Armament: 1 x 1 - 6 pound.

0 m   5 m   10 m

Newfoundland banks. These were, in fact, a target, and the German submariners had come prepared to adopt an entirely new tactic in their attacks against the fishing fleets.

Moving northeast parallel to the coast, *U-156* was some 110 kilometres south-southwest of Cape Canso at noon on the 20 August when its crew captured the Canadian fishing trawler *Triumph*. Arming the trawler with a three-pounder gun they had brought with them for the purpose and sending its Canadian crew off in a lifeboat to row for shore, the Germans set about capturing and sinking four more fishing vessels that afternoon. After spending the night of 20–21 August steaming northeast at the trawler's top speed, *U-156* and *Triumph* captured and sank two more fishing vessels at dawn on the 21st, 80 kilometres east-southeast of Cape Breton Island. The trawler in all probability was scuttled during the morning of the 21st, and the German submarine disappeared until 0130 hours on 25 August when it attacked the British steamer *Eric* about 115 kilometres west-northwest of the French island of St. Pierre. Then around 0600 hours *U-156* overtook the Newfoundland schooner *Wallie G.* 40 kilometres west of Saint-Pierre.

Turning south-southwest, the U-boat had travelled approximately 30 kilometres when it spotted a group of four fishing schooners at anchor about a kilometre apart from each other. As *U-156* was in the process of boarding and sinking the schooners, however, the vessels were spotted from the bridge of HMCS *Hochelaga*, part of a four-ship Canadian patrol searching for the German submarine. Rather than steering directly for the enemy, however, *Hochelaga*'s captain, Lieutenant R.D. Legate, turned back to the flotilla leader, urging caution and suggesting they await reinforcements. Ignoring Legate's timidity, the flotilla leader in HMCS *Cartier* steamed at top speed for the U-boat's reported position only to find that it had submerged after sinking the remaining schooners. Having failed immediately to close with the U-boat upon sighting it, *Hochelaga*'s captain was placed under arrest and court-martialled at Halifax in early October. In view of the overwhelming evidence of a loss of nerve in the face of the enemy, Legate was found guilty and sentenced to dismissal from the navy with the forfeiture of his commission, war service gratuity, medals, and other benefits. Following this easy evasion of the Canadian flotilla, *U-156* boarded and sank another Canadian fishing schooner, *Gloaming*, 118 tonnes, 130 kilometres southwest of Miquelon Island on 26 August before heading for home. Alone among the U-boats that operated off the North American coast in 1918, however, *U-156* failed to return safely to Germany, disappearing on 25 September, most likely a victim of the British mine barrage to the west of Fair Isle. Nevertheless, Legate's actions on 25 August were a rather sorry conclusion to the RCN's only direct encounter with an enemy warship during the course of the war.

Even as the East Coast escort fleet was fanning out across the fishing banks to warn schooners of the presence of *U-156*, a second U-boat appeared off Nova Scotia. After operating south of New York, *U-117* began its homeward voyage, stopping the Canadian schooner *Bianca* approximately 275 kilometres southeast of Halifax on 24 August. But the attempt to sink the vessel with bombs failed when its tobacco cargo swelled with seawater and plugged the holes in the hull. *Bianca* was taken in tow by a Boston fishing schooner three days later and successfully brought into Halifax. The delay in survivors reaching shore, occasioned by the greater distance *U-117* was operating from the coast, meant that naval authorities could not organize an effective response to its activities. By the time Halifax received word of the attack on *Bianca*, for instance, the U-cruiser had already sunk the American fishing trawler *Rush* on the morning of the 26 August, about 260 kilometres east-southeast of Canso and 170 kilometres south-southwest from where *U-156* sank *Gloaming* that same morning. The next day *U-117* torpedoed and sank a 2,320-tonne Norwegian merchant ship 175 kilometres southwest of Cape Race. On the evening of 30 August, the U-boat overhauled two Canadian fishing schooners travelling in company and sank them with bombs 450 kilometres northeast of St. John's. Fortunately, the abandoned fishermen were picked up by a passing steamer two days later and brought ashore while the submarine arrived safely in Germany in late October.

The Canadian Navy's meagre anti-submarine forces also received a welcome reinforcement at the end of August. Throughout the spring and summer NSHQ had been attempting to organize a naval air service to operate patrol aircraft along the coastal shipping lanes. Since Canadian naval airmen had to be trained for the new service, the U.S. government agreed to send U.S. Navy aircraft and crews to Nova Scotia to man airbases at Halifax and Sydney in the meantime. An advance party of Americans arrived at Halifax on 5 August. They brought portable hangers with them to begin the task of establishing a temporary aerodrome at Baker Point, on the Dartmouth side of the harbour. After receiving four Curtiss HS-2L flying boats by rail from the United States, the American airmen began air patrols off Halifax at the end of August. Meanwhile, a similar detachment of U.S. Navy flying boats assigned to the Sydney air station, began their first air patrols off Cape Breton in mid-September. While the American patrols were being organized, the call for Canadian recruits for the new air service was sent out to newspapers on 8 August, even though the government did not officially approve the Royal Canadian Naval Air Service (RCNAS) until 5 September. Sixty-four RCNAS volunteers were sent to the Massachusetts Institute of Technology in Boston in late September and early October to commence aircrew training, while a third contingent of RCNAS cadets followed at the end of October. Another 12 RCNAS cadets and six RCN petty officers sailed to Britain in early October to begin

The Halifax Explosion of 6 December 1917 devastated the harbour, but *Niobe* amazingly survived and can be seen raising steam at the right of this photo.

Library and Archives Canada C-019953

airship training. The war ended, however, before any of the RCNAS airmen could complete their training.

Even as *U-156* and *U-117* departed Canadian waters at the end of August, the *U-Deutschland*, refitted and recommissioned as *U-155*, arrived in mid-September and laid a series of mines some 10 to 15 kilometres southwest of Chebucto Head and Sambro Island, at the entrance to Halifax Harbour. As well as being hampered by the fog that normally occurred off Nova Scotia during the summer months, the German submarine recorded having to interrupt its work after spotting destroyers and patrol vessels in the shipping lanes off the Sambro lightship — undoubtedly *Grilse*, deployed in the approaches along with the three USN submarine chasers as part of the port's defences. After lying 20 kilometres off the coast during the night of 18–19 September, the U-cruiser made its way to Sable Island in an effort to cut some of the telegraph cables linking Canada to Britain, but did not waste much time on the effort, cutting only one cable before heading for U.S. waters. On 17 October, *U-155* sank the 6,130-tonne U.S. freighter *Lucia* as it was steaming in an unescorted convoy from New York to Marseilles, France, making it the last ship sunk in North American waters during the war.

In view of the complete absence of destroyers from the Canadian Navy's order of battle, the fact that German submarines did not sink a single ship in convoy is a testament both to the effectiveness of shifting Halifax convoys to Quebec and to the RCN's ability to get the most out its armed yachts, submarine chasers, trawlers, and drifters. The three merchant ships actually sunk in Canadian waters were all attacked while proceeding independently as, indeed, were most of the ships sunk off the U.S. coast. The only other victims in Canadian waters were the 15 small fishing schooners and trawlers sunk by *U-156* and *U-117* between 20 and 30 August. While there is no denying the success achieved by shifting the convoy assembly port to Quebec, the decision was an obvious one for the naval authorities to have made. With over 80 percent of Canadian-bound transports and liners having to journey up the St. Lawrence to load at Montreal in any event, the use of Halifax as an assembly port made little sense within the Canadian transportation network — of which the convoy system was an extension — and simply added 650 kilometres to a merchant ship's voyage, all of it in the very waters that were most exposed to U-boat attack. Protecting the fishing fleets, however, was more problematic. Lacking radios, the unarmed schooners could not alert naval authorities of events until the crews rowed ashore, 12 to 24 hours after they had been attacked. As a consequence, the Canadian Navy could only see that word of the threat was spread across the various fishing banks even as their inability to intercept any U-boats (aside from *Hochelaga*'s encounter) made the RCN appear useless to many in the Maritimes. Nonetheless, Canadian naval officers were privately relieved that the U-boats had attacked vulnerable fishermen while ignoring the far more valuable Canadian convoy traffic.

Throughout the First World War, the RCN was squeezed between the Admiralty's relative indifference to Canadian naval defence and Prime Minister Borden's unwillingness to accept NSHQ's advice unless it had London's stamp of approval. The result was the situation in which the Canadian Navy found itself in 1918, facing the six-inch guns of U-cruisers with a fleet composed primarily of slow trawlers and drifters armed with weapons half the size of the enemy's. Despite the handicaps imposed on it, the RCN's war experience

Department of National Defence CN-6508

Naval Air Station Dartmouth was established in the summer of 1918 as a base for the planned RCN Air Service, but only U.S. Navy HS-2L flying boats such as this were available before the war ended.

was not without some success. From the tiny, prewar remnants of Laurier's navy, a total of 8,826 Canadian personnel served in the RCN during the war: 388 RCN officers and 1,080 RCN ratings, and 745 RNCVR officers and 6,613 RNCVR ratings. Another 90 RN and RNR officers and 583 ratings served with the RCN for a grand total of 9,499 sailors. Of these totals, 190 men in RCN service were killed in action, died of wounds, or died of disease or accident, the latter category including those sailors who were killed in the Halifax explosion. Although a much smaller service, the First World War navy's fatality rate of two percent was, in fact, identical to that sustained by the RCN in the Second World War. While the prewar cruisers *Niobe* and *Rainbow* were the navy's largest warships, the RCN employed 130 commissioned vessels on the East Coast during the war and another four in the Pacific. Nonetheless, there was no escaping the fact that the RCN emerged from the war with a tarnished reputation in the eyes of the Canadian public. Not only had the navy been saddled with a portion of the blame for the Halifax explosion, but the decision by the Germans to attack the fishing fleet also amounted to a direct, if unintended, attack on the RCN's already limited public credibility. As the officer who would lead the post-war Canadian Navy for a decade and a half, Captain Walter Hose recalled in later life that the navy had to endure "scathing — you might say scurrilous — ridicule for years in the press and in parliament, against the navy itself, which was trying its best, making bricks without straw, to maintain the highest efficiency possible and which could not defend itself, it was indeed discouraging."[8] The discouragement reflected in Hose's statement, however, also served to foster a determination among many of the RCN's younger officers to see that the navy would never again be relegated to the status of afterthought in future Canadian conflicts.

Notes

1. DHH, 81/520/1440–5, Vol. IV, "Defensive Measures — 1914. Reports on Situation. Copies for Chief of Staff," 12 August 1914.
2. DHH, 81/520/8000, "HMCS Rainbow," Vol. 2, Hose to Senior Naval Officer Esquimalt, Report of Proceedings, 17 August 1914.
3. Aglionby's account is quoted in Gilbert N. Tucker, *The Naval Service of Canada (I)* (Ottawa: The King's Printer, 1952), 243–44.
4. DHH, 81/520/8000, HMCS *Protector* [Base], W. McLaurin to E.C. Russell (Naval Historian), 11 February 1963.
5. LAC, RG 24, Vol. 4020, Kingsmill, Memorandum for the Deputy Minister, 17 April 1916.
6. LAC, RG 24, Vol. 4031, Colonial Secretary to Governor General of Canada, 11 November 1916.
7. LAC, Admiralty to Naval Ottawa, 16 March 1918.
8. DHH, Hose, BIOG file, Rear-Admiral Walter Hose, "The Early Years of the Royal Canadian Navy," 19 February 1960.

CHAPTER 3

The Interwar Years

Bill Rawling

I arrived in London by train on the morning of November 11th, 1918. As my taxi drove past Selfridge's, a large sign was being hoisted into place, "Armistice Signed at Five A.M." This news took some time to circulate, and it wasn't until 11 a.m., when the Armistice actually came into force, that all hell broke loose ... With one accord, everyone in sight broke into wild cheering, women wept openly, flags appeared in all directions. London literally went mad! Every taxi, every passing car, were boarded by men in uniform, in civvies, by girls of all shapes and sizes — anyone who could get in, or even on the roofs. Motor lorries and trucks were commandeered and careened through the streets, the clinging passengers cheering and waving flags, palm leaves snitched from hotel lobbies, their own hats, other people's hats, even articles of underwear. A remarkable example of spontaneous relief and joy.
— FRANK LLEWELLYN HOUGHTON, MEMOIRS

A then-young RCN officer, Frank Llewellyn Houghton, recorded these memories decades after the event, but they remained fresh to him. The carnage that had been the First World War had come to an end, but for the institution that was the Royal Canadian Navy peace meant an evaluation of its place in Canadian government policy — and its priority in the federal budget. The main naval threats, especially Germany, had been disposed of, and although Great Britain and the United States were clear rivals at sea (in

John Horton, *West Coast Squadron Leaving Esquimalt*.

regards to trade) the possibility of full-scale conflict between those two countries was simply too slim to serve as a basis for naval planning. Furthermore, the deaths of 60,000 Canadians on the battlefields of Europe had touched untold numbers of families, who were understandably sceptical of what had been purchased for the price, and hesitated to make any further sacrifice, whether on land or at sea. As historians Michael Hadley and Roger Sarty have observed, "Canada lacked the national will to develop a navy and had no myths of glory and empire with which to nourish the idea. The parliamentary debates on the Naval Service estimates of May 1919 subjected the Canadian Navy's performance in the Great War to harsh scrutiny and often unjustified scorn." As we have seen in the previous chapter, the RCN had performed its duty, but had not captured the public imagination and had even taken some of the blame for the Halifax explosion: "Offering an unsensational past, the navy seemed to provide no justification whatever for future development. Naval prestige was not a Canadian issue."[1] If the Canadian Expeditionary Force that indisputably had covered itself in glory could be disbanded, it is understandable that members of the RCN looked to the future with some apprehension.

Not so much, however, as to preclude planning. Admiral of the Fleet Lord Jellicoe, visiting various colonies of the empire in the immediate post-war period, recommended that, for protecting Canada's trade and ports, it needed three light cruisers, a flotilla leader, a dozen torpedo craft, and eight submarines with a parent ship. He also made recommendations for a fleet unit that could become part of the Royal Navy in time of emergency, but the Imperial Conference of 1921 resolved "That while recognizing the necessity of co-operation among the various forces of the Empire to provide such Naval Defence as may prove to be essential for security and while holding that equality with the Naval strength of any other power is a minimum standard for that purpose, this Conference is of opinion that the method and expense of such co-operation are matters for the final determination of the several Parliaments concerned…." Dominion autonomy won out over naval centralization, and

The Canadian fleet in 1921: HMC Ship *Aurora* (foreground) and destroyers *Patriot* and *Patrician* in Esquimalt Harbour.

the best the Royal Navy could get at the time were "a number of useful consultations" with several dominions and India, "at which were discussed such matters as local co-operation of each Dominion in regard to the provision of oil tanks, local Naval Defence, etc."[2]

"Local Naval Defence" may have had a Laurier-like ring to it, and the peace was less than a year-and-a-half old when a Conservative Canadian government acquired a Laurier-like navy: on 24 March 1920, it accepted the British offer of a light cruiser and two destroyers, which would be commissioned respectively as HMC Ships *Aurora*, *Patriot*, and *Patrician*. The result, somewhat ironically, was that the RCN would be more capable in time of peace than it had been during the Great War, as none of the vessels it had operated during that conflict could be characterized as "warships." These newly-acquired vessels would operate out of Halifax and Esquimalt, as would trawlers, the latter later reclassed as minesweepers. For the immediate post-war era all these vessels would remain close to home for training and operations, with fisheries patrols a large part of the latter. The Naval Service had taken over responsibility for some of this work from the Department of Marine and Fisheries in the early days of its existence, and would play an important role in protecting natural resources at sea for the remainder of the century and beyond. It did so at its own expense, since it was an opportunity for training, so that in 1921–22, it spent $325,000 on such duties, while Marine and Fisheries expended $350,000. Given the nature of the laws that governed resource exploitation, enforcement could be extremely intricate. The Captain's monthly report for *Thiepval* on 5 March 1920, noted for example,

> while cruising off Cape Scott, a fishing boat was sighted picking up her dories, she
> was stopped and the Capt ordered on board as she proved to be the La Paloma
> of Seattle, Capt informed that he was suspected to be inside the 3 mile limit, took
> the boat in tow, and proceeded to the inside buoy, and by careful Sextant angles fixed
> her at three and one half miles from the West Haycock Isl. The ship was then released,
> and told to get farther off shore, as this was the same man Capt Hurley, who in
> 1914, in the U.S. boat Malola, was warned off Rose Spit, by the Malaspina.[3]

As for the three largest warships of the RCN, they were commissioned on 1 November 1920. Equipment having been installed and tested, they sailed from the British Isles on 1 December, though by 1800, as reported by *Aurora*'s captain, H.G.H. Adams, "all Ships were hove to with a Southerly gale blowing.... The sea-going behaviour of all Ships was a matter of congratulations, but a good deal of discomfort was experienced by small leaks in upper deck, etc which were easily put right by the Ships Staff."

Words like "unfamiliarity" were used frequently in reports on the ships' personnel. For example, *Aurora*'s complement of 323 included 47 ordinary seamen and boys recruited in Canada who had no previous experience. "This number is practically as high as there is room for in the Ship," which was sailing with less than the optimum complement of artisans, being short two ordnance artificers, one electrical artificer, one plumber, one joiner, and one light director layer (for *Patriot*). Furthermore, Adams felt that "it is necessary for efficiency of the Destroyers that 1 Ordnance Artificer, 1 Electrical Artificer and 1 Shipwright be carried in addition as the work on the Destroyers is more than the Staff of *Aurora* can cope

Marine Museum of Great Lakes at Kingston

The trawler *Thiepval* coaling at Petropavlovsk, 31 July 1924.

with." Such work, in this part of the cruise, included range finding exercises on all working days, though "The Gun Circuits, etc, have still a good deal of work to be carried out before firing can safely take place, and … I do not anticipate being ready for any serious firing program before two months. Meanwhile training is taking place daily."[4]

As everyone involved expected, improvement came with practice. *Aurora* and other vessels conducted convoy and harbour defence exercises before a year was out, and played a role in the international arena in 1921. The stage was Costa Rica, during a cruise by *Aurora, Patriot,* and *Patrician* in the spring and summer. A hint of things to come came in a message of 6 June, when the Admiralty advised that Puerta Culebra, a possible port of call for the Canadian warships, "is unsuitable for visit of His Majesty's Canadian Ships as usual salutes and other International courtesies cannot be accorded at that port. British Minister at Costa Rica suggests Punta Arenas as port of call which is in direct railway communication with Capital." The ships arrived on 6 July, and after the usual courtesies (including an exchange of salutes), reported *Aurora's* captain,

> The British Minister arrived down [sic] in a special train during the afternoon
> with a deputation from the British Residents of San Jose and was my guest on
> board during his stay at the Port.…An invitation was extended to 12 officers of

*the Squadron to visit San Jose the following day and remain up there for 2 nights,
which I accepted especially as the Minister thought that this visit would strengthen
his hands in negotiations with the Costa Rica government over claims of the Royal
Bank of Canada and the re-granting of oil concessions to a British Company
which had been taken away.[5]*

Negotiations ended successfully. The highlight of the operation being a night at the opera,
it was more of a trade mission than gunboat diplomacy, but a sure sign that Canada's small
navy could play a role in the empire's affairs.

The 1921 election of William Lyon Mackenzie King's Liberals, however, forced the Canadian Navy to re-evaluate establishments and capabilities. From $1.2 million in 1919, the navy's
budget had risen to almost two million in the two fiscal years that followed, but the new
government called for a limited, $1.5 million navy budget. The director of the naval staff,
now Commodore Walter Hose, who had replaced Kingsmill in 1920, quickly concluded that
such would be insufficient to keep a capable navy, no matter how small, at sea. The service
would therefore rely on reserves to maintain its existence, and the plan he submitted on 19
April 1922 (and was swiftly approved on the 24th) decreed that *Aurora* would be laid up and
Canada's naval college closed, although the two destroyers could remain in commission.

It was at that time that Lieutenant Frank Houghton returned from eight years of service with the Royal Navy, joining *Patriot* as second-in-command. The captain was Lieutenant
Howard Emerson Reid, "one year older and six months senior to me." It was not a happy
moment, as "I was returning to the RCN at a time when it was at its lowest ebb. I shall
always remember the farewell party given to my predecessor, Lieutenant Cuthbert Robert
Holland Taylor.... I can still hear in my mind the last words he managed to articulate before
he quietly and appropriately passed out: 'I've seen a Navy die, boys! I've seen a Navy die!'"[6]
Such words may seem melodramatic, but the RCN was not just an institution, but a society and a community as well. Still, as a member of that society, Walter Hose seemed far less
angry and far more optimistic, at least after some time had passed. In August he wrote one
of his colleagues, who had retired before the cuts, that,

*As you may imagine, we have had to go through an anxious time as regards the
Canadian Navy, but although I very much deplore the arbitrary cut of $1,000,000
in our appropriation, still I have by no means lost hope as regards the future, and I
hope within the next couple of years to have an efficient reserve of at least 1,500
men organized and trained by the nucleus of the permanent force, and I still believe
that from that we shall expand into a seagoing Service again.[7]*

He was right. He was also a level-headed leader who preferred logical argument to
emotional outbursts while explaining how the RCN served the nation's interests. In an
October 1922 report to Cabinet, he asked policy makers to consider that:

*our geographical position, particularly on our Pacific Coast, makes the advent of
assistance from the remainder of the Empire a matter for considerable time. This*

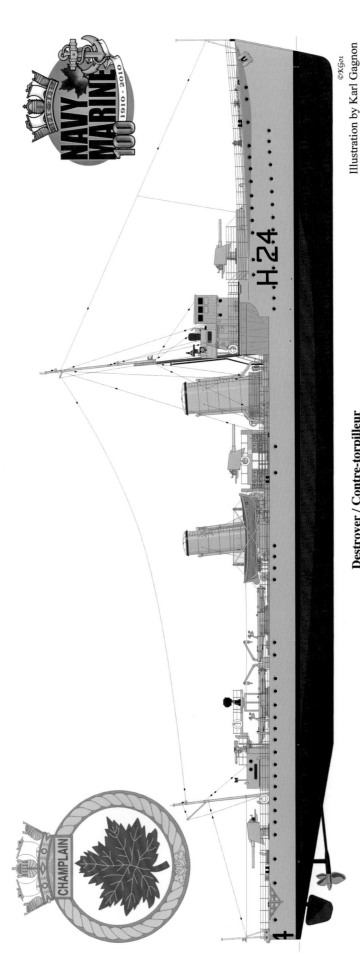

H.24

Illustration by Karl Gagnon

Destroyer / Contre-torpilleur
Classe S Special Class

0 m   5 m   10 m

H.M.C.S. CHAMPLAIN (I)
1932

(ex H.M.S. TORBAY)
Launched 06 March 1919. Built by Thornycroft, Southampton.

01 March 1928 - 25 November 1936

Dimensions: 84.2 m x 8.3 m x 3.2 m

Displacement: 1,087 tons   Speed: 32 knots   Crew: 90
Armement: 3 x I - 102 mm; 1 x I - 2-pound; 2 x II - 533 mm TT.

N.C.S.M. CHAMPLAIN (I)
1932

(ex H.M.S. TORBAY)
Lancé le 06 mars 1919. Construit par Thornycroft, Southampton.

01 mars 1928 - 25 novembre 1936

Dimensions: 84.2 m x 8.3 m x 3.2 m

Déplacement: 1 087 tonnes   Vitesse: 32 noeuds   Équipage: 90
Armement: 3 x I - 102 mm; 1 x I - 2 livres; 2 x II - TLT de 533 mm.

©KG01

*applies even more forcibly to our maritime enterprises, the immense capital embarked
in our fisheries, our merchant ships, our sea commerce and their allied industries on
shore, than to our territory…*

The need to defend trade rather than land was a recurring theme in Hose's analysis. He
noted, for example, that economic relations with countries other than the United States
were worth $695 million:

*This sum is just the actual value of the goods and takes no account of the distress
occasioned all over the Dominion — to the farmer and the lumberman, the artisan
and the fisherman, resulting from the dislocation of such an immense volume of
trade in all commodities.*[8]

All such endeavours together added up to $796.5 million. Similarly, the Canadian Navy had
to take militia requirements into account, since the transportation of troops overseas, as
had occurred during the First World War, required naval escort.

Indeed, naval budgets expanded year by year throughout Mackenzie King's tenure of
office, rising to a high of almost $3.6 million in 1930–31, allowing the operation of bases
at Esquimalt and Halifax, of two destroyers (*Patriot* and *Patrician*), and of four minesweepers
(*Festubert, Ypres, Armentières*, and *Thiepval*). Two reserve systems were developed, the first
being the Royal Canadian Naval Reserve (RCNR), made up of officers and sailors of
the merchant marine who could train a few weeks a year for potential service with the
RCN; by the autumn of 1923 there were registrars in such potential recruiting areas as
Charlottetown, Quebec City, Saint John, Halifax, Montreal, Lunenburg, Prince Rupert,
Victoria, and Vancouver. The second system, the Royal Canadian Naval Volunteer Reserve
(RCNVR), for its part, had by 1926–27 reached a strength of 24 officers and 577 ratings,
if one only counted those who attended training. Its members required no previous naval or
merchant marine experience, and its half-companies and companies scattered in cities across
Canada served not only to prepare officers and sailors, but as a means to advertise the RCN
in communities hundreds and even thousands of kilometres from the sea. The ultimate experience for a member of the RCNVR was to attend an RCN cruise. In September 1924, for
example, about 50 of them embarked in ships of the North America and West Indies Squadron
as they executed a wide variety of evolutions in Canadian and Newfoundland waters.

Perhaps the most interesting operation of the Royal Canadian Navy in the 1920s, however, was carried out in the Pacific Ocean. In the spring of 1924 the minesweeper *Thiepval*
left Esquimalt to complete two main tasks. The first was to support a British "Round
the World Aeroplane Flight" by establishing caches of fuel at various locations between the
Aleutians and Japan. The second was to gather information, following an observation by
the RCN's intelligence officer that the forthcoming cruise would be the opportunity of
a lifetime for collecting intelligence. Returning from its travels on 21 August, the ship provided a 30-page report (quite detailed for that period) on several ports in the Aleutian and
Pribiloff Islands of Alaska, the Kamchatka Peninsula and the Komandorski Islands of Soviet
Russia, and the Japanese Kurile Islands. It noted that in the Aleutian and Pribiloff Islands,

British & Canadian Destroyers.

Esquimalt Naval Museum VR2004.459.081

"General health conditions are good," that "Oil seepages have been discovered near Ugashik and Becherof Lakes, in the Alaskan Peninsula," and that "There is a church" in Oestkamchatka in the Kamchatka Peninsula, a sign that atheism had not completely taken hold in that part of the Soviet Union. A different part of the report provided information on wireless stations, including a photograph, the name of each, the name of the nearest town, latitude and longitude, its height above sea level, the type of station, and the number of masts and their type, for a total of 21 pieces of data.[9]

The Royal Canadian Navy, therefore, although totally incapable of fighting a war, was nonetheless able to carry out useful operations in peacetime, and not only of the fisheries patrol and lifesaving variety. By the

RCN and RN destroyers on fleet manoeuvres in the Caribbean in the late 1930s.

end of the 1920s, the RCN had established itself as an instrument of Canadian government policy, whose role in wartime would be to defend the focal points of Canadian trade. To that end, Commodore Hose advised, "it is more important to have *numbers* than individual unit size and offensive power," for though a cruiser "is more than powerful enough to deal with an armed merchant raider," it could only handle one such threat at a time, whereas "two or three destroyers would render the position decidedly dangerous, especially in the case of a night attack, for a light cruiser. Each would be a match for most armed raiders. For search purposes they would cover a large radius of effective action and concentration on any point could be achieved with rapidity." Also, "For submarine hunting they are practically essential."[10] The RCN would therefore be a destroyer-centred navy.

The destroyers *Champlain* and *Vancouver*, named for famous explorers of the Canadian East and West, had replaced *Patriot* and *Patrician*. While the minesweepers focused on fisheries patrols and lifesaving operations, the destroyers spent more time training in the use of their guns and torpedoes as well as showing the flag in various cities, towns and villages on Canada's coasts and up its wider and deeper rivers; cruises to southern climes were still part of their routine. The two destroyers had been acquired as temporary stop-gaps, the King government signing contracts for the construction of *Saguenay* and *Skeena* in 1929, and as brand new vessels they would incorporate some of the latest developments in ship design. The vessels were commissioned in 1931, and followed the same operational schedule of training, showing the flag, and southern cruises that had occupied their predecessors.

A cruise of January 1932 proved to be an exception. Economic hardship in El Salvador led to revolt, for which the local communist party took credit, although the violence had far more to do with material wants than with ideology. The British Consul, concerned that insurgents would attack such British interests as the railways, requested naval assistance, and

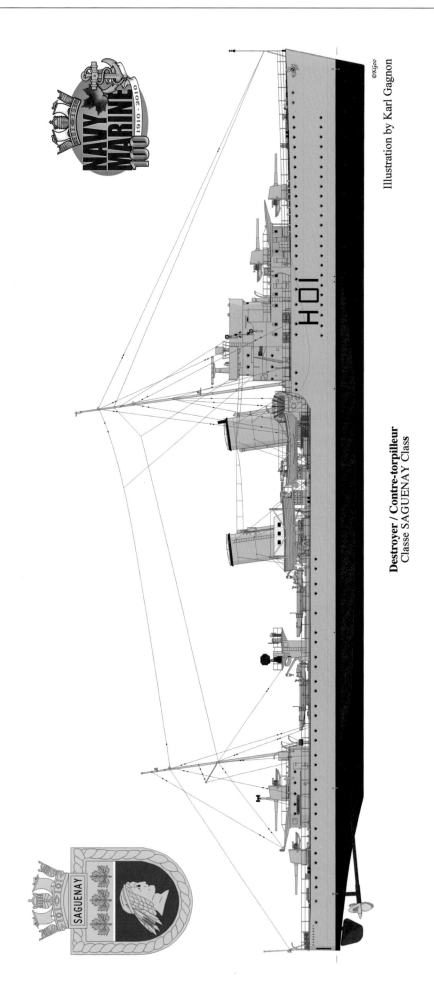

Illustration by Karl Gagnon

Destroyer / Contre-torpilleur
Classe SAGUENAY Class

0 m 5 m 10 m

H.M.C.S. SAGUENAY (I)
1932

Launched 11 July 1930. Built by John I. Thornycroft & Co. Ltd., Southampton.

22 May 1931 - 30 July 1945

Dimensions: 97.5 m x 9.9 m x 3 m
Displacement: 1,337 tons   Speed: 36 knots   Crew: 181
Armament: 4 x I - 120 mm; 2 x I - 2-pound; 2 x IV - 533 mm TT; depth charges.

N.C.S.M. SAGUENAY (I)
1932

Lancé le 11 juillet 1930. Construit par John I. Thornycroft & Co. Ltd., Southampton.

22 mai 1931 - 30 juillet 1945

Dimensions: 97,5 m x 9,9 m x 3 m
Déplacement: 1 337 tonnes   Vitesse: 36 noeuds   Équipage: 181
Armement: 4 x I - 120 mm; 2 x I - 2 livres; 2 x IV - TLT de 533 mm; grenades sous-marines.

as it turned out His Majesty's Canadian Ships *Skeena* and *Vancouver* were on a cruise in the region. *Skeena's* orders, received by radiotelegraph as the ships made their way to the port of Acajutla, were clear and concise, in keeping with such matters in the RN and RCN:

> *On arrival get in touch with British Consul or other British authority and ascertain*
> *what can be done. Failing that enquire from constituted San Salvador authority and*
> *ascertain if assistance required to protect British lives and property. At same time*
> *get in touch with United States authorities and work in co-operation with them*
> *ascertain if any Canadian residents no overt act should be taken unless actual and*
> *immediate imperative necessity to save lives of British subjects.[11]*

The ship accommodated five British women who were concerned for their safety, while the captain, Victor Gabriel Brodeur, and his executive officer, the ubiquitous Frank Houghton, went ashore to conduct a reconnaissance.

What they found was a peasant population in full revolt but avoiding damage to churches, railways, and those farms that paid higher than the normal wage. The Salvadorean military restored order, executing some 20,000 people in doing so, and the insurrection was crushed by the end of the month. An important lesson for the RCN was confirmation of the need to install a modern wireless telegraphy station in Ottawa, as messages from *Skeena* were being passed through Bermuda to Halifax, which had been out of communication with Ottawa all day on 25 January and in poor communication on the 26th and 27th, mainly due to atmospheric interference. There was a facility at the Ottawa suburb of Rockliffe, but:

> *The small power of the transmitting apparatus at Rockliffe was a great drawback....*
> *A number of messages were received direct but could not be acknowledged till some*
> *hours later, giving rise to a certain amount of congestion and unnecessary W/T*
> *traffic, since the same messages were re-transmitted by an intermediate station....*
> *In particular it would have assisted Bermuda greatly if Ottawa had been able to*
> *acknowledge messages as soon as received.... Communication would also have been*
> *much facilitated if Ottawa had been able to transmit direct to Skeena during the*
> *whole period Skeena was audible at Ottawa.[12]*

Rockliffe should, according to the director of naval intelligence, Commander W.B. Hynes, RN, be Canada's first priority in re-equipping W/T stations. The lesson was clear — the RCN of 1932 was not a coastal force.

As Walter Hose and the naval staff contemplated such modernization and expansion, they were unaware that the next year the institution they served would suffer a near-death experience. The country was going through one of the worst economic downturns in its history, and as historian Desmond Morton has noted, "In Ottawa, politicians and officials ransacked budgets for economies. Defence was an obvious place to look. Warned of widespread Communist organizing among the unemployed, the cabinet decided not to cut deeply into the militia or the permanent force [army]. The other services were more vulnerable."[13] As Chief of the General Staff General Andrew McNaughton explained at the time, "The situation with which we are now faced involves a very large reduction in the funds to be made available for Defence and to distribute these reductions over all the Forces would result in weakness everywhere." Therefore, it would be best to "narrow our purpose" to "the forces necessary for the maintenance and support of the Civil Power," and to "the creation of a minimum deterrent to seaborne attack." A small navy would not serve such a purpose, at least not in General McNaughton's thinking:

> On the other hand Air Forces even in small numbers are a definite deterrent in narrow waters and on the high seas in the vicinity of the shore; they can be developed with considerable rapidity provided a nucleus of skilled personnel in a suitable training organization is in existence; pilots engaged in civil aviation can be quickly adapted to defence purposes; civil aircraft are not without value in defence, and any aircraft manufacturing facilities are equally available to meet military as well as civil requirements. [14]

Placed in an extremely difficult position, McNaughton rightly or wrongly opted to support the Royal Canadian Air Force (RCAF), if necessary at the cost of the RCN.

McNaughton's threat to do away with the navy was considered seriously elsewhere in bureaucratic Ottawa. Hose, now with the title of chief of the naval staff, reminded Treasury Board that, although the Great Depression might force a reduction in government spending, it had not changed global-strategic considerations. He also threatened to resign. It is unknown which of these initiatives convinced the president of the Treasury Board to change his mind, but that did happen: the Canadian Navy's budget was reduced (not deleted) from almost $3.6 million in 1930–31 to a little over $3 million the following year; it would be reduced further, to $2.2 million, by 1933–34, but its existence would never again be put into doubt. When Walter Hose retired on 1 January 1934, he had reason to be satisfied.

His successor was Percy Nelles, a member of the first class of cadets who had joined in 1908 even before the RCN was created. By late 1935 he was chief of the naval staff of a permanent organization of 102 officers, 804 ratings, and four destroyers, the 1937–38 budget providing funds to acquire two more destroyers. Then, in the period from 1935 to 1939, the defence budget increased more than four-fold, while the navy's main role gelled somewhat, evolving from a general requirement to defend against surface raiders to the more specific function outlined in the army's Defence Scheme No. 2, of protecting Canadian neutrality in a war between the United States and a third power — most likely Japan. The navy would therefore concentrate mainly on the West Coast, even as the Italian invasion of Abyssinia (Ethiopia) in October 1935 provided a forum to determine what would be the RCN's logistical requirements on the first day of a European war. Although the Canadian government had no intention of intervening, the naval service was unaware of that, and attempted to prepare to operate what few vessels it had. In order of priority, it needed: ammunition for four-inch and 12-pounder guns to be mounted in auxiliary vessels, totalling $20,000 dollars; two anti-submarine nets at $32,500; a general stock of ammunition at $110,000; five torpedoes (half of an outfit) at $70,000; two wireless sets at $30,000; minesweeping maintenance stores at $15,000; two fire control clocks at $30,000; and, at the bottom

Esquimalt Naval Museum VR999.758.103

The commissioning of HMCS *Fraser* at Chatham, United Kingdom, on her transfer from the Royal Navy, 17 February 1937.

of the list of priorities, the other half of the torpedo outfit, at another $70,000. The grand total came to $377,500. In the event, Italy was not opposed in any real sense in its annexation of Ethiopia, so the stores and equipment were not purchased, but it had perhaps been a useful exercise in logistical planning.

More concrete was the acquisition of *Fraser* and *St. Laurent* in 1937, and in early 1938 Cabinet authorized a complement of 1,582 ratings, making a more than three-fold increase since the immediate post-war period. To the RCNR, with registrars in all of Canada's larger ports, and the RCNVR, with divisions in every major city in the country, was added the Fisherman's Reserve, an exclusively West Coast organization whose role would be to keep an eye on its thousands of bays, inlets, and rivers, still with the aim to maintain Canadian neutrality in keeping with Defence Scheme No. 2. Fisheries and lifesaving patrols continued to be an important part of the RCN's routine, to which were added experiments in ice breaking and reconnaissance operations in Canada's Far North. *Ottawa* and *Restigouche* were commissioned in 1938, and training, particularly on the West Coast, was conducted with war clouds on the horizon, especially after Japan's invasion of China in 1937.

Then in 1938 Adolf Hitler demanded that Czechoslovakia's Sudetenland, in which over a million ethnic Germans lived, be annexed to the Third Reich. A conference was organized to take place in Munich, the main players being France, Britain, and Germany, but pending its outcome it was reasonable to assume that war was imminent. As *Fraser's* captain reported:

> *While the ships were at Cypress Bay the international situation became tense. The only news available was the unofficial press news received on the main W/T set and various broadcasts heard on private radio sets in the ship. On Tuesday evening, 27th September, the Commanding Officer decided to bring ships to a state of preparedness for war, except that items which would involve large expenditure of stores and were not absolutely essential should not be taken in hand … The work was commenced at 0600, Wednesday, 28th September, and continued until dark. The longest item was the preparation of eight torpedoes and fitting of warheads in Fraser. This was not completed until noon on Thursday, 29th September.* [15]

Like the Abyssinian crisis, it proved to be more of an exercise than a necessity, but it was the first time since the 1918 Armistice that Canadian vessels prepared for an all-out conflict.

Training was therefore conducted with an added level of seriousness, as Frank Houghton later remembered:

> *In spite of, or perhaps because of, the international situation, which since Munich (where part of Czechoslovakia was handed over to Germany) was becoming increasingly ominous, we proceeded on the usual Spring Cruise to the Caribbean in January 1939, during which we carried out war exercises with the cruisers of the North American and West Indies Squadron.* [16]

Exercises were realistic and rehearsed RCN ships in the types of operation they were expected to carry out in time of war. "I shall always remember one particular exercise when the two cruisers represented enemy armed raiders whose object was to sink British merchant shipping in the western Caribbean." The job of the Canadian flotilla was to find and sink them. It was all rather heady, as:

> *This involved a lot of steaming at high speeds over a vast area, an ideal setting for such an exercise at that time of year. At one period the destroyers were spread out at just visibility distance of each other, searching for the "enemy." Towards evening, nothing having been sighted by then, Captain (D[estroyers]) recalled all destroyers to join him for a night sweep. Just at that moment, however, based on certain information I had been able to intercept on my wireless, I was almost sure I was on the track of one of the cruisers, so I decided to take a calculated risk and disobey the recall signal.*

About half an hour later, "to my enormous relief," the Canadians "sighted the topmasts of a cruiser just peeking over the horizon. We immediately turned away to avoid being

King George VI presents the King's Colour to the Royal Canadian Navy during a ceremony in Beacon Hill Park, 30 May 1939.

sighted ourselves and I sent off an enemy report. About two the following morning all destroyers, having rejoined Captain (D), were able to carry out a surprise attack on the cruiser and 'sink' her with torpedoes." Houghton was not reprimanded for ignoring orders.

Hitler's forces invaded Poland on 1 September 1939, France and Britain declared war on the 3rd, and Canada followed suit on the 10th. The RCN began the Second World War with a much more coherent force and a much better sense of what was expected of it than it had at the beginning of the previous global conflict, mainly because its leadership was rarely distracted from essentials. There being too little funding in the early 1920s to maintain a cruiser and two destroyers, the former was sacrificed, emphasis was placed on the reserves to maintain a link with communities across the country, and the naval service carried on as best it could. Facing budgetary disaster in the early 1930s, it cogently and coherently explained its role in the defence of Canada, namely to protect the ports where so much of the country's trade was imported or exported, and the trade routes that led to those harbours. Throughout the interwar period, it had ships to operate, namely destroyers, so that it could lay claim to being a true navy as opposed to a mere roll of names on reserve lists sometimes operating small, unwarlike trawlers and other vessels. It was not the fleet of battlecruisers and supporting vessels that some had envisaged in the early years following the First World War, but it was a realistic little force, with no little experience of operating ships at sea, and able to conduct itself well. In a country that was not very large in population to begin with, and that had spent years in the midst of a depression that threatened the very foundations of its economy and society, the institution that was the Royal Canadian Navy in 1939 was no small accomplishment.

Notes

1. Michael L. Hadley and Roger Sarty, *Tin-Pots and Pirate Ships* (Montreal: McGill-Queen's University Press, 1991), 301.
2. A. Temple Patterson (ed.), *The Jellicoe Papers: Selections from the Private and Official Correspondence of Admiral of the Fleet Earl Jellicoe, Vol. 2* (London, 1968), 370–71, 374–76, and 378.
3. LAC, RG 24, Vol. 5687, HMCS *Thiepval*, "Captain's Monthly Report for March 1921."
4. LAC, RG 24, Vol. 3887, Captain *Aurora* to Secretary of the Naval Service, 17 December 1920.
5. LAC, RG 24, Vol. 5632, HMCS *Aurora*, "Letter of Proceedings," 14 July 1921.
6. Houghton, *Memoirs*, 91.
7. DHH, 2001/112, C11, Hose Papers, Walter Hose to Capt H.E. Holme, 10 August 1922.
8. LAC, RG 26, J1, Vol. 77, King Papers, Walter Hose to William Lyon Mackenzie King, 26 October 1922.
9. LAC, RG 24, Vol. 11924, Director of Naval Intelligence to District Intelligence Officer Esquimalt, 27 September 1924.
10. LAC, RG 24, Vol. 4046, Chief of the Naval Staff, "The Naval Defence Policy in Canada," 21 August 1930.
11. LAC, RG 24, Vol. 1598, Chief of the Naval Staff to *Skeena*, 23 January 1932.
12. LAC, RG 24, Vol. 6198, Director of Naval Intelligence to Chief of the Naval Staff, 12 February 1932.
13. Desmond Morton, *Canada and War*, 97.
14. LAC, MG 30, E133, Vol. 12, Chief of the General Staff to Minister of National Defence, 1 June 1933.
15. LAC, RG 24, Vol. 5684, HMC Ships *Fraser* and *St Laurent*, "Reports of Proceedings," 1 to 30 September 1938.
16. Houghton, *Memoirs*, 136-37.

Maritime Research and Development in the Interwar Period, 1919–39

Harold Merklinger

Although the interwar time was a period of near disaster for the RCN, seeds planted before and during the Great War for the navy's technical development continued to grow. The organizational relationships between government, universities and to some extent industry were formalized and developed.

Foremost among Canada's universities was Montreal's McGill, where Canada's premier soldier, Arthur Currie, became principal in 1920. However, it was Currie's wartime artillery commander (and former McGill student and professor), Andrew McNaughton, who as president of the National Research Council from 1935 began to forge relationships among NRC, universities, Canadian industry, and the Department of National Defence.

McNaughton applied his early research into cathode ray tubes toward post-war work in support of air navigation, leading to the invention of the cathode ray radio direction finder, which would later impact both anti-submarine techniques and radar. During his tenure as president of NRC from 1935–39 he fostered the interchange of personnel between DND and NRC, and between Canadian industry and NRC, positioning Canada to make solid technical contributions from the very beginning of the coming war effort.

Oceanographic work was continued largely under the aegis of fisheries research sponsored by the Biological Board of Canada. In 1928 H.B. Hachey was appointed as the first physical oceanographer to the Atlantic Biological Station at St. Andrews, New Brunswick, and in 1931 J.P. Tully arrived at the station in Nanaimo, British Columbia, where much of his pioneering work in a similar capacity was supported by RCN funding. Sponsorship of this work was transferred to the Fisheries Research Board when it was established in 1937.

Charles F. Goodeve (1904–80) of Winnipeg was a junior officer in the RCNVR in 1927 when he received a scholarship to study chemistry at the University College, London. Having then joined the RNVR, by 1939 he was a lieutenant-commander at HMS *Vernon*, the Royal Navy torpedo and mining establishment. His early achievements included degaussing methods and the "Double-L sweep" for protection against mines. As the wartime director of the Department of Miscellaneous Weapons Development he would be instrumental in development of the "Hedgehog" anti-submarine mortar. Later, as Britain's deputy controller of research and development, he fostered the rational tracking and prioritization of research and development efforts, including those of allies. For his achievements he was awarded an Order of the British Empire (in 1942) and a Knighthood (1945).

Another Canadian, Frederick G. Creed, in 1938 proposed to the British Admiralty an aircraft carrier design based on his "Small Waterplane Area Twin Hull" (SWATH) principle. This design had to wait until 1968 to see fruition, but remains a promising ship concept to this day.

As war became a certainty, government processes were found to be too slow and unwieldy to fund timely research and development. Concerned wealthy individuals and corporations offered to donate funds — in total about $1.3 million — to kick-start high-priority developments. This "Santa Claus Fund" was to give the Canadian scientific war effort a significant head start.

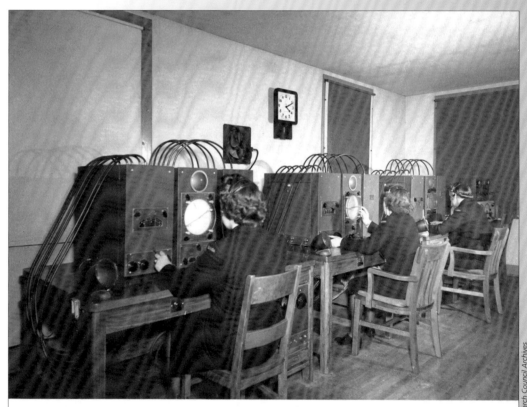

The "Cathode Ray Direction Finder" was developed by the National Research Council and had several military applications, including radar and the location of radio transmitters, such as those on submarines (pictured here).

C.R.D.F. RADIO DIRECTION FINDING EQUIPMENT (BANDS 'A' & 'B' & 'C') IN OPERATION

National Research Council Archives

CHAPTER 4

"Stepping Forward and Upward": The Royal Canadian Navy and Overseas Operations, 1939–45

Donald E. Graves

Up to Kola Inlet, back to Scapa Flow,
Soon we shall be calling, for oil at Petsamo.
Why does it always seem to be, Flotilla No. 23,
Who plough the Arctic Ocean and thrash the Barents Sea?

When we get to Scapa, do we get a rest,
All we have is signals invariably addressed.
"Dear ALGONQUIN" with love from "D,"
Why are you here? Get back to sea!

Over in our mileage, due for boiler clean,
When we're not with convoys, there's practice in between,
Now as you have surely guessed,
We do our best, but need a rest.
— 23RD FLOTILLA SONG[1]

Canadian War Museum 19880046-001

Donald Connolly, *Finale*, picturing the action in Onagawa Bay, Japan, 9 August 1945, from which Lieutenant Robert Hampton Gray, VC, DSC, was posthumously awarded the RCN's only Victoria Cross.

The Royal Canadian Navy's greatest contribution in the Second World War was the role it played in the Battle of the Atlantic, the grim and unrelenting struggle against the German U-boats, which is the subject of the next chapter. What is often overlooked, however, is that the RCN also manned a variety of warships, from light cruisers to landing craft, which carried out many different tasks in European and Pacific waters. The RCN's participation in surface warfare in these theatres was primarily driven by the ambition of Naval Service Headquarters in Ottawa to build up a "balanced fleet" or "blue water navy" that would be the foundation of a post-war service so strong that never again would it face possible dissolution as it had in the 1920s.

When war broke out in September 1939, NSHQ viewed the most dangerous threat as being large surface raiders, not submarines, and to counter this threat it wished to obtain powerful fleet destroyers of the Tribal class. In the winter of 1939–40 an arrangement was made with the Admiralty in London for Canada to produce escort vessels for the Royal Navy in return for British construction of four Tribal-class vessels in the United Kingdom. Until these ships were completed, NSHQ arranged for the conversion of three large passenger ships — *Prince David*, *Prince Henry*, and *Prince Robert* — as auxiliary cruisers, and while the seven destroyers of the pre-war fleet were employed on convoy duty in the Atlantic the "Prince" ships mainly operated on the Pacific coast. When the fall of France in June 1940 brought the U-boats to the Atlantic littoral, the RCN became increasingly involved with the North Atlantic but NSHQ never entirely relinquished its ambition to man larger warships.

As the first of the Tribals would not commission until late 1942, this ambition could not be realized in the short term. During the early part the war, however, many Canadian naval officers and seamen gained valuable experience by serving with the Royal Navy. The full story of their activities has never been properly told, but it should be emphasized that Canadian sailors served at sea in every theatre of war in appointments ranging from the conventional to the extreme.

To provide just a few examples, Midshipman L.B Jenson, RCN, was in the battlecruiser HMS *Renown* when it engaged the German capital ships *Scharnhorst* and *Gneisenau* off Norway in April 1940. Lieutenant R.W. Timbrell, RCN, received a Distinguished Service Cross (DSC) for his service at Dunkirk in June 1940 while Sub-Lieutenant G.H. Hayes, RCNVR, survived being sunk in the same evacuation. Sub-Lieutenant G. Strathey, RCNVR, was a radar officer on the cruiser HMS *Ajax* when it sank three Italian destroyers in the Mediterranean in October 1940. Lieutenant S.E. Paddon, RCNVR, was a radar officer in the battleship HMS *Prince of Wales* when it fought the *Bismarck* in the spring of 1941 and

HMCS *Prince Robert*, one of three Canadian National Steamship liners converted into armed merchant cruisers by the RCN as a stopgap in 1940, is pictured here, in a British drydock in January 1944, after later conversion as an anti-aircraft cruiser.

survived his ship's sinking off Malaya seven months later. Five Canadian officers were lost in the cruiser HMS *Bonaventure* when it was sunk off Crete in March 1941 and Lieutenant C. Bonnell, DSC, RCNVR, died in a Chariot "human torpedo" during a raid on Sardinia in December 1941. Surgeon-Lieutenant W.J. Winthrope, RCNVR, was killed in the daring commando attack on Saint-Nazaire in March 1942. Lieutenant J.H. O'Brien, RCN, witnessed the massive Allied amphibious landings in Sicily and Italy in 1943. Sixty Canadian ratings were serving in HMS *Belfast* when it participated in the sinking of the *Scharnhorst* in the Barents Sea in December 1943. Lieutenant R.H. Lane, RCNVR, served in the British heavy cruiser HMS *Glasgow*, Lieutenant-Commander F.H. Sherwood, RCNVR, was captain of the submarine HMS *Spiteful* operating in the Indian Ocean in 1945, while Captain H.T.W. Grant, RCN, commanded the cruiser HMS *Enterprise* in 1943–44. Lieutenant F.R. Paxton, RCNVR, was radar officer in the destroyer HMS *Venus* in May 1945 when it detected the Japanese heavy cruiser *Haguro* at the extreme range of 55 kilometres, a contact that ended with the enemy's destruction. Perhaps one of the most unusual wartime jobs was that of Lieutenant-Commander B.S. Wright, RCNVR, as commander of a special operations detachment in central Burma in 1945 whose job was to swim across the Irawaddy River at night to raid the enemy.

Two branches of the Royal Navy in which Canadians formed a substantial presence were coastal forces and naval aviation — largely because NSHQ permitted Britain to recruit in Canada for these specialties. By 1943 more than 100 RCN officers were serving in coastal forces, commanding small but heavily-armed fast attack craft in the Channel and the Mediterranean. Their exploits were remarkable. Lieutenant-Commander T.G. Fuller, RCNVR, was awarded the DSO and two bars for operating against enemy warships in the Adriatic, while Lieutenant R. Campbell, RCNVR, participated in commando raids on Rommel's troops in North Africa. Four young RCNVR officers, Lieutenants J. Davies, W. Johnston, R. MacMillan, and J.M. Ruttan, became responsible for mine clearance in Tobruk during the siege of 1941–42, while Lieutenant-Commanders G. Stead and N.J. Alexander, RCNVR, each commanded British coastal forces flotillas in the Mediterranean. One of the most outstanding feats accomplished by a Canadian was the action fought in May 1943 between *MGB 657*, commanded by Lieutenant-Commander J.D. Maitland, RCNVR, and a surfaced German U-boat — not only did Maitland beat off the enemy's attack but so distracted the submarine's bridge crew that it accidentally rammed another U-boat, sinking both vessels. Lieutenant A.G. Law, RCNVR, took part in an attack on the German battlecruisers *Scharnhorst* and *Gneisenau* when they made the "Channel Dash" in February 1942. As Law attempted to avoid the attentions of German E-boats and destroyers that were determined to sink his fragile motor torpedo boat (MTB) before he got within torpedo range, his coxswain drew his attention to the sky: "Sir, aircraft with two wings — they must be British!"[2] And they were, for overhead were five Swordfish torpedo planes flying in to make their own effort against the enemy battle cruisers. All five were shot down (and the German battlecruisers made it through).

Lieutenant-Commander G.C. Edwards, RCNVR, flew one of the antiquated aircraft that made this attack but survived to eventually command a squadron of Swordfish in the Fleet Air Arm. Edwards not only survived crashing a "Stringbag" (as these biplanes were

Library and Archives Canada PA-204587

The war the navy expected: recruits at HMCS *York*, February 1942, doing close order drills in front of a full-size mock-up of a King George V–class battleship.

termed) in the Mediterranean, he was one of the few pilots to survive a ditching in the frigid Arctic Ocean when his carrier escorted a Murmansk convoy. Lieutenant-Commander D.R.B. Cosh, RCNVR, commanded a squadron of the more modern Wildcat fighters in the escort carrier HMS *Pursuer* that participated in a strike against the German battleship *Tirpitz* in April 1944. Lieutenant-Commander R.E. Jess, RCNVR, commanded a Fleet Air Arm squadron of Avengers operating with the British Pacific Fleet against Japanese targets in 1945. There were a number of Canadian naval fighter pilots in the Pacific. Lieutenants D.J. Sheppard, RCNVR, and W.H.I. Atkinson both scored five kills in this theatre, and three of Atkinson's victories were difficult night interceptions. Lieutenant D.M. Mcleod, RCNVR, survived miraculously almost unscratched when the engine of his Corsair failed on take off, with the result that it cartwheeled several times — nose over wing over tail — on the water. Lieutenant A. Sutton, RCNVR, was posted missing in his Corsair during a raid on Sumatra in 1945. Lieutenant R.H. Gray, RCNVR, also flew Corsairs and his courageous attack on a Japanese destroyer in August 1945 brought a posthumous award of the only Victoria Cross earned by the RCN during the war. One of Gray's squadron mates, Lieutenant G.

Anderson, RCNVR, was killed in the same attack when his badly-damaged Corsair crashed while landing on their carrier, HMS *Formidable*. Anderson was the last member of the Canadian Navy to die in the Second World War.

The RCN also made a substantial contribution to the Combined Operations service, the organization created to carry out raids on occupied Europe and develop the specialized techniques required to conduct the large amphibious landings that marked the latter years of the war. In early 1942, 50 officers and 300 ratings proceeded to Britain to form two flotillas of landing craft. On 19 August 1942, 15 officers and 55 ratings from this group were with British landing craft flotillas that participated in Operation Jubilee, the ill-fated raid on Dieppe that cost the Canadian army nearly 3,000 casualties, or about 65 percent of the troops that took part. In a letter home written shortly afterward, Sub-Lieutenant D. Ramsay, RCNVR, provided a dramatic kaleidoscope of the images he had witnessed that terrible day, including:

> a German armed trawler blown clear out of the water by one of our destroyers; a five-inch shell right through from one side to the other on the boat next to me without exploding; the boat officer, Skipper Jones, RNR (ex-Trawlerman as you can guess) screaming invectives at the Jerry and coming out once in a while with the famous Jonesian saying, "get stuffed;" a large houseful of Jerry machine gunners pasting hell out of anybody who dared come near the beach; a Ju 88 whose wing was cut in half by AB [Able-Bodied Seaman] Mitchinson of Ontario in the boat astern; a plane swooping down low behind a destroyer and letting go a 2000 lb. bomb, which ricocheted over the mast and burst about 10 yards on the starboard bow; peeking over the cox'ns box and looking into the smoking cannon of an Me 109. I'm here to state that that was close.[3]

Organized as four distinctly RCN flotillas, Canadian Combined Operations personnel then took part in Operations Torch (the landing in North Africa in November 1942), Husky (the Sicily landing in July 1943) and Baytown (the Italy landing that September). The achievements of the Canadian flotillas were almost unknown in Canada, much to the chagrin of NSHQ, which became determined that the same case would not apply with the RCN's Tribal-class destroyers when they entered service.

The first of these warships, HMCS *Iroquois*, was commissioned in November 1942 and was followed, over an eight-month period, by HMC Ships *Athabaskan*, *Haida*, and *Huron*. Armed with six 4.7-inch guns, two four-inch high-angle guns, four 21-inch torpedo tubes, and a variety of smaller anti-aircraft weapons, these big, graceful and powerful destroyers were intended not only to be the RCN's striking force overseas, but also the nucleus of a post-war fleet. As it was, NSHQ narrowly stickhandled around a proposal by Prime Minister Wiliam Lyon McKenzie King that the Tribals be either employed on the North Atlantic convoys or for the defence of the Pacific Coast. "The Tribal is essentially a fighting Destroyer," advised Commander H.G. DeWolf, Director of Plans, and would be wasted in any task other than that for which it had been designed. It was his opinion that the best course was to put the Tribals "under British operational control" where they could "contribute to the general cause."[4] Fortunately, this logic won the day and the four ships spent their wartime career with the RN's Home Fleet where they carved out an impressive fighting record.

After working up and overcoming technical and personnel problems, *Athabaskan* and *Iroquois* saw their first action in the Bay of Biscay. The "Biscay Offensive" of the summer of 1943 was intended to catch and destroy U-boats transiting from their French bases to the North Atlantic but it enjoyed mixed success, particularly as Allied warships were within range of German shore-based aircraft. On 27 August, *Athabaskan* was operating in company with the destroyer HMS *Grenville* and the sloop HMS *Egret* when it was attacked by a new weapon — a radio-controlled "glider bomb," actually a missile launched and guided by aircraft. As *Athabaskan's* commanding officer, Lieutenant-Commander G.R. Miles, RCN, reported, 19 Dornier 217 bombers approached and,

> the three leading aircraft dropped their rocket bombs almost simultaneously; two were failures and the third, never deviating from its course for an instant, came straight for Athabaskan's bridge. It was a magnificent shot and no dodging it. Striking the port side at the junction of B gun deck and the wheelhouse, it passed through the chief petty officers' mess and out the starboard side where it exploded when twenty to thirty feet clear of the ship.[5]

Another bomber targeted *Egret*, which was hit and sunk. Suffering heavy damage but mercifully few casualties, *Athabaskan* was able to limp back to Plymouth to spend a lengthy period in drydock before being again fit for service.

In November 1943 the three operational Tribals were ordered north to Scapa Flow, the barren and isolated Home Fleet base in the Orkneys, to work the "Murmansk Run," escorting and screening convoys from Britain to Russia. From their inception in August 1941 to the end of the war, these convoys were the most dangerous operations carried out by the Allied navies, and losses in both merchant and warships were heavy as they took place within easy range of German bases in Norway. The Arctic convoys faced not only U-boats and aircraft, but also major fleet units — including the battleship *Tirpitz*, sister ship to the *Bismarck* — as well as terrible weather, rough seas, and extreme cold. Although the Murmansk Run was vital to the Russian war effort, it was not a popular service and Lieutenant P.D. Budge, RCN, of *Huron* explains why:

> It seemed that gales were forever sweeping over the dark, clouded sea. The dim red ball of the sun barely reaching the horizon as the ship pitched and tossed, the musty smell of damp clothes in which we lived, the bitter cold, the long, frequent watches that seemed to last forever. This on a diet of stale bread, powdered eggs and red lead [stewed tomatoes] and bacon. The relief to get below for some sleep into that blessed haven — the comforting embrace of a well-slung hammock. There was no respite on watch for gun, torpedo or depth-charge crews as every fifteen minutes would come the cry "For exercise all guns train and elevate through full limits" — this to keep them free of ice..... The watch below would be called on deck to clear

the ship of ice — the only time the engine room staff were envied. Each trip out and back seemed to last an eternity with nothing to look forward to at either end except that perhaps mail would be awaiting us at Scapa Flow.[6]

In late December 1943, *Haida*, *Huron*, and *Iroquois* formed part of the covering force for Convoy JW 55B, which was attacked by the German battlecruiser *Scharnhorst*. The Canadian vessels were not directly involved in the action but were long-distance witnesses by radio of the destruction of the *Scharnhorst* on Boxing Day 1943. When they anchored in the approaches to Murmansk two days later, their ships' companies held a belated Christmas celebration, and in *Haida* one of its officers remembered, "the whole mess deck was draped with signal flags; a bottle of beer at each man's plate; the candles throwing a pleasant light; and practically everyone drunk."[7]

The powerful Tribal-class destroyers *Haida* and *Athabaskan* steam in formation in the English Channel, spring 1944.

As the Tribals began operations during 1943, NSHQ made impressive strides toward achieving its plan of creating a balanced fleet that would survive inevitable post-war defence cutbacks. The RCN's progress toward this bright, shining goal was accelerated by four factors. First, 1943 saw the climax of the Battle of the Atlantic and Allied dominance over the

Library and Archives Canada PA-151742

U-boats, allowing the RCN for the first time since 1940 to "draw breath" and contemplate the future. Second, recruiting for the Canadian Navy had reached the stage where there was a surplus of personnel, many waiting to man new escort vessel construction not yet completed. Third, in contrast, the RN was experiencing a severe personnel shortage and had more ships than it could man. Fourth, and most important, the time was approaching when the Western allies would have to undertake a major cross-Channel invasion, an operation that would require not just hundreds but thousands of ships and smaller craft.

These factors became apparent at the Quadrant conference attended by the leaders of Britain, the United States, and Canada at Quebec City in September 1943. In meetings with Admiral Dudley Pound, the First Sea Lord of the RN, and Vice-Admiral Louis Mountbatten, the head of combined operations, Vice-Admiral Percy Nelles, the Canadian chief of the naval staff, confessed his concern that the Canadian Navy "did not finish the war as a small ship navy entirely."[8] Far from that, he informed his British counterparts, his intention was to create a post-war fleet of five cruisers, two light fleet aircraft carriers, and

Crew of the V-class destroyer *Algonquin* sponging out their 4.7-inch (12-centimetre) gun after bombarding German shore defences in the Normandy beachhead.

three flotillas of fleet destroyers. Nelles asked for British assistance in achieving this ambitious objective and he got it. With the help of Britain's Winston Churchill in some very adroit manoeuvring around Canadian Prime Minister Mackenzie King, who was ever suspicious of defence expenditures, Nelles came away with happy results. It was agreed that the RCN would take over and man two escort carriers, two light cruisers, two fleet destroyers, three flotillas of LCI (Landing Craft, Infantry), and also contribute a beach commando — an amphibious traffic control unit — for the forthcoming invasion.

Other initiatives undertaken in 1943 and early 1944 increased the RCN's presence in European waters. The three Prince ships, no longer required as auxiliary cruisers, were taken in hand throughout the year and rebuilt: *Prince David* and *Prince Henry* were converted into landing ships, each of which would carry a landing craft flotilla, while *Prince Robert* was rebuilt as an anti-aircraft defence ship. The strong Canadian presence in Coastal Forces led to a British proposal that the RCN man two MTB flotillas for the invasion and the first personnel were on their way overseas by October 1943. In early 1944, a British request for minesweepers was met by the dispatch of 16 Bangor-class vessels. In all, the Canadian contribution to Operation Neptune, the naval component of the planned Normandy landing, would be 126 vessels of all types and no less than 10,000 officers and seamen. Apart from the boost this would give the Allied cause, NSHQ firmly believed that participation in the most crucial operation of the war would enhance the RCN's prestige and increase its profile among the Canadian people. Neptune would be the culmination of the wartime growth of Canada's navy and it would involve the cream of that service.

In January 1944, much to the satisfaction of their ships' companies, the four RCN Tribals were transferred from Scapa to Plymouth. Here they formed, along with RN Tribals, the 10th Destroyer Flotilla, which had the task of carrying out "Tunnel" operations to reduce the strength of major German surface units in the Channel. Commencing in late February, the 10th Flotilla patrolled at night, searching for enemy destroyers and torpedo boats (actually small destroyers) based in Le Havre and Cherbourg. This work continued through March and into April, without any contact, causing the crews to term the Tunnel patrols as "FAFC," an acronym that can be rendered most tactfully as "Fooling Around the French Coast." Things changed on the night of 25–26 April 1944 when *Athabaskan*, *Haida*, and *Huron*, along with British vessels, encountered three large German torpedo boats, *T-24*, *T-27*, and *T-29*, and began a gun and torpedo battle that evolved into a long chase as the enemy tried to escape. *T-27* and *T-24* got away — although the former was badly damaged by accurate Canadian gunnery — but *T-29* was not as fortunate. The Canadian destroyers circled it at close range hitting it with every weapon they could bring to bear until it was scuttled by its crew, becoming the largest warship to be sunk by the RCN up to that time in the war.

Two nights later, guided by radar, *Athabaskan* and *Haida* again caught up with *T-24* and *T-27* and damaged the latter vessel so severely that its commanding officer ran it aground. Unfortunately, *Athabaskan* was hit by a torpedo fired by one of the German vessels causing a magazine to explode, igniting fuel oil that set it on fire and quickly sank it. The disaster unfolded very fast. Leading Seaman B.R. Burrows, manning the destroyer's gunnery radar, ran out on the starboard side of the stricken vessel and later recalled:

I just got blown over the side. Instinct told me, "Get the hell out of here, fast!" so I
swam as fast as I could. Diesel fuel is very volatile and I got showered with diesel
fumes [oil] — they burnt me from stem to stern. I didn't know it at the time — it
hit me so fast that I just kept on swimming. Also, although I didn't know it at the
time, I was swimming through Bunker C fuel, the black sticky stuff used in the ship's
boilers to drive the main engines. I got covered in it.[9]

Most of the *Athabaskan's* crew were able to get off the destroyer before it went down, but the explosions had destroyed almost all its boats and floats. DeWolf in *Haida*, seeing his comrades' plight, brought his ship near the men swimming in the water and proceeded to pick up survivors, thus placing his own destroyer in peril. Seeing this, Lieutenant-Commander Stubbs, the captain of *Athabaskan*, in the water with his men, shouted "get away, *Haida*, get clear!"[10] and DeWolf regretfully had to leave the scene after picking up only 42 men, although he left his own boats and floats for their succour. Of *Athabaskan's* ship's company of 261 officers and men, 128 did not survive its sinking, among them Lieutenant-Commander Stubbs. The loss of *Athabaskan* was not in vain — by the end of April 1944, as the Allies began the final preparations for the invasion, German destroyer strength in the Channel had been reduced to just five vessels.

By this time, the various Canadian naval units that would participate in Operation Neptune had begun to assemble in southern British ports. The 16 Bangor-class minesweepers arrived in April to commence training in sweeping, a new activity for their ships'

Department of National Defence GM-2016-R

The 29th Motor Torpedo Boat
flotilla races across the Channel.

69

companies. They did not impress their British instructors, who commented on the Canadians' nonchalant attitude that minesweeping was "child's play." That attitude was quickly knocked out of them during six weeks of intense work-ups lasting until late May when they were judged by the RN as being "efficient, keen and competent."[11] Eight of the Bangors formed the 31st RCN Minesweeping Flotilla under Commander A.G. Storrs, RCN, the remainder being divided up among British flotillas.

The two Canadian MTB flotillas, and the landing ship and landing craft flotillas, had fewer problems as they possessed a nucleus of veteran officers and warrant officers who knew their business. *Prince David*, *Prince Henry*, and the 260th, 262nd, and 264th LCI(L) Flotillas participated in the major amphibious exercises held in April and May, although to its dismay Beach Commando W learned that it would not be part of the assault forces but would come ashore at a much later date. The 29th RCN MTB Flotilla under Lieutenant-Commander A.G. Law, RCNVR, manning 20-metre "Short" boats armed with a two-pounder (40 mm) gun and 18-inch torpedoes, and the 65th RCN MTB Flotilla under Lieutenant-

The strain still evident on his face, Commander Harry DeWolf, captain of *Haida*, with Commander-in-Chief Plymouth, discussing the action of earlier that morning (29 April 1944) in which *Athabaskan* was lost.

Commander J.R.H. Kirkpatrick, RCNVR, manning the larger and more heavily-armed Fairmile D Type "Dog Boat" craft worked up at Holyhead throughout April and May. Law was horrified when the 29th Flotilla's torpedo tubes were removed and replaced with small depth charges. "Mere words," he later commented, "cannot explain the effect on the Flotilla's morale: the bottom dropped out of everything, and our faces were long as we watched our main armament and striking power being taken away."[12] Law lobbied hard to get the torpedoes back but it would take two months before they returned.

In late May, two of the fleet destroyers acquired from the RN after the Quadrant discussions of the previous September, HMCS *Algonquin* and HMCS *Sioux*, arrived in Portsmouth. Although given Tribal names, the newcomers were from the more modern "V" class and, although somewhat smaller and less heavily armed (only four 4.7-inch guns as opposed to six 4.7-inch and two four-inch guns in the Tribals), they were sturdy ships with longer range. After commissioning and work ups both destroyers had been sent to Scapa Flow in April where they served as screening vessels in two carrier air strikes against the *Tirpitz*. They acquitted themselves well but the ships' companies were happy to be ordered south to provide shore bombardment for the Normandy landing. They did not have long to wait. At 1500 hours on 5 June 1944, Lieutenant-Commander D.W. Piers, RCN, *Algonquin's* commanding officer, assembled his officers and men on the destroyer's quarter-deck to inform them that the invasion would take place on the following day and that *Algonquin* had "been chosen to be in the spearhead." As Leading Seaman K. Garrett remembered,

> Everyone there gave a low moan about being in the spearhead of the invasion, but Debbie [Piers] had more to say, which stunned everyone there. He mentioned that also we had been chosen to be the point on the end of the spear. I said to my fellow shipmates, "A spear sometimes gets blunted." Then the Captain had more to say. He said, "If our ship gets hit near the shore, we will run the ship right upon the shore and keep firing our guns, until the last shell is gone."
>
> I was scared no longer. With a spirit like this, we couldn't lose. I felt right then and there, "We will succeed."[13]

Three hours later, HMCS *Algonquin* sailed for France.

The armada assembled for Operation Neptune consisted of 6,900 vessels, ranging from battleships to merchant ships, including 63 Canadian warships, and no fewer than 4,100 landing ships or craft, of which 46 were manned by the RCN. The first Canadian sailors to see action in the operation were the 16 Bangor-class minesweepers, which had the crucial task of clearing corridors through the German defensive mine belt so that landing craft could reach the beaches. The 31st Flotilla commenced its work in the early evening of 5 June, sweeping and marking a channel to the American landing site dubbed "Omaha Beach," and completed it by dawn on 6 June. As the sweepers turned out to sea, they could see hundreds of landing craft approaching the coast under the cover of a heavy shore bombardment carried out by battleships, cruisers, and destroyers to neutralize the German shore defences.

Algonquin and *Sioux* participated in this bombardment. Their initial task was to fire at shore batteries located on the eastern side of Juno Beach and both destroyers commenced shooting shortly after 0700. *Sioux* engaged a shore battery for 40 minutes before ceasing fire as the first landing craft approached the beach. Lieutenant L.B. Jenson, RCN, the executive officer of *Algonquin*, recalled that the destroyer hoisted its White Ensign before opening fire at a shore battery near the village of Saint-Aubin-sur-Mer. Forty-five minutes later, when *Algonquin* checked fire, the "sea was getting a little choppy and the hundreds of landing craft going in looked rather uncomfortable."

"So far," Jenson remembered,

> *no shells or bombs had come our way and we had the privilege of a grandstand view of British and Canadian forces in this incomparable assault. Fires were burning on shore and some landing craft also appeared to be on fire, while soldiers were clambering out of other landing craft and moving ashore without noticeable opposition.*[14]

The two destroyers stood off the coast until the assault troops had secured the beaches, after which they provided fire support on call from forward observation officers who landed with the infantry. At 1051 *Algonquin* destroyed two German self-propelled guns with its third salvo.

The Canadian LCI flotillas and the two LCA (Landing Craft, Assault) flotillas carried by *Prince David* and *Prince Henry* had a less happy time. The 529th Flotilla from *Prince David* transported troops of the 3rd Canadian Infantry Division into Juno Beach, but a 10-minute delay in landing meant that a rising tide covered many of the beach obstacles and seven of the eight LCAs in this flotilla were lost either from mines or German fire. The 528th Flotilla operating from *Prince Henry* suffered not only from shore fire but also explosive charges attached to obstacles and lost one LCA when the craft hit a mine. The 260th LCI Flotilla encountered similar perils when its seven craft landed later in the morning, as well as a German aircraft, which dive-bombed *LSI 285* without effect. All of this flotilla's craft managed to get off the beach, but the 262nd LCI Flotilla was forced to leave five of its 12 craft on the beach after they suffered mine damage. The 10 LCIs of the 264th Flotilla transported British troops to Gold Beach and, as the captain of each craft was anxious to win the £10 in the flotilla pool for the LCI that touched on shore first, they "jammed" their craft "full-ahead" with the result that some hit the beach at such speed that they could not get off again.[15] Otherwise this flotilla had a rather quiet time.

Neptune was a complete success and when darkness came on 6 June 1944 just over 150,000 Allied troops were in France — at a cost of 9,000 casualties, of which 1,081 were from the Canadian Army and Navy. Having got the initial wave ashore, the Allied navies' task was to guard their vulnerable seaborne lines of communication. Toward this end, the 29th MTB Flotilla was the first Canadian naval unit to see action. On the night of 6 June, Lieutenant-Commander Law and four of his boats engaged German fast attack craft attempting to lay mines on the eastern flank of the beachhead. A swift and hard-fought little action followed in which the 29th Flotilla, along with British MTBs, sank one of the German craft and damaged others. On the following two nights, Law's boats encountered and engaged

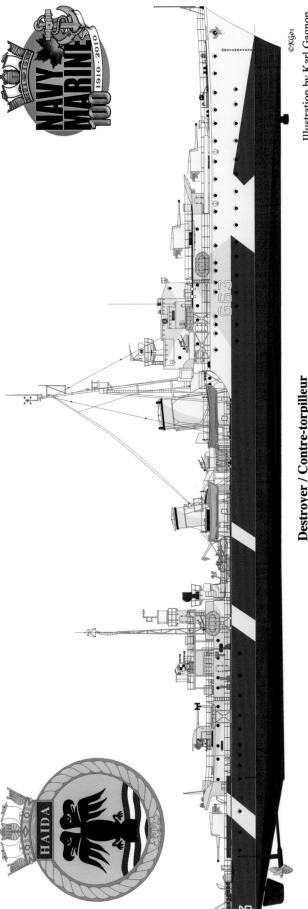

©Kg01

Illustration by Karl Gagnon

Destroyer / Contre-torpilleur
Classe TRIBAL Class

0 m   5 m   10 m

H.M.C.S. HAIDA
1944

Launched 25 August 1942. Built by Vickers-Armstrongs Ltd, Newcastle-on-Tyne.

30 August 1943 - 11 October 1963

Dimensions: 114,9 m x 11,4 m x 3,4 m
Displacement: 1,927 tons   Speed: 36 knots   Crew: 259
Armament: 3 x II - 120 mm; 1 x II - 102 mm; 1 x IV - 2 pound;
6 x II - 20mm; 1 x IV - 533 mm TT; depth charges.

N.C.S.M. HAIDA
1944

Lancé le 25 août 1942. Construit par Vickers-Armstrongs Ltd, Newcastle-on-Tyne.

30 août 1943 - 11 octobre 1963

Dimensions: 114,9 m x 11,4 m x 3,4 m   Équipage: 259
Déplacement: 1 927 tonnes Vitesse: 36 noeuds
Armement: 3 x II - 120 mm; 1 x II - 102 mm; 1 x IV - 2 livres;
6 x II - 20mm; 1 x IV - TLT de 533 mm; grenades sous-marines.

several small German destroyers prowling around the beachhead. Although seriously over-matched and cursing the fact that their torpedoes had been removed, the Canadian MTBs engaged the enemy vessels with their two-pounder guns and managed to scare them off before they did any serious harm.

The *Kriegsmarine*, however, was just getting started. On the night of 8–9 June, a powerful German surface force consisting of three destroyers (*Zh-1, Z-24, Z-32*) and a torpedo boat (*T-24*) attempted to attack shipping in the western side of the beachhead. Fortunately, the German movement was betrayed by signals intelligence, which permitted the 10th Destroyer Flotilla of eight vessels, including the *Haida* and *Huron*, to make an interception. Contact was made in the early hours of 9 June and a ferocious night-time engagement with guns and torpedoes ensued. Dodging a German torpedo attack, *Haida, Huron*, and their British consorts opened fire with their main armament, inflicting serious damage on the enemy. In just over an hour, *ZH-1* was sunk and the three surviving German warships broke off contact and made for Brest, unwittingly steaming through a minefield, which hampered pursuit. Regaining contact with *Z-32, Haida* and *Huron* fired at the hapless destroyer, which had become separated from the other two enemy ships, with accurate radar-controlled gun fire until its captain deliberately ran it aground. This highly successful action, which saw the Canadian Tribals achieve the destruction of their third large German warship in two months, completely fulfilled NSHQ's hopes that RCN surface warships would garner positive publicity.

Throughout the summer of 1944, Canadian ships continued to watch the seaward flank, as the Allied armies gradually expanded their bridgehead. The two MTB flotillas saw the most consistent action. Lieutenant-Commander Kirkpatrick's 65th Flotilla arrived in Normandy on 11 June to operate on the western side of the beachhead, and for the next two weeks the flotilla's Fairmile "Dog boats" fought a number of actions against German coastal convoys, sinking several small escort vessels. Perhaps the high point came on the night of 3–4 July when Kirkpatrick took his command into the port of Saint-Malo and shot up two German patrol boats before withdrawing unscathed under heavy fire. Thereafter things settled down on the western flank and the 65th Flotilla enjoyed a relatively quiet summer until it was withdrawn to Britain in early September.

Matters were more hectic on the eastern side. The 29th Flotilla rejoiced when it was re-armed with torpedoes in mid-June as they now had an effective weapon against the German "Night Train" operations that saw enemy surface ships, including destroyers, torpedo boats, E-boats, and small minesweepers attempting to break into the beachhead area. During the latter part of June and well into July, the 29th Flotilla fought several nighttime actions including a particularly dangerous one against nine German E-boats attempting to sortie from Le Havre on the night of 4–5 July that encountered three of Law's MTBs off Cap D'Antifer. As he remembered:

> *Simpson, the radar operator, soon picked up echoes at 2,000 yards dead ahead, and*
> *Footsie signalled the frigate that we had picked up the enemy. Sure enough, nine*
> *E-Boats, hugging the coast, were moving toward our position, and I grimly imagined*
> *their surprise when they found the opposition so well established in their hideaway.*

459 moved off, steadily increasing speed, followed closely astern by Bobby and Bish. The enemy were now 1,500 yards from us, and both sides were closing dead ahead. It was exactly at midnight when our three boats opened fire at 1,400 yards, and at 1,200 yards all guns were blazing away at the leading E-Boat. We then switched targets to the third E-Boat in line, and under our concentrated volley it burst into flames and was left in a sinking condition. His comrades quickly made smoke, obscuring our view, but we could still see the glow of the fire through the haze, and I very much doubt if the craft could have made Le Havre.[16]

Darkness hours were often livened by attacks from the *Luftwaffe*, which rarely managed to hit anything but interfered with everyone's sleep. Some of these aircraft, however, dropped "Oyster" pressure mines, which were virtually unsweepable. HMCS *Algonquin*, which, along with *Sioux*, had continued to engage shore targets at the request of the army in the weeks following D-Day, had a close call on 24 June when it came to anchor off the beachhead. Lieutenant L.B. Jenson, RCN, officer of the watch, spotted a floating mine and was granted permission to sink it with gunfire. As he recalled:

I decided to do it personally, using my Sten gun. Looking back, we were a bit too close and this was an unusually stupid thing to do. I did not stop to reflect that mines can blow up and shower you with shrapnel. God was with me. The mine with all its horns intact quietly sank.

[The British destroyer, HMS] Swift snootily signalled us, "While you play around, may I anchor in your billet and you anchor in mine?" I signalled, "Yes, please," and she steamed ahead to what had been our spot. I watched in my binoculars as she let go her anchor and was immediately enveloped in a cloud of white spray. There was a second explosion, her back was broken and she started to sink.[17]

Fifty-seven British sailors died in this incident, but that did not stop the hard-bitten "Algonquins" from sending boats over to the wreck to salvage useful items of equipment, including a quantity of rum stored in the petty officers' mess. Shortly thereafter, their bombardment tasks completed, the two "V"-class destroyers withdrew to Britain.

The cross-Channel invasion having been accomplished, the RCN's participation in combined operations began to wind down. The three LCI flotillas were paid off in July just as Beach Commando W landed in Normandy where it remained for two months handling waterborne and vehicle traffic on Juno Beach before it too was paid off. *Prince David* and *Prince Henry*, with their attached LCA flotillas, left Normandy in late July and headed for the Mediterranean where they formed part of the Allied naval force assembled for Operation Dragoon, the invasion of southern France. This was successfully carried out on 16 August and the two ships were then employed in the eastern Mediterranean, ferrying troops and supplies to Allied forces operating in Yugoslavia and Greece until the end of the year.

The Canadian Tribals with the 10th Flotilla continued to be active in the Normandy area throughout the summer. On 27–28 June, *Huron* sank a heavily-armed German minesweeper

RCN infantry landing craft heading for the beaches, 6 June 1944.

and several patrol boats with gunfire before leaving for Canada for a refit. In the late summer *Iroquois* and *Haida* began to carry out offensive sweeps in the Bay of Biscay to clear out German coastal traffic. On the night of 5–6 August, the two destroyers engaged an enemy convoy of eight ships south of Saint-Nazaire, sinking two escorting minesweepers before starting to shell the remaining vessels. *Haida* had just started on this work when a round prematurely detonated in a gun of its "Y" turret, killing and wounding several members of the gun crew. Able Seaman M.R. Kerwin, though blinded and dazed by the explosion and wounded by splinters, went into the blazing turret and succeeded in dragging a gun crew member to safety, which brought him the award of a Conspicuous Gallantry Medal. This accident forced *Haida* to withdraw for repairs leaving *Iroquois* as Canada's representative in the Biscay.

In the early hours of 16 August, *Iroquois*, in company with the cruiser HMS *Mauritius* and the destroyer HMS *Ursa*, encountered a large convoy near the mouth of the Gironde River. The enemy escort, consisting of the old adversary, *T-24*, an aircraft tender, and several minesweepers, put up a stiff fight. After dodging torpedoes launched by *T-24*, *Iroquois* responded with a torpedo attack of its own, but Force 27 had to withdraw to seaward after coming under fire from heavy German coast batteries. It later returned, and *Ursa* and *Iroquois* between them sank or drove aground three minesweepers and two other vessels. The enigmatic *T-24* escaped but was later sunk by British and Canadian aircraft. The commanding officers of both *Mauritius* and *Ursa* had high praise for *Iroquois'* gunnery, the captain of *Ursa* reporting that the action reflected the greatest credit on its commanding officer, Commander James Hibbard, RCN. *Iroquois* remained with Force 27 until early September when it was

withdrawn, as by this time German naval forces in France had nearly ceased to exist, either sunk at sea or destroyed in port by air bombardment.

The 16 Canadian minesweepers continued with their undramatic but important work in the Channel. It was not until early 1945 that they were returned to escort duties, but the end of the war saw them return to minesweeping when an international effort was made to clear European waters of the deadly items. The Canadian Bangors only ceased this task in September 1945, but mine clearance continued for many years after the shooting had ended.

After the Allied armies broke out of Normandy in mid-August to liberate Paris and the Low Countries, Canadian naval units continued to protect their seaward flank. Throughout the autumn, the 29th and 65th MTB Flotillas, based in southeast England, interdicted E-boat raids and harassed German coastal traffic. For the Canadian MTBs, the high point of this period was the amphibious landing on Walcheren Island in the Scheldt Estuary, which was carried out in early November. Shortly thereafter Lieutenant-Commander Law's 29th Flotilla had the misfortune to run into the "Four Horsemen of the Apocalypse," a force of four German flak trawlers armed with deadly 88 mm guns that enjoyed legendary status in Coastal Forces. As Law recalled,

> *Although I had not come in contact with these uncouth gentlemen since 1943 when I had been working off the Dutch coast, I knew that these bullies were far from gentle.... We spent the remainder of the night playing a game with each other which consisted mainly of batting shells back and forth. No one was getting hurt, but it was a frighteningly dangerous game. As soon as we had manoeuvred into a possible torpedo position and were ready to pull the lever, what would happen? The Four Horsemen would alter course toward us, and just to keep the game lively they would slam out a few more 88 mms..... The game went on; and at the end of the period there was still no score.*[18]

In December, the 29th Flotilla was glad when it was transferred to the liberated port of Ostend as it meant less transit time in the Channel. On Valentine's Day 1945, however, Law's command met an untimely end when an accident in the crowded harbour led to the destruction by fire of 12 MTBs and the deaths of 64 officers and sailors, including 29 Canadians. As only four, very worn, Canadian MTBs survived the disaster, it was decided to disband the 29th Flotilla. It was replaced at Ostend by the 65th Flotilla, which served there until the end of the war.

The two Canadian "V"-class destroyers, meanwhile, returned to northern waters. To reduce the German naval threat to the Murmansk convoys, a series of operations were undertaken to sink the remaining German capital ships based in Norway. *Algonquin* and *Sioux* joined a Home Fleet destroyer flotilla based at unlovable Scapa Flow and participated in Operation Mascot on 17 July, screening carriers that flew off aircraft in an unsuccessful attempt to sink the dreaded *Tirpitz*. Subsequent strikes on the German battleship proved

Department of National Defence PMR92-554.

The safe return to Scapa Flow of the Canadian-operated aircraft carrier HMS *Nabob*, after being torpedoed by a U-boat on 22 August 1944, was an amazing feat of seamanship.

no more profitable, and it remained a threat until November when Royal Air Force (RAF) Lancaster bombers destroyed it with 5,450 kilogram "Tallboy" bombs.

Before that, in August, *Algonquin* and *Sioux* were joined by HMS *Nabob*, the Canadian-manned escort carrier. Carrying 13 Grumman Avenger torpedo-bombers and eight Wildcat fighters, *Nabob* saw its first action in Operation Offspring, an aerial minelaying operation in Norwegian coastal waters on 9 August and performed well. Then came Operation Goodwood, a planned air attack on the *Tirpitz* carried out by the fleet carriers, HM Ships *Formidable*, *Furious*, and *Indefatigable*, combined with a minelaying strike by *Nabob* and another escort carrier in the waters of the Altenfjord, the German battleship's lair. Bad weather hampered Goodwood and most of the air strikes and minelaying attacks were cancelled. Unfortunately for *Nabob*, late in the afternoon of 22 August it was hit by torpedo fired by a U-boat that blasted a hole that measured 10 by 15 metres in its starboard side. As his ship began to settle by the stern, the commanding officer, Captain H.N. Lay, RCN, commenced damage control efforts and evacuated all non-essential personnel to waiting destroyers, including *Algonquin*. Within four hours, however, the flooding was brought under control and *Nabob* was able to raise steam and get under way, although down by the stern. Over the next five days, the wounded carrier slowly limped the 1,600 kilometres to safety at Scapa, even flying two Avengers off its sloping flight deck to harass a U-boat that was trailing it. For *Nabob*'s largely Canadian crew it was an impressive piece of seamanship, but the vessel's fighting days were over — its company was paid off and the carrier was cannibalized for spare parts.

In September and October, *Algonquin* and *Sioux* resumed escort duty on the Murmansk Run. It was, as one officer recalled, a return to the "most hazardous and horrible place for naval operations" to take place, which had to be carried out in the face of not only pack ice, ferocious storms, "perpetual night in winter, perpetual day in summer," but also German submarines and aircraft.[19] In November, *Algonquin* got some relief from this onerous duty when it participated in Operation Counterblast, an attempt to interrupt enemy coastal traffic, transporting vital iron ore from Norway to Germany. In company with British cruisers and destroyers, *Algonquin* intercepted a large convoy off Stavanger on 12 November and, as its commanding officer, Lieutenant-Commander D.W. Piers, RCN, reported:

> *Many targets were plainly visible and quickly engaged. ALGONQUIN opened fire on an escort vessel at an initial range of 5400 [yards or 4937 metres] at 2314 and obtained a hit with the first salvo. This target was also being engaged by other ships ahead; it burst into flames within a minute. Fire was shifted at 2317 to a merchant ship at an initial range of 8000 yards [7315 metres]. Using No. 2 gun (B) for starshell illumination and the remainder of the armament firing S.A.P [Semi-Armour-Piercing round] this second target was also reduced to flames by the first few salvoes.[20]*

The result of Counterblast was that two of four German merchant ships and five of the six escorts were sunk. Unfortunately, however, similar operations carried out over the winter garnered minimal results.

When *Algonquin* left for refit in Canada in January 1945, *Sioux* continued serving on with the Murmansk Run. If anything, things got worse when the *Luftwaffe* deployed a large force of torpedo bombers to northern Norway — air attacks now became frequent and, inevitably, losses became heavier. On 10 February, *Sioux* was with Convoy JW-64 outward bound to Murmansk when it came under heavy air attack. As its commanding officer, Lieutenant-Commander E. Boak, RCN, reported, the *Luftwaffe* pressed its attacks home:

> *a JU 188 appeared from a bearing of Green 90 …, about 50 feet off the water and 3000 yards [2743 metres] away, flying directly towards the ship. At about 1500 yards [1371 metres] the plane dropped a torpedo and banked away to starboard, flying-up between HMCS SIOUX and HMS LARK…. [My] Ship went "Full ahead together, hard-a-port," and steadied up on a course 060, Starboard [20 mm] Oerlikons opened up on the plane just before the torpedo was dropped and followed him out of range, and also one round from "B" gun was fired at him but was short. Enemy's port engine was seen to be smoking heavily before he disappeared into a snow flurry.[21]*

The return convoy, RA-64, encountered terrible weather. One of *Sioux*'s officers recalled that "abused engines broke down, cargoes shifted, decks split, steering gear went wonky, ice-chipped propellers thrashed," while the seas "continued at awful heights, spindrift streaming from boiling crests."[22] The weather did not stop the Germans: not only was RA-64 attacked by torpedo bombers but also by a large force of U-boats that managed to sink two of the escorts while losing one of their own. On 19 February, the *Luftwaffe* appeared overhead and, at one point:

> *One of the planes closed to torpedo [merchant ship] number 103. Fire was opened and aircraft released torpedo which eventually exploded at end of run between 9th and 10th columns [of merchant ships]. The plane went down the port side being heavily engaged with close range weapons. At the same time a plane coming in from the starboard quarter was also engaged and driven away.*[23]

Throughout these two convoys, *Sioux* was almost in constant action and the efforts of its commanding officer and ship's company were marked by the award of a Distinguished Service Order (DSO) to Lieutenant-Commander Boak. Shortly thereafter it departed for Canada for a well-deserved and needed refit.

Sioux was replaced by *Haida*, *Huron*, and *Iroquois*, returning from their own refits, as well as the second Canadian-manned escort carrier, HMS *Puncher*. This ship enjoyed better luck than *Nabob* and participated in four operations in February, March, and April against Norwegian targets, flying off its Wildcat fighters to provide air cover for shipping strikes and minelaying operations, before withdrawing for boiler cleaning. During these last few months of the war — although *Iroquois* participated in one coastal convoy attack, sinking a tanker — the major activity for the Tribals was the seemingly interminable Arctic convoys and perhaps no sailors in the RCN were happier when the surrender of Germany in May 1945 brought an end to the war in Europe and relieved them of this burdensome task.

One enemy remained. From 1943 onward, when it became clear that the Battle of the Atlantic and the war in Europe were moving toward a favourable conclusion, NSHQ had turned its attention to planning for the Pacific. The intent was to demonstrate that the RCN was more than an ASW escort force and affirm the objective NSHQ had doggedly pursued since 1939 — to make a major contribution in terms of surface ships to act as the foundation for the balanced blue water post-war fleet. The Navy's ambitious plans were thwarted only in part by Mackenzie King, who not only kept a careful eye on costs but was ever suspicious of getting Canada entangled in British colonial problems. After much discussion and a considerable amount of political manoeuvring between the government, NSHQ and the RN, it was ultimately agreed that the RCN would man two light fleet carriers with four Canadian air squadrons on board, two light cruisers, four Tribal-class destroyers, two "V"-class destroyers, eight new Crescent-class destroyers, the anti-aircraft ship *Prince Robert*, and no less than 44 anti-submarine warfare (ASW) vessels. In terms of personnel, this

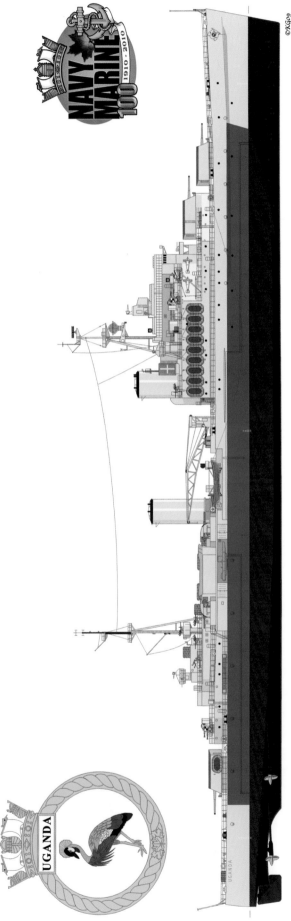

Illustration by Karl Gagnon

Cruiser / Croiseur
Classe UGANDA Class

0   5   10 m

H.M.C.S. UGANDA
1945
(ex H.M.S. UGANDA)
Launched 07 August 1941. Built by Vickers-Armstrong Ltd., Newcastle-on-Tyne.

21 October 1944 - 13 June 1956

Dimensions: 169.4 m x 19.2 m x 5 m
Displacement: 8,800 tons   Speed: 30 knots   Crew: 730
Armament: 3 x III - 152 mm; 4 x II - 102 mm; 3 x IV - 2-pound;
2 x IV - 40 mm; 4 x II - 20mm; 8 x I - 20 mm; 2 x III - 533 mm TT.

N.C.S.M. UGANDA
1945
(ex H.M.S. UGANDA)
Lancé le 07 août 1941. Construit par Vickers-Armstrong Ltd., Newcastle-on-Tyne.

21 octobre 1944 - 13 juin 1956

Dimensions: 169,4 m x 19,2 m x 5 m
Déplacement: 8 800 tonnes   Vitesse: 30 noeuds   Équipage: 730
Armement: 3 x III - 152 mm; 4 x II - 102 mm; 3 x IV - 2-livres;
2 x IV - 40 mm; 4 x II - 20mm; 8 x I - 20 mm; 2 x III - TLT de 533 mm.

commitment would total about 37,000 officers and seamen, serving both afloat and ashore — nearly half the RCN's strength in late 1944.

The RCN took greatest pride in the two light cruisers provided to Canada by Britain as a free gift. Armed with nine six-inch guns, eight four-inch high angle guns and many smaller 20 and 40 mm guns, these ships were intended to bolster the anti-aircraft defences of the British Pacific Fleet in which they would serve. HMCS *Uganda*, the first cruiser to enter service, was commissioned in Charleston, South Carolina, on Trafalgar Day (21 October) 1944. An impressive array of American, British, and Canadian dignitaries and senior officers attended the ceremony and the British ambassador reported that Canadian naval officers were "all labouring happily under a feeling of excitement and anticipation caused by the acquisition of what they called in their official leaflet 'the first Canadian cruiser….' It was as though," he continued, "the Canadian Navy was reaching manhood and that, through its Navy, Canada herself was stepping forward and upward."[24] In early February 1945, following work ups, *Uganda* sailed for the Pacific, while the second cruiser, HMCS *Ontario*, commissioned in April and immediately sailed to join it.

In May *Uganda* participated in the shore bombardment of the Sakashima Islands, part of the invasion of Okinawa, but its normal role with the British Pacific Fleet was to act as an anti-aircraft guard, a duty it performed in June and July during a number of airstrikes on the Japanese home islands. In July, however, *Uganda*'s war and NSHQ's plans for a major Pacific force came to a somewhat ignominious end, because of the federal government's policy that only volunteers would serve in the Pacific and that all service personnel who volunteered would receive 30 days clear leave in Canada before being sent to that theatre. This meant that, if *Uganda*'s ship's company did not volunteer *en masse*, the ship would have to return to Canada to re-commission with an all-volunteer crew. On 28 July 1945 the vote was held in *Uganda* and 80 percent of its officers and seamen opted not to volunteer. This being the case, *Uganda* departed for Esquimalt and arrived there shortly before the dropping of atomic bombs on Hiroshima and Nagasaki brought an end to the Pacific conflict. Consequently, no Canadian warship was present in Tokyo Bay when representatives of the Japanese government unconditionally surrendered to the allied powers on board the American battleship USS *Missouri*.

The Canadian Navy's role in surface warfare during the Second World War has been overshadowed by its major contribution to victory in the Battle of the Atlantic. During the long years of that seemingly interminable struggle, however, the RCN achieved an outstanding record of success in conventional naval operations in Europe and the Pacific, operations that would prove a very useful foundation for the post-war service.

Notes

1. DHH, NHS 1650, Ship files, HMCS *Algonquin* Ship file.
2. C.A. Law, *White Plumes Astern* (Halifax: Nimbus Publishing Ltd., 1989), 11.
3. Quoted in W.A.B. Douglas, Roger Sarty, Michael Whitby, *A Blue Water Navy* (St. Catharines, ON: Vanwell Publishing, 2007), 111.
4. LAC, RG 24, Vol. 6797, Captain H.G. De Wolfe, "Employment of Tribal Destroyers," 7 December 1942.

5. United Kingdom National Archives [UKNA], ADM 199/1406, Report of Proceedings, HMCS *Athabaskan*, 30 August 1943.

6. DHH, BIOG file, Address by Rear-Admiral P.D. Budge, 19 September 1981.

7. R.D. Butcher, *I Remember Haida* (Hantsport, NS: Lancelot Press, 1985), 36–37.

8. UKNA, ADM 205/31, Minutes of Meeting, Quebec, 11 August 1943.

9. P.R. Burrows, "Prisoners of War," *Salty Dips, Vol. 3* (Ottawa: Naval Officers' Association of Canada, 1988), 171.

10. Len Burrow and Emile Beaudoin, *Unlucky Lady: The Life and Death of HMCS Athabaskan* (Toronto: McClelland & Stewart, 1982), 125.

11. DHH, Commander, Fleet Minesweeping Office, Devonport, to Captain, Minesweeping Command, 22 April 1944.

12. Law, *White Plumes Astern*, 37.

13. Quoted in L.B. Jenson, *Tin Hats, Oilskins and Seaboots* (Toronto: Robin Brass Studio, 2000), 222.

14. Jenson, 226.

15. J.M. Ruttan, "Race to Shore," *Salty Dips, Vol. 1* (Ottawa, 1985), 193.

16. Law, 104.

17. Jenson, 233.

18. Law, 148.

19. Jenson, 213.

20. LAC, RG 24, DDE 224, Report of Proceedings, HMCS *Algonquin*, 13 November 1944.

21. LAC, RG 24, DDE 225, Narrative of Air Attack, HMCS *Sioux*, 10 February 1945.

22. Hal Lawrence, *A Bloody War* (Toronto: Macmillan of Canada, 1979), 168–69.

23. LAC, RG 24, DDE 225, Report of Air Attack, HMCS *Sioux*, 20 February 1945.

24. UKNA, ADM 1/18371, Sir Gerald Campbell to Director of Operations, 30 October 1944.

Maritime Research and Development in the Second World War

Harold Merklinger

Once hostilities commenced, scarcely any aspect of warfare escaped the attention of NRC. Naval research undertakings included seasickness (with minor success), training methods, radio communications, radio direction finding, and diffused lighting to reduce ship visibility at night. One of the more offbeat projects, codenamed "Habbakuk," involved the use of a refrigerated ice-sawdust mixture (called Pykrete) to build a mid-Atlantic aircraft landing platform.

An early naval problem was the German magnetically-triggered mine. NRC approached Dalhousie University to investigate the issue on a part-time basis. The resulting effort was the beginning of a small unit that became the Naval Research Establishment (NRE) under direct navy control in January 1944, and "degaussing ranges" were established at several locations to systematically measure and de-magnetize ships of their natural magnetic fields. When German submarines began using acoustic homing torpedoes in September 1943, NRE promptly developed an effective countermeasure — the CAAT towed noisemaker.

NRC's greatest effort was the development of radar, which had many applications including ASW. In September 1939, NRC began work on a simple surveillance radar for Halifax harbour, and in the spring of 1941 the "Night Watchman" system was in place — the first operational radar in North America. NRC's first shipboard radar system was the anti-submarine SW-1C 1.5-metre radar. Its long wavelength limited its effectiveness against submarines, but by 1944 NRC had developed the successful Type 268 three centimetre radar for use against smaller targets. Canadian radar expertise was manifest in another way in the war at sea: through an unusual arrangement with NRC, most of the "RN" officers involved in radar training and serving as radar officers in major British warships were Canadians. NRC also worked on ASW weapons, developing a system for the gyro-stabilization of the Hedgehog ASW mortar, permitting its operation in rough weather.

Although it had been widely expected that sonar would solve the anti-submarine problem, it proved nearly worthless in Canadian waters. The bathythermograph, which measures temperature changes with depth, now revealed the problem — the complex temperature-salinity structure in the surface layers where submarines were operating.

Tully and Hachey were seconded to conduct oceanographic research from HMC Ships *Ehkoli* and *Moncton*, leading to a better understanding of the tactical implications of ocean water conditions.

A number of naval challenges also benefitted from the adoption of an Operations Research discipline in Canada. "OR" had been developed in the United Kingdom initially as a mathematically based technique for analyzing and optimizing air defence but it was quickly applied to other warfare areas. A team of six mathematicians was established at NSHQ headed by Dr. J.H.L. Johnstone and assisted by a smaller Halifax-based group at NRE, with most of their work focused on ASW tactics and statistics.

While the return to peace saw the reduction of defence staffing — NRE was down to just seven people by 1946 — the wartime experience left Canadians with a confidence that they could address technology problems as well as anyone else. It bequeathed a legacy of technological success and national competence in nuclear physics, electronics, oceanography, naval engineering, aviation science, and medicine that would find its expression in post-war development.

An early form of the CAAT noisemaker, a simple but effective acoustic torpedo decoy.

Defence Research and Development Canada Atlantic

The U.K. Type 271 radar (looking like a smokestack above the bridge) and the Hedgehog ASW spigot mortar (below the bridge wing) as mounted on the corvette *Sackville*.

H. Merklinger.

CHAPTER 5

Fighting the U-Boats, 1939–45

Marc Milner

The reputation of the RCN in this war depends
on the success or failure of the NEF ...
— COMMODORE L.W. MURRAY, RCN,
FLAG OFFICER, NEWFOUNDLAND
FORCE, OCTOBER 1941

The war against the U-boats from 1939 to 1945 was the formative experience for the Royal Canadian Navy in the twentieth century. Fought largely by reservists in small ships built in Canada and operating from Canadian bases, the defence of North Atlantic trade against the submarine menace defined a naval role for Canada within a much larger alliance. After 1945 the RCN became the best anti-submarine warfare (A/S or ASW as it is now known) navy in the world as part of the North Atlantic Treaty Organization (NATO). But it was not an easy or direct path.

In 1939 the RCN expected submarines to be a manageable problem. As Chief of the Naval Staff, Commodore Percy Nelles observed in 1937, "If international law is complied with, Submarine attack should not prove serious." However, should submariners again resort to unrestricted attacks, Nelles felt that "the means of combating the Submarines are considered to have so advanced that by employing a system of convoy and utilizing Air Forces, losses to Submarines would be very great and might compel the enemy to give up this form of attack."

Convoys and airpower had reduced the effectiveness of the submarine in 1917–18, but the optimism of naval officers about the submarine problem was fired by the perfection

John Horton, *Halifax — The Spring Board*, in which the flurry of dockyard activity during the Second World War is clearly evident.

of "asdic" (now called sonar). This active "pinging" acoustic locating device allowed warships to attack submerged targets effectively. It had never been used extensively under operational conditions, but interwar trials and training suggested that few subs — expected to operate inshore and submerged — would now escape the deadly combination of asdic and depth charges.

When the liner SS *Athenia* was sunk by *U-30* on 3 September 1939, the day the war began, it was assumed that the Germans had resumed an unrestricted submarine campaign against Allied shipping. Convoys were instituted immediately, and the first to sail from Halifax, HX-1, left with an escort of HMC Ships *Saguenay* and *St. Laurent* on 16 September. The destroyers protected the convoy from submarines inshore. Once HX-1 was well out to sea, larger vessels arrived to shield it from surface raiders — a threat which lingered well into 1941. The primary function of the convoy system was safe and timely arrival of the ships, and the object of its passage was avoidance of the enemy. At times special intelligence (called Ultra), provided by breaking the German operational codes for the North Atlantic, permitted highly effective routing. But the subs could not always be avoided and the convoy system provided the focal point for much of the RCN's war with the U-boats.

There was little in the first year of the war to suggest that submarines were a major issue. When the Canadian Navy ordered its initial wartime shipbuilding program in early 1940, its main vessel — the corvette — was completed as a jack-of-all-trades, but would prove to be master of none. This included complete minesweeping equipment, a single magnetic compass and the most basic of asdic, the type 123A. In 1940 none of this seemed to matter.

Under operational conditions submarines proved remarkably difficult to locate and destroy, but what really confounded the Allies was the adoption of new tactics by Germany's U-boats. In the late summer of 1940 the U-boats, operating from new bases in France, began to employ "pack attacks" on Allied convoys on the high seas. The deployment of U-boats into a long patrol line solved the problem of locating convoys in the vastness of the ocean, while the U-boats themselves attacked the convoy on the surface at night like motor torpedo boats — submerging only to escape Allied forces. What followed was the U-boats' first "Happy Time," when they roamed the Atlantic with impunity, overwhelming the tiny escorts of transatlantic convoys and creating a generation of U-boat aces.

The RCN participated modestly in this early phase. The bulk of the navy's destroyers were already overseas guarding Britain against invasion. These destroyers soon joined escort forces for convoys in the Western Approaches. It was during these operations that HMCS *Ottawa* shared in the destruction of the Italian submarine *Faa' di Bruno* on 6 November — the first time the RCN destroyed an enemy at sea.

The ex-USN "four-stackers" were not the best ASW platforms, but they were good enough for the critical years of 1940–41. Here *St. Croix* returns to Halifax after a harsh winter crossing.

What ultimately drew the whole RCN into the war against the U-boats was the extension of pack attacks westward. By the spring of 1941 the British had pushed A/S escort of transatlantic convoys to south of Iceland, leaving a gap between there and the limits of RCN escorts on the Grand Banks. In May 1941 the British asked them to fill that gap in transatlantic A/S escort of convoys. As a result, the Newfoundland Escort Force (NEF) was born and with it the commencement of the RCN's war on U-boats.

The burden of this new role fell on the RCN's corvettes, those jacks-of-all-trades built for local work. In the spring of 1941 their great value lay in seakeeping and operational range, thereby allowing the convoy system to be completed. The keys to effective trade defence were evasive routing based on good intelligence — and the British battle fleet, which sank *Bismarck* in May. The close escort only fought if the system failed. So in 1941 using newly commissioned and ill-equipped Canadian corvettes with poorly trained crews in the mid-ocean was a fair risk.

Besides, there were some in the RCN who thought the corvette was an excellent ASW vessel, especially the Senior Officer, Canadian Corvettes, Lieutenant-Commander James Douglas "Chummy" Prentice, RCNR. A Canadian who had retired from the RN in 1934, Prentice thought that the nimble and highly manoeuvrable corvette was more than a match for the U-boat, and he taught their crews to launch "quick attacks." These called for a steady 12-knot speed during both the search and the final depth charge attack. This allowed contact to be maintained until the last possible moment, and eliminated the sudden burst of speed in the final attack run that would alert the U-boat. Enthusiasm for attacking and sinking U-boats were the hallmarks of Prentice's training schemes throughout the war, and it may account for the success of Canadian corvettes in destroying U-boats.

However, what was wanted from 1941 to 1943 was less the ability to sink U-boats than skill at defending convoys, and equipment shortages made this task especially difficult. Good convoy defence required good tactical intelligence, excellent leadership and teamwork, and effective communications. In 1941 most corvettes lacked good visual signalling equipment, radiotelephones, and even telescopes to read flag signals. Escort groups were often *ad hoc*, leadership was inconsistent, and group training non-existent — because no permanent group training establishment existed.

These problems were manifest in all the operations of the NEF, especially in the battle for SC-42 in September 1941. The slow eastbound convoy was escorted by the destroyer HMCS *Skeena* and three corvettes, with support from now-Commander Prentice's training group, *Chambly* and *Moose Jaw*. During the initial confused night action of 8–9 September, when seven ships were lost, the escort caught only glimpses of the attackers. When *Kenogami* fired its four-inch gun at a U-boat, the blast left everyone temporarily night-blind and the sub escaped. Meanwhile, *Skeena* pursued a U-boat inside the convoy just as the convoy started an emergency turn. While *Skeena* swerved to avoid collisions, the U-boat raced by it on an opposite course drawing fire from every gun within range. Both *Skeena* and the U-boat escaped unharmed.

Canadian fortunes were redeemed the next night when Prentice's *Chambly* blew *U-501* to the surface right in front of *Moose Jaw*. When *Moose Jaw* ran alongside the submarine, the U-boat's captain blithely stepped from his conning tower to the corvette's fo'c'sle. Then

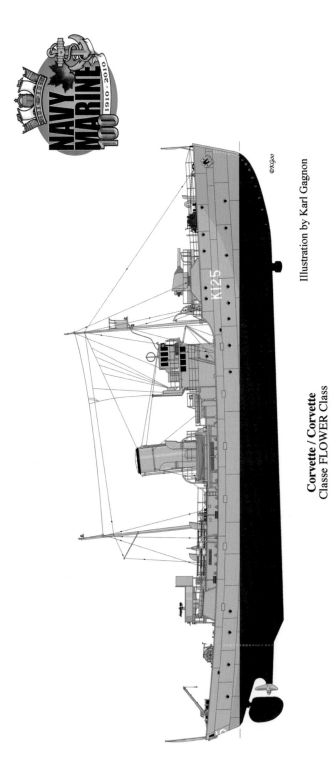

©XGoo

Illustration by Karl Gagnon

Corvette / Corvette
Classe FLOWER Class

0 m   5 m   10 m

H.M.C.S. KÉNOGAMI
1941

Launched 05 September 1940. Built by Port Arthur Shipbuilding Co. Ltd., Thunder Bay.

29 June 1941 - 09 July 1945

Dimensions: 62.5 m x 10.1 m x 3.5 m
Displacement: 950 tons   Speed: 16 knots   Crew: 85
Armament: 1 x I - 102 mm; 2 x II - 7.62 mm machine-guns; depth charges.

N.C.S.M. KÉNOGAMI
1941

Lancé le 05 septembre 1940. Construit par Port Arthur Shipbuilding Co. Ldt., Thunder Bay.

29 juin 1941 - 09 juillet 1945

Dimensions: 62,5 m x 10,1 m x 3,5 m
Déplacement: 950 tonnes   Vitesse: 16 noeuds   Équipage: 85
Armement: 1 x I - 102 mm; 2 x II - mitrailleuses de 7.62 mm; grenades sous-marines.

U-501 got underway. *Moose Jaw* eventually rammed it, then used its guns to keep the Germans from manning their armament. Most of the crew was captured before the U-boat sank: *U-501* was the RCN's first confirmed U-boat kill, and its first single-handed destruction of an enemy warship.

In the end, 16 merchant ships were lost from SC-42. In reaction, the RCN increased the size of escort groups, and scrambled to acquire new equipment like radiotelephones and radar. But this all took time. Only 15 early model radars were fitted to Canadian corvettes before the end of the year, and communications remained a major impediment: in mid-October *Shediac* missed a flag signal ordering a change in convoy course and the next morning found itself alone at sea. Through the fall of 1941 NEF operations remained plagued by poor equipment, too few destroyers and escort group commanders, no training, and an operational cycle between Newfoundland and Iceland that was unbearable as winter set in. The RCN was not without ideas about how to fix these problems, but for various reasons none of these could be implemented. What saved the struggling NEF was the sudden transformation of the war itself on 7 December 1941.

The entry of the United States into the war opened-up a vast new theatre for enemy operations, and by the end of January 1942 U-boats were probing the U.S. coast. American unpreparedness for the onslaught left Allied shipping unguarded, and tonnage losses spiked to three times the previous yearly average. Canada was spared much of this calamity because of the rapid introduction of convoys along the East Coast, such that the RCN even ran oil tanker convoys to South America through the carnage without loss.

But the expansion of the war in 1942 resulted in two defeats for the RCN that year. The root cause of both was the lingering problem of outdated equipment, but this was exacerbated by the over-commitment of the RCN to operations in support of it allies.

The first area to feel this inflexibility was the Gulf of St. Lawrence. The Canadian Navy had long anticipated U-boat attacks in the Gulf. The moment came in May, when *U-553* sank the steamers *Nicoya* and *Leto* between Gaspé and Anticosti Island. By the time *U-132* arrived in the St. Lawrence River in early July traffic was moving in convoys. But in the "slot" between Father Point and Cap Gaspé the river confined their movements to an easily intercepted route. *U-132* discovered this on the bright moonlit summer night of 6–7 July, not far from Rimouski, when it sank three ships from the Quebec-Sidney convoy QS-15. The escorting Bangor-class *Drummondville* caught *U-132* on the surface and tried to ram it; however, the U-boat crash-dived successfully. *Drummondville* then bracketed the sub with depth charges, inflicting serious damage, but no asdic contact was obtained.

The real damage was done by *U-517* and *U-165*. In the early hours of 27 August, in the northern gulf, *U-517* sank the American troopship *Chatham* (only 13 of the 562 passengers and crew were lost), while *U-165* attacked the main body of the convoy sinking one ship and leaving another foundering to be sunk by *U-517*.

U-517 then escaped destruction when it entered Forteau Bay and ran afoul of the corvette *Weyburn*, which was unable to get an asdic contact. Those same poor acoustic conditions saved *U-517* several days later after it attacked the little Quebec-Labrador convoy NL-6. *Weyburn* stumbled onto *U-517* as it took aim at the *Donald Stewart*, driving the sub underwater just as the torpedoes were fired. As the steamer sank, *Weyburn* looked in vain for the U-boat. Tony German, a junior officer on *Weyburn*'s bridge, later recalled, "It is a fact that *Weyburn* didn't get a sniff of him on asdic although we'd seen him twice, as large as life."[1]

In September, *U-517* and *U-165* moved into the St. Lawrence River and let the convoys come to them. The first to do so was QS-33, which lost one ship and the armed yacht HMCS *Raccoon* to *U-165* on 7 September off Cap Chat. The next day *U-517* sank three ships from the convoy off Cap Gaspé. German radio gloated over the victory, describing Canada's escort fleet as third rate. Four days later *U-517* destroyed the corvette *Charlottetown* in broad daylight off Cap Gaspé. Then on 15 September *U-517* attacked SQ-36 by using the eastward flow of the river and the forward motion of the convoy to drift silently down

A depth charge attack in progress.

Library and Archives Canada PA-133246

on its victims in the darkness, sinking two ships. *U-165*, informed of the convoy's progress, later hit three ships in a submerged daylight attack.

No naval counterattacks were effective against these two intrepid submariners. In many instances the escorts were right on top of U-boats and watched them submerge. And yet the searching asdics failed to penetrate the complex water layers. As one German U-boat captain later observed, once down into the Gulf through the 15-metre depth "layer" they were as "safe as in the bosom of Abraham."[2]

The Canadian Navy had to admit defeat and the government closed the Gulf to oceanic shipping in September 1942. Actual losses to Gulf shipping were negligible: for the QS-SQ series only 1.2 percent. Moreover, the decision was made late in the shipping season and other ports could handle the traffic. Nonetheless, both the navy and the government took intense public criticism for their inability to keep the nation's main artery open in the face of enemy attack.

Perhaps for that reason, problems in the navy's other major effort, in the mid-ocean, remained a secret for 40 years. The elimination of Iceland as an escort relay point in February (to free escorts for elsewhere) forced convoys to travel a predictable route across the Atlantic by the spring of 1942. The advantage for the RCN was that its four Newfoundland-based escort groups gained access to excellent facilities in Northern Ireland, including training. When the U-boat packs returned to the mid-ocean briefly in May, to see what was going on, they easily found Canadian escorted convoys but did not find them easy targets.

Nonetheless, serious equipment shortfalls remained, especially the lack of modern radar. Although the RCN was adapting to 1.5-metre sets known as the SW-1C, the British were already fitting the shorter wavelength (and hence more precise) 10-centimetre radar, the type 271. It could detect small targets on the sea at considerable ranges. The RCN was also short of destroyers and shipboard high frequency direction finding (HF/DF) radio-interception gear. Destroyers provided escorts with the speed needed to "put down" shadowing U-boats, forcing them to submerge and so drive off the enemy. Only the RCN's pre-war River class and the ex-American "four-stacker" St. Croix class had the range to operate in the mid-ocean. In theory, the British made up for the shortfall of destroyers in Canadian groups. But the RN destroyers assigned were often mechanically unreliable and in the fall of 1942 Canadian mid-ocean groups frequently sailed with only one destroyer.

The importance of destroyers was enhanced if their sweeps were directed by HF/DF. HF/DF could fix the direction and rough distance of a U-boat wireless transmission, and two sets could fix the sub's location by triangulation. If this was done early and well enough, destroyer sweeps might help the convoy escape entirely. At the least, HF/DF-directed sweeps reduced the number of U-boats the escort had to fight. In 1942 the only Canadian ship fitted with HF/DF was *Restigouche*.

The RCN also understood the need to reinforce threatened convoys, especially in the fog shrouded waters of the Grand Banks. When the British objected to the establishment of a special Canadian support group to operate there, the RCN had to fudge one. In April 1942 "Chummy" Prentice's training group was re-established and during the next four months he trained over a score of corvettes and supported nearly as many convoys east of Newfoundland. When his group dissolved in August due to increased operational commitments, the Americans and British soon established the "Western Support Force" to fill the need.

There was no question that RCN escorted convoys needed all the help they could get in late 1942, for they were still slaved to slow convoys. In the last half of 1942, the RCN escorted 14 out of 24 slow eastbound convoys, while the RN protected the fast HX series. The British escorted more than their share of the slow westbound convoys (17 out of 21), but westbound speeds were nominal: all ships steaming in ballast against prevailing winds were slow. This meant that Canadian escorted convoys — roughly 35 percent of the traffic — were more easily intercepted, more easily attacked, and spent longer in the danger area.

Attacks against convoys in the mid-ocean began in earnest in early June, when ONS-100, the hundredth slow convoy returning from the United Kingdom to Halifax, was attacked while escorted by C-1. The next slow convoy, ONS-102, escorted by the "American" group A-3 of two U.S. Coast Guard cutters, a USN destroyer, the Canadian destroyer *Restigouche*,

The RCN-RCAF combined operations room at St. John's.

and three RCN corvettes, reinforced by Prentice's training group of *Chambly* and *Orillia*, fared much better. In one day alone *Restigouche* used its HF/DF set to locate and drive off five U-boats as they made their sighting reports: two were damaged. Meanwhile, Prentice operated as distant cover and a "striking force" around ONS-102. In the end only one daring submariner slipped into the convoy, sinking one ship.

These battles confirmed the need for modern equipment, but there was little the RCN could do to acquire it before the year ended. Moreover, convoy battles in July and August were not without success for the RCN. In the battle around the fast UK to New York convoy ON-113 at the end of July two ships were lost, but *St. Croix* sank *U-90*. In the battle for ON-115 a week later, C-3 fought the "wolf pack" to a stalemate for most of the passage. In the absence of HF/DF, the group used its medium frequency direction finders (fitted for navigational purposes) to locate the MF homing beacons of shadowing U-boats. It was only partially successful, and it may simply have been the aggressive patrolling by *Saguenay* and *Skeena* during the transit that kept the pack at bay. Sweeps also led to the destruction of *U-558* on 31 July by *Skeena* and the corvette *Wetaskiwin*.

ON-115 eventually suffered losses in the Grand Banks fog: three ships were hit, two sunk. Had the rump of C-3 been fitted with modern radar they could have turned the poor visibility to advantage. The corvette *Sackville* had three close encounters with U-boats on the night of 31 July–1 August. At the time it was believed it killed one and seriously damaged another. But none was sunk. Even British staff officers concluded afterward, "*Sackville's* two [*sic*, actually three] U-boats would have been a gift if it had been fitted with RDF [radar] type 271."[3]

Two more U-boat kills followed that summer. The most dramatic was *Assiniboine's* memorable battle with *U-210* in the fog around SC-94 in August after a wild hour-long running gun battle. While *Assiniboine* tried to ram and the U-boat tried to steady on course long enough to dive, they traded gunfire. *U-210's* conning tower was riddled with holes and littered with dead; *Assiniboine's* upper decks and bridge were cut-up by German 40mm fire, and small fires started in its superstructure. Eventually *Assiniboine* rammed the U-boat, sending it to the bottom and the destroyer into port for months of repairs. The British corvette *Dianthus* helped even the score around SC-94 by ramming and sinking another sub.

The RCN killed one more U-boat in the summer of 1942 (but it was not credited until 1982), when *Morden* sank *U-756* in the battle for SC-97 on 1 September. That marked the end of a successful summer for Canadians on the North Atlantic Run. Of the five U-boats destroyed in the mid-ocean since May, Canadians sank four. One can only wonder at what the C groups might have accomplished had they been properly equipped. But when they stopped sinking U-boats the RCN mid-ocean effort came to be judged by its ability — or inability — to defend convoys.

The crisis began in September with the passage of ONS-127, during which aggressive sweeps by *St. Croix* and *Ottawa* could not prevent the loss of seven ships and *Ottawa* itself with heavy loss of life. Canadians congratulated the escort of ONS-127 for a difficult job well done, blaming the losses directly on the lack of modern radar. Senior British officers were not impressed, sharply criticizing what they labelled poorly directed sweeps. The British had

long suspected that the Canadians were aggressive but misguided and ONS-127 seemed to confirm that.

With the loss of *Ottawa*, and with *Assiniboine* and *St. Laurent* in refit, the RCN was now down to one destroyer for each of its four mid-ocean groups. While the RCN looked for ways of acquiring more escort destroyers, it finally removed the bureaucratic hurdles to fitting modern equipment in British ports and hoped that the British destroyers assigned to the C groups were able to steam. And to make matters even worse, the Germans now had a radar detector to warn of first generation — metric wavelength — sets. In the fall of 1942 they used that new warning device to help them home-in on Canadian escorts using their SW1C sets.

In contrast to the struggling Canadians, the British groups in the mid-ocean sank U-boats and put up effective radar barriers around their convoys. In the most serious British battle of the fall, for SC-104 in mid-October, eight losses to the convoy were balanced by two U-boat kills by RN destroyers. If Canadian ships could no longer sink U-boats, they

Rear-Admiral L.W. Murray, Flag Officer Newfoundland, greets the crew of the destroyer *Assiniboine* at St. John's after their sinking of *U-210* on 6 August 1942; the ship's captain, Lieutenant-Commander John Stubbs (right), would be lost with his next ship, *Athabaskan*.

must at least protect shipping. The tragic passage of SC-107 in early November suggested that they could no longer do that, either.

SC-107, escorted by *Restigouche* and six corvettes, was intercepted while still west of Cape Race. Seventeen U-boats were directed to attack. One was sunk by the RCAF early in the battle, while *Restigouche* used its HF/DF to help drive off shadowers. But with only one destroyer, and with only *Restigouche* and the British corvette *Celandine* with modern radar, the escort was overwhelmed. Eight ships went down in the first furious night of battle; seven more followed over the next week. No U-boats were sunk by the naval escort. It was a devastating blow to Canadian prestige and morale.

In contrast, ONS-144 coming the other way a week later and defended by only six corvettes, five Norwegian and one British, of group B-6 was also beset by a large pack. Fortunately, all the escorts carried type 271 radar and by forming a tight barrier around the convoy they fought it through with only six ships lost.

Quite apart from Canadian shortcomings, the British were anxious about the mid-ocean by November for other reasons. The landings in North Africa on 8 November resulted in the suspension of the eastern Atlantic convoys, making the mid-ocean the only way in or out of Britain. Moreover, much of the shipping lost in 1942 was British or British chartered, and the North African campaign strained what remained.

By November the Allies were also operating in the Atlantic without the benefit of Ultra intelligence. Since the previous February Allied cryptanalysts had been unable to read the signals of Atlantic U-boats. Through most of 1942, with the U-boats attacking inshore, this was not a serious problem. However, by late 1942, the U-boats began to concentrate in the mid-ocean again. The decisive battle of the Atlantic war was looming and any weakness in Allied escort forces had potentially disastrous consequences.

SC-107 pointed to the Canadians as the weak link in the mid-ocean. Training, maintenance, leadership, and equipment all seemed to be inadequate. Even the Americans confided to the British their concerns about the ability of the Canadians. Obscure warnings about "fairly drastic" measures to sort out the mid-ocean reached Ottawa in early December. The RCN was aware of the need for action, too. In November *Saguenay* was damaged in a collision and *St. Croix* went into refit, leaving Canadian mid-ocean groups desperately short of destroyers. In early December the government appealed to the British for the loan of at least 12 escort destroyers.

The British were not convinced that destroyers were the solution. They believed that the RCN had expanded too rapidly, taken on too many tasks, was poorly trained and badly led. Something had to be done. The British solution was to get the RCN out of the embattled mid-ocean. On 17 December 1942 Winston Churchill made a formal request to the Canadian government asking that the C groups be withdrawn.

The Canadian naval staff rejected the British claims. Equipment shortages were crucial, as was the unreliability of the RN destroyers assigned to Canadian groups, and the burden of escorting slow convoys. Even Lieutenant-Commander P.M. Bliss, RN, recently arrived in Ottawa from St. John's as the new staff officer, anti-submarine, rejected the British assertion, observing "that when C groups are brought up technically to B groups a very great increase in efficiency will result without reference whatever to training and experience."[4]

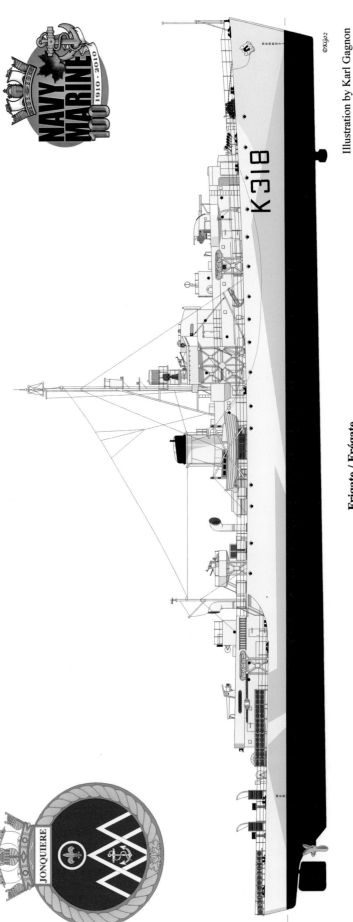

Illustration by Karl Gagnon

©XGo2

Frigate / Frégate
Classe RIVER Class

0 m	5 m	10 m

N.C.S.M. JONQUIÈRE
1944

Lancé le 28 octobre 1943. Construit par Davie Shipbuilding & Repairing Co. Ltd., Lauzon.

10 mai 1944 - 04 décembre 1945
20 septembre 1954 - 12 septembre 1966

Dimensions: 91,9 m x 11,1 m x 3,9 m
Déplacement: 1 445 tonnes   Vitesse: 19 noeuds   Équipage: 141
Armement: 1 x II - 102 mm; 1 x I - 12 livres; 4 x II - 20 mm;
Hedgehog; grenades sous-marines.

H.M.C.S. JONQUIÈRE
1944

Launched 28 October 1943. Built by Davie Shipbuilding & Repairing Co. Ltd., Lauzon.

10 May 1944 - 04 December 1945
20 September 1954 - 12 September 1966

Dimensions: 91.9 m x 11.1 m x 3.9 m
Displacement: 1,445 tons   Speed: 19 knots   Crew: 141
Armament: 1 x II - 102-mm; 1 x I - 12-pound; 4 x II - 20 mm;
Hedgehog; depth charges.

JONQUIÈRE

Bliss was right. However, events at sea undermined the Canadian case. In late December ONS-154, escorted by C-1, was routed through the widest portion of the air gap, battered by the tail end of a hurricane, and beset by 20 U-boats. The escort had much new equipment aboard, but the radars and HF/DF sets were not yet calibrated and the assigned British destroyer failed to show. C-1 fought blind, holding the U-boats to a draw for the first two days, sinking *U-356* in the process (not awarded until after the war). Then the defence was overwhelmed and ONS-154 lost 15 ships, with no apparent retribution exacted upon the enemy.

On 6 January 1943, the Canadian Cabinet agreed to the temporary withdrawal of Canada's mid-ocean escorts. "This is another real good turn you have done us," Winston Churchill replied. Indeed, it was. The RCN had been driven to the brink of collapse in 1942, in the face of enormous enemy pressure. As the RN's *Monthly Anti-Submarine Report* for January 1943 conceded, "The Canadians have had to bear the brunt of the U-Boat attack in the north Atlantic for the last six months, that is to say, of about half of the German U-boats operating at sea…." That they did so with a fleet manned largely by reservists who "put up a good show is immensely to their credit." In short, during the last half of 1942 the Canadian Navy shouldered the weight of the U-boat war. Sadly, subsequent historians of the Atlantic war failed to notice.

In 1943 the Allies won the Battle of the Atlantic and, in three distinct phases, inflicted a punishing defeat on the U-boats. The RCN was not really a part of this great Allied offensive: it remained tied primarily to close escort work. In the spring of 1943 victory around the transatlantic convoys was won by a combination of better weather, improved intelligence, increased air support, and designated "support groups" that were able to hunt and kill U-boats. The RCN had a front row seat for this offensive when its escorts returned to the mid-ocean in March and early April, but attempts by the Canadians to again field a support group did not come to fruition until late May. By then the carnage in the mid-ocean had ended and the Germans had temporarily abandoned pack attacks.

The Allied offensive over the summer consisted of air assaults in the Bay of Biscay, and by USN escort carriers off northwest Africa and south of the Azores. By the time EG-5 (Escort Group-5), the first RCN support group, got into the Biscay to help the air force the battle had escalated to include surface vessels and heavy reinforcement from the German air force. As a result, EG-5's first foray off northwest Spain nearly ended in catastrophe, when the Germans employed their new glider-bombs to attack the ships (including the new RCN Tribal-class destroyer *Athabaskan*, as described in the previous chapter). Surface ship ASW operations in the area were subsequently abandoned.

Meanwhile the second RCN support group, EG-9, arrived in the UK. Its first assignment also encountered a new weapon that effectively destroyed the group. In September the Germans planned to blast their way back into North Atlantic convoys using increased anti-aircraft fire and a new acoustic homing torpedo. In late September 20 U-boats equipped with this new equipment lay in wait for ONS-18/ON-202, two convoys that joined together as they approached the pack. EG-9 was sent to help.

By the time EG-9 arrived on 20 September a full battle was underway. The British frigate *Lagan* of C-2 already had its stern blown-off by a homing torpedo, and while conducting a sweep *St. Croix* of EG-9 was struck by a homing torpedo that left it shattered. EG-9's senior officer arrived in HMS *Itchen* just in time to see the second torpedo strike *St. Croix*, which disappeared in a towering explosion. When a torpedo detonated in *Itchen*'s wake, it set off to screen the rescue operation of the corvette *Polyanthus*. All that *Itchen* ever found of the corvette was wreckage and a single man clinging to it: *Polyanthus*, too, had been completely destroyed by a single homing torpedo. It was early the next morning before *Itchen* returned to pluck 100 survivors of *St. Croix* from the sea and headed back into the battle.

Despite intense air support and the sinking of one of the attackers, 10 U-boats remained in contact with ONS-18/ON-202 at dusk on 22 September. That night EG-9's corvettes *Morden*, *Chambly*, and *Sackville* all dodged homing torpedoes, but *Itchen* was not so fortunate. It disappeared in a shattering blast caused by a torpedo detonating just below its magazine. Only three men survived: two from *Itchen* and one who had been rescued from *St. Croix; Polyanthus*'s lone survivor perished.

The Germans claimed a great victory in the battle for ONS-18/ON-202, but the truth was quite different: three escorts and six merchant vessels were lost, but so were two U-boats. An RCN success of sorts in this battle was the quick response to the homing torpedo. Production of CAAT equipment began on 21 September, the day after *St. Croix* was sunk and while the battle still raged. By the time ONS-18/0N-202's escorts arrived in St. John's their new CAAT gear was waiting. Meanwhile, the final German pack assault on the transatlantic convoys fizzled out, hounded and beaten by Allied naval and air power — and watched again from the sidelines by the RCN. It was not until November that the first U-boat kill fell to an RCN support group, when *Snowberry* of EG-5 sank *U-536*.

If 1943 was arguably the worst year of the war for RCN ASW, then 1944 was the best. The sinking of *U-536* in November 1943 marked the start of a year-long period in which the Canadian Navy was second to none in finding and sinking submarines. Over the winter of 1943–44, much of the support group effort around transatlantic convoys fell to the Canadians, including EG-6, EG-9, and C-2. They did extremely well, with a concentration of successes in the open ocean in the late winter and early spring. Indeed, between the sinking of *U-257* by the new River-class frigate[5] *Waskesiu* on 27 February 1944 and the end of April, the RCN sank four out of 14 U-boats claimed by surface vessels in the North Atlantic.

Among these winter victories was *U-744*, pursued by C-2 for 32 hours on 5–6 March — the second longest hunt of the war. C-2 was operating in support of HX-280 when *Gatineau* picked-up *U-744* on asdic at a great depth. Its captain was no ordinary submariner, and attacks during the day achieved nothing. C-2 circled the U-boat that night, maintaining asdic contact and waiting for first light to renew its attacks. The next morning the pounding began. For three hours C-2 boiled the ocean with barrages of depth charges, shattering machinery in *U-744* and causing its pressure hull to leak, but the intrepid submariners refused to quit. After a pause for several hours, and amid deteriorating weather, C-2 attacked again in the late afternoon. Then suddenly *U-744* bobbed to the surface near *Chilliwack*. The corvette smothered the U-boat in gunfire, blowing off the sub's anti-aircraft gun and riddling the conning tower with holes. When the firing stopped a boarding party was sent away to try to salvage the U-boat. Thirty-nine Germans were rescued, but *U-744* — slowly filling with water — was torpedoed and sunk.

A boarding party from the corvette *Chilliwack* comes alongside *U-744*, 6 March 1944.

The sinking of *U-744* was a classic deep water ASW operation of the period: a large group of ships holding a deep contact, pounding it relentlessly with masses of depth charges and hoping that a lucky attack or sheer exhaustion in the submarine would end the action. Meanwhile, British support groups, equipped with newer equipment and in some cases (like EG-2) directed by special intelligence, scored with greater ease. The net result, however, was much the same: the RCN proved to be effective U-boat hunters in the first months of 1944.

That trend continued over the summer, as the best of the North Atlantic ASW veterans — ships as well as men — concentrated in British waters to support the Allied landings in France that started on 6 June. Besides the Channel-clearing effort described in the previous chapter, the RCN committed four support groups to this campaign. The veteran River-class destroyers were combined into groups EG-11 and -12 and assigned to work in the middle of the English Channel along with two British groups. Two groups of RCN River-class frigates, EG-6 and -9, joined three British groups to form an outer barrier to the English Channel between Brest and the south of Ireland.

These groups faced a "new" challenge: inshore ASW in tidal waters that were often mined, and invariably strewn with shipwrecks, while under constant threat of attack by the enemy. ASW veterans soon understood that proper classification of the contact was all-important — and extremely difficult. Until they learned to anticipate the impact of tidal currents on their own movements and on water passing quickly over bottom features, it was not unusual to have reports of large boulders moving at considerable speed along the bottom. This was complicated by the unexpected tendency of U-boats to lie on the bottom when being hunted.

So learning a new form of ASW and sorting out the enemy from the background clutter became the story of the summer of 1944. The best at doing this was EG-11, which sank three U-boats, the best score of any group over the summer. EG-11's skill owed a great deal to the tenacity, patience, and inventive genius of its officers and men. They perfected systems for classifying bottomed contacts, including profiling them using their navigational echo sounder. Snagging the contact with a grappling hook on a wire, and sliding a depth charge down the wire to "cook off" against the target achieved further "classification." EG-11 called this "tin opening." If the debris — especially bodies or parts thereof — was fresh and German it was probably a sub. RN officers found this particularly distasteful, although highly effective.

The RCN continued to enjoy success in its ASW operations in the fall of 1944, when things were generally very quiet as the Germans adjusted to the loss of bases in France. The RCN achieved a pinnacle of sorts in October when the frigate *Annan* of EG-6 sank *U-1006* north of the Shetlands. They had given up on an asdic contact and were miles away when *Annan*'s radar operator took one final peek astern and found *U-1006* on the surface. The frigate raced back and sank the U-boat after a brief but fierce gun battle. *U-1006* was the only U-boat sunk by the Allied navies in the North Atlantic in October 1944.

Unfortunately, none of the expertise displayed by the RCN inshore in British waters in 1944 transferred easily to Canadian waters. The area was vast by comparison, there were too few support groups in Canada, and the RCN struggled with complex inshore water conditions to the very end of the war. The U-boats therefore achieved some success off Canada in 1944, torpedoing the frigate *Magog* in the St. Lawrence River and the corvette *Shawinigan* off Port aux Basques in the fall of 1944.

Worse followed that winter. *U-806* sank the minesweeper *Clayoquot* just off Halifax on Christmas Eve, and then, in early January, *U-1232* began a successful cruise off Nova Scotia. On 4 January it sank three

An RCN crew handles the surrendered *U-889* off Shelburne, Nova Scotia, as a Royal Canadian Air Force (RCAF) Canso flying boat passes overhead.

Library and Archives Canada PA-116720

ships near Egg Island, then attacked convoy BX-141 in the very entrance to Halifax harbour during a blizzard, sinking two ships and damaging a third. *U-1232* was lining up for another shot when the frigate *Ettrick* ran over it by accident, smashing the conning tower, rolling the U-boat over and snagging the sub with its CAAT gear. No one in *Ettrick* knew what had struck it until the hull was examined in drydock and bits of *U-1232* removed; the sub, however, survived. Asdic conditions had been so poor that contact could not be made on the freighter *British Freedom*, which lay on the bottom with its bow pointed skyward.

Apart from atrocious weather and water conditions, the bottom off Halifax was so boulder strewn that asdic echoes bounced in all directions and ships often unwittingly tracked themselves. Only constant air patrols and operations by USN forces in deep water beyond the Canadian zone provided an effective check on U-boat depredations in the RCN's own front yard in the last winter of the war.

The situation overseas was better. RCN groups continued to sink U-boats until the end of March 1945, even if they were unable to keep up with the RN. Under pressure to crush the U-boat fleet before the war ended or Germany could deploy the radically new type-XXI and XXIII subs in large numbers, the British increasingly put their better-equipped groups in the hot spots. The key components of this very late war ASW were the latest asdic and radar. In particular, the three centimetre radar of RN Captain-class frigates could detect the snorkel masts of U-boats. So radar searches became the key to initial detection, and British groups got the high probability areas as a result. Ironically, the RCN's last "kill" of the war, *U-1003*, occurred when a snorkelling U-boat collided with *New Glasgow* on a dark night. The U-boat was subsequently abandoned and the RCN was awarded credit.

The RCN destroyed 33 enemy submarines during the war: three Italian and the rest German. It was, in the end, a very small proportion of the 1,000 U-boats sunk by the Allies between 1939 and 1945, and a very modest portion of the 500 of these claimed by naval vessels. But the real measure of the RCN's war against the U-boats lay in the shipping safely escorted. Indeed, a huge proportion of the 25,000 ships brought safely across the Atlantic during the war moved under Canadian escort. That work was not glamorous, and it made no compelling history. However, it did make Allied victory in 1945 possible. And in the Atlantic war against submarine adversaries, the RCN found its niche for the next 50 years.

Notes

1. As quoted in Michael L. Hadley, *U-Boats Against Canada: German Submarines in Canadian Waters* (Montreal/Kingston: McGill-Queen's University Press, 1985), 115.
2. Hadley, 228.
3. As quoted in Marc Milner, *North Atlantic Run: The Royal Canadian Navy and the Battle for the Convoys* (Toronto: University of Toronto Press, 1985), 140.
4. As quoted in Milner, 199.
5. The class designation followed British usage; Canadian frigates generally were named after Canadian towns, with destroyers taking river names.

CHAPTER 6

Naval Art of the Second World War

Pat Jessup

The vessel slices through swells or rough water, which spreads water-colour washes most unexpectedly; and the vibration from her powerful engines and propellers is frequently so great that putting a line or brush stroke on paper or canvas is often an exciting gamble as to its ultimate position or character. Add to this that the ship rolls all the time, and is zigzagging with a convoy....

The big convoy which we are helping to protect is a beautiful sight rolling and plunging in a heavy sea with white water coming aboard and gorgeous sky over all. It seems like a very thrilling performance put on for our special benefit with war far away, — until "action stations" are sounded as possibly somebody "gets it."

— ROWLEY MURPHY, "AN ARTIST WITH THE
ROYAL CANADIAN NAVY," *MARITIME ART*
(DECEMBER 1942/JANUARY 1943)

Illustrating the Royal Canadian Navy's war at sea presented unique challenges not experienced by those who documented the action of either the Canadian Army or the Royal Canadian Air Force. Sustaining creativity within an inhospitable environment while battling the tedium of long and rolling ocean crossings, eight artists participated in the naval

Rowley Murphy, *Convoy in Rough Weather*.

program from 1943 to 1946: Commander Harold Beament; Lieutenant-Commanders Donald Cameron Mackay and Tony Law; and Lieutenants Rowley Murphy, Tom Wood, Michael Forster, Leonard Brooks, and Jack Nichols (Captain Alex Colville, normally employed with the Army program, enjoyed a brief sojourn on loan to the RCN in the Mediterranean theatre in the latter part of 1944).

Canada is largely credited with pioneering the production of war art during the First World War through its Canadian War Memorials Fund (CWMF). Sir Max Aitken (later Lord Beaverbrook) initiated the CWMF to address a perceived shortcoming on the battlefront. A journalist foremost, Aitken recognized that Canadians would be better served with graphic representations of the war effort in Europe. As a consequence, he hired civilian artists, primarily British, to document the Canadian contribution, although the participants

included such notables as A.Y. Jackson and other members of what would become the Group of Seven.

A generation later, during the Second World War, Prime Minister Mackenzie King's government did not immediately warm to the notion of employing artists as was done in 1917 and the program had a slow start. Eventually, a similar program known as the Canadian War Records (CWR) was introduced, this time with military artists commissioned to portray Canada at war. The style adopted by the Group of Seven, and attributed to European influences of the First World War, overwhelmingly influenced the decision makers for Canada's Second World War program. For the most part, this "national" style was an underlying prerequisite for selection and the artists chosen were predominately well established, from central Canada, and — most importantly — capable of producing exhibition quality work.

During the First World War, the CWMF artists produced paintings and sculptures on a grand scale. Comparatively, the *Instructions to War Artists* charged the Second World War

Harold Beament, *St. Lawrence Convoy.*

CWR artists to depict war "vividly and veraciously"[1] but in a smaller and more manageable style. Indeed the official naval paintings and drawings (no sculptures were produced) many times were completed on-the-spot and presented a more spontaneous, bolder-in-style, and non-traditional view of war.

Although the government delayed for nearly three years into the war before undertaking official sponsorship of a war art program, interest within the cultural community remained strong and behind the scenes communication kept the notion alive. Naval officers played their part.

Commander Harold Beament for one, a veteran of the First World War, was already serving in the RCNVR in 1939 when he wrote his friend H.O. McCurry, director of the National Gallery of Canada (NGC), regarding the start of a program similar to the CWMF. "I gather that some attempt is being made to get things organized in the direction of War Records," he wrote, making it clear that he wanted to "get in on the Naval end of it" if one got started. A member of the Royal Canadian Academy of Arts (RCAA), Beament saw that "really important stuff [is] going on here that should be recorded. Unfortunately in the job that I am doing at present, it is impossible to find time to do anything."[2] As senior officer of the River Patrol based out of Rivière-du-Loup, Beament was in charge of two armed motor launches and one yacht in the lower River and Gulf of St. Lawrence. His job "was to rush from one place to another down the Gulf hoping to give the impression that there were dozens of little vessels waiting to devour any marauding German ships"[3] — a notion portrayed vividly in his *St. Lawrence Convoy* (CWM 19710261–1049).

Fredericton native Donald Cameron Mackay saw a war art program as an opportunity to paint: "It was practically impossible to make a living as an artist unless you were a successful portrait painter. In the 1920s and 1930s, artists made money as teachers, illustrators, commercial artists, or as consultants in some field related to the arts, but they had little time to produce paintings."[4] Mackay's artistic training was under Henry M. Rosenberg at the Nova Scotia College of Art (NSCA), himself a student of James Abbott McNeill Whistler, the American famed for his strong and harmonious composition more popularly known as *Whistler's Mother*. The importance of balance through colour and linear design was passed from teacher to student and subsequently to Mackay, as illustrated in his *Convoy, Afternoon* (CWM 19710261–4208) and *Signal Flag Hoist* (CWM 19710261–4251). In addition to studies at NSCA, Mackay taught with Arthur Lismer of the Group of Seven at the Art Gallery of Toronto. Already in the RCNVR as a yachtsman, Mackay entered active service the day that Great Britain declared war on Germany on 3 September 1939. While primarily employed within the Intelligence Branch, Mackay managed to get to sea to "do some drawing and painting and a little work on camouflage as well."[5]

Another artist who kept McCurry up to date with his naval comings and goings was Rowley Murphy, RCAA. A Torontonian who joined the RCNVR in 1940, he had spent his early years on the city waterfront sketching schooners and passenger ferries, and was a lecturer at the Ontario College of Art before the war. He became a recognized marine painter whose accolades included a prize in the First Victory Loan Poster Competition in 1940 and illustrations in *Saturday Evening Post, Maclean's, Canadian Magazine, Canadian Home Journal, Toronto Star Weekly*, and *Toronto's Hundred Years*. Murphy initially was employed by the

Canadian Navy to develop camouflage patterns for its warships (one of his designs was HMCS *Hamilton*, painted with different patterns on each side). He lamented in an exchange of notes with McCurry in the spring of 1941 that he had to bear the brunt "of ratings taking great delight" in bothering him: "I have been from the start of the war greatly interested in drawing and painting naval war records; and to that end have been permitted to go sea … at my own expense." The result was "the production of a good deal of work, though I have always been hampered by my unofficial status." While sympathetic, McCurry wrote back: "Cannot help with your very worthy desire to record the doings of the navy.... I am afraid it is all tied up with the Government's policy of war records in general...."[6]

Rowley Murphy figured prominently among a gathering of 150 well-known members of the artistic community at Queen's University in Kingston, Ontario, in 1941. Outraged at the indifference displayed by the government during the first two years of the war, with the war raging over the skies of Europe and at sea in the North Atlantic, they formed *The Federation of Canadian Artists* to pressure Mackenzie King into making a decision on a war art program. Simultaneously, McCurry was pressing for a government program, equating the

Donald Cameron Mackay,
Convoy, Afternoon.

value of a war art program as being "worth many ships, tanks and guns,"[7] and incidentally because it would offer employment to artists affected by the interwar Depression.

With the added voice of the Honourable Vincent Massey, Canadian High Commissioner to Great Britain, and the tireless petitioning of the government by the formidable A.Y. Jackson, Mackenzie King finally acquiesced. Cabinet approved the formation of the Canadian War Records late in 1942, with Massey appointed chair and a War Artists Advisory Committee headed by McCurry and consisting of representatives from the Historical Branches of the RCN, RCAF and Canadian Army to administer the program. McCurry's selection committee quickly gathered to adjudicate the 32 artists nominated by the three services to participate. The committee resolved that those selected for the program would have exemplary qualifications, preferably that they should be members of the RCAA, have national and international credentials, and serve on faculty in a university art program. The first artists were selected by February 1943 and generally remained "embedded" within their military environment for the duration of their contract. In accordance with the *Instructions to Artists* also compiled by the committee, the artists were expected to record "significant events, scenes, phases and episodes in the experience of the Canadian Armed Forces" and engage in "active operations" in order to "know and understand the action, the circumstances, the environment, and the participants." The artists would be required to produce paintings and field drawings "worthy of Canada's highest cultural traditions, doing justice to History, and as works of art, worthy of exhibition anywhere at any time."[8] In a six-month period, they were required to produce a daunting collection made up of two 40×48-inches and two 24×30-inches oil paintings; 25 watercolours, 10 measuring 22×30-inches, the rest, 11×15-inches; and their field sketches. In the event, this schedule proved to be too demanding, and the numbers were adjusted down to accommodate bad weather, lack of subject matter, and bureaucratic red tape.

McCurry drew upon the expertise of advisers from the wider artistic community including, A.J. Casson, Edwin Holgate, Charles Comfort, and, specifically, A.Y. Jackson (Holgate and Comfort later signed up for active duty and were employed as war artists with the army). Jackson played a key role in the selection process for the program. "As far as possible the most capable artists in the country were given the opportunity to participate," he recalled, with "professional artists already in the armed forces" given first consideration.[9] For this reason, Harold Beament, Donald Cameron Mackay, and Rowley Murphy were offered the first navy billets in the program.

Another serving officer who caught Massey's eye in England was Lieutenant-Commander C. Anthony ("Tony") Law. Commander of the 29th Canadian Motor Torpedo Boat Flotilla renowned for engaging with enemy coastal convoys off France, and twice Mentioned-in-Dispatches for this highly dangerous and stressful activity, Law professed to paint "to keep sane."[10] Born into a life of privilege in 1916 to parents living in London during the Great War, Law grew up in Quebec City but moved to Ottawa in 1935, where he was captivated by the Group of Seven collection in the old National Gallery (the building that is now the Museum of Nature). This visit was followed by a membership in the Art Association of Ottawa and studies under Franklin Brownell, Frederick Varley, and Frank Hennessy. Critics of his first solo exhibit in Quebec City in 1937 noted his "strong, virile treatment" and "typical

Charles Anthony ("Tony") Law,
*Motor Torpedo Boats Leaving for
Night Patrol Off Le Havre.*

Canadian character,"[11] and the next year he was awarded the prestigious Jessie Dow Prize, given for excellence of work in oil and watercolour. He enrolled in the RCNVR on the outbreak of war in 1939, and his previous sailing and powerboat experience earned him an immediate posting to England and the Royal Navy's coastal fleet driving MTBs. The Canadian high commissioner was quite taken by the young commander's work and attempted to entice him to paint full time with the CWR. Law wanted to remain in action and declined. While awaiting the delivery of new MTBs destined for the RCN in 1943, however, Law agreed to a temporary assignment. For two-and-one-half months he painted RCN ship portraits before joining his new Flotilla (e.g., *His Majesty's Canadian Ship Huron*, CWM, 19710261–4086). A second and permanent assignment took place later in the war.

As for other candidates, Jackson knew most of the potential artists personally and acknowledged that, while there was much interest in the program from the art community, "it was not possible to gamble on the mere promise of potentialities."[12] He thought Leonard Brooks, a member of the Arts and Letters Club in Toronto, would do well as a naval artist. Jackson and Brooks had worked outside together on painting expeditions: "He can stand cold weather. Good out-door guy."[13]

Another to receive Jackson's approval was Michael Forster. Born in India but raised in England, Forster immigrated to Canada in the middle of the Depression, and found employment with The Grip, a commercial art firm in Toronto, painting backdrops for the T. Eaton Company's College Street department store windows, where he came under Jackson's eye. Forster had studied under the modernists Bernard Meninsky and William Roberts in London and Paris, and his decidedly avant-garde style appealed to Jackson.

Artists recruited for the program, if not already serving, underwent obligatory basic training as junior officers. In the case of Beament, Law, Mackay, and Murphy, contracts were offered commensurate to their existing rank. For naval artists newly recruited to the RCN, the war art scheme offered full-time employment at the junior rank of sub-lieutenant for a probationary six-month period. A promotion to lieutenant, a pay increase of 75 cents a day and a longer contract followed if the artist's work pleased the committee. Commissioned in 1944, Leonard Brooks was thrilled with the appointment as he now could paint with

Michael Forster, *Wreckage on Beach Near Newhaven, England.*

abandon "with no other thought in mind."[14] Rowley Murphy, with 40 years experience onboard yachts and time with the merchant and Canadian navies, thought otherwise. Bemoaning the junior rank, Murphy wrote:

> *If there has been any officer whose ignorance or incompetence was outstanding aboard some of the vessels mentioned, it was that of Sub-Lieutenant. They are considered the lowest form of animal life in some ship! … I can't think of any rank more detrimental to carrying out successfully the work I'm so anxious to produce. The [sub-lieutenants] … among proper seamen are unwelcome everywhere …*[15]

When Michael Forster (contracted earlier by the NGC to depict the Merchant Navy) was offered a commission, he hesitated. Concerned that he would be hamstrung by rules and regulations and tied down to a conventional style of painting, Forster wrote McCurry: "If they are looking for minutely factual drawings of great technical clarity and detail, then I am not their man."[16] McCurry's response was relaxed and encouraging: "It has always been a problem with the chair of the War Artists Committee to secure for the artists freedom to paint in their own way but this has been achieved in all cases…. My reason of course for recommending you is because I like your approach."[17]

Forster joined the RCNVR after D-Day and was tasked to record the post-invasion activity in the Channel and France. While he did not sketch "on-the-spot," Forster worked up his studio canvasses from visual notes and photographs. Particularly interested in the wreckage of war, his images of bomb-shattered Brest, beached ships, submarine pens, and the artificial Mulberry Harbour at Arromanches are strong in composition and distinctive by their monochromatic palette (e.g., *Submarine Pens at Brest*, CWM 19710261–6169, or *Wreckage on Beach Near Newhaven, England*, CWM 19710261–6171).

Ottawa native Thomas Wood waited until he was almost 30 before volunteering for war duty. For the most part self-taught, the hard times of the Depression made him hesitate to leave a good paying job as a commercial artist, which at least enabled him to take classes at the Ottawa Art Association with the celebrated Canadian masters Franklin Brownell and Frederick Varley. Joining the RCNVR on 23 May 1943 at HMCS *Carleton* in Ottawa, Wood served within the Directorate of Special Services at naval headquarters in Ottawa designing propaganda posters and pamphlets. Six months after joining, he sailed for England in a troop carrier as a newly minted RCN war artist.

In Southampton prior to D-Day, Wood's reduced palette of burnt sienna and grays captured the solemnity of the preparations, and a leaden sky set the tone for his work (e.g., *Third Canadian Division Assault Troops*, CWM 19710261–4917). On 6 June, Wood landed with the Canadians three hours after the first troops made land. The voyage across in a British landing craft was far from boring:

> *It was a colossal chunk of history and I of course was involved with how as an artist was I going to interpret this thing in terms of the technical and emotional forces that I had…. The craft was pitching around too roughly to permit any sketching, so I stood up and took pictures with a borrowed camera … Snipers*

Thomas Charles Wood, *Corvette Entering St. John's Newfoundland.*

were firing at us, but their aim was poor; only one man in our whole flotilla was wounded.[18]

Even though Wood was surrounded by the dead and dying, he resisted yielding to his "emotional forces." Instead, his *D-Day 1944* (CWM 19710261–4857) portrayal of jaunty landing craft bedecked with pennants blowing in a brisk breeze and rushing toward shore, belies the devastation and human cost of the day. Save for faint flashes from distant German shore batteries, the painting could be of a regatta with boats racing across the finish line.

Sent to St. John's after D-Day, Tom Wood was confronted with "utterly atrocious" weather in the isolated port: "We have had every variety … that I suppose exists, except sunshine. It has sleeted, rained, and snowed, and fog, fog, fog, all the time!" All the same, Wood found the port city picturesque with "great jagged rock formations enclosing the harbour like a bowl,"[19] as demonstrated in his *Corvette Entering St. John's, Newfoundland* (CWM 19710261–4853), painted from a bleak vantage point on the south bank of the harbour. Later, Wood, found himself in a fortuitous situation when *U-190*, having surrendered to the RCN off of Cape Race, was escorted into Bay Bulls on 14 May 1945. Convincing authorities to take him to where the crew was being held, Wood spent several hours taking photographs of the sailors, which he later used to paint *German Prisoners Leaving Their U-Boat, Bay Bulls* (CWM 19710261–4870).

Painting at sea presented a new range of challenges even to artists used to working *en plein air*. Rowley Murphy seemed particularly exasperated when he described, in the passage quoted at the opening of this chapter, the typically trying conditions that made painting at sea a frustrating experience: "as the vessel slices through swells or rough water, which spreads water-colour washes most unexpectedly; and the vibration from her powerful engines and propellers is frequently so great that putting a line or brush stroke on paper or canvas is often an exciting gamble as to its ultimate position or character. Add to this that the ship rolls all the time, and is zigzagging with a convoy …"[20] Despite the aggravation, watercolour was the medium of choice at sea, because, as D.C. Mackay pointed out: "even at sea, nobody liked the smell of turpentine if you were painting in oils. Turpentine clings to woollens and uniforms, particularly in dampness. No matter what rugged seadogs the sailors were, they were all apt to get a little queasy in heavy weather …"[21]

Later, far from the Battle of the Atlantic, Rowley Murphy fared no better ashore in British Columbia. His studio, an unheated firebrick storage shed, was unsuitable to art making: "The almost daily rain makes interior damp so great that water colours are impossible to use … and some oil sketches made indoors early this month are still not dry enough for shipment," he complained.[22] Later a malfunctioning sprinkler system wreaked havoc on his paintings.

And then there was the very nature of their subjects. Time was needed to make the transition, as Tom Wood characterized it, from the "Gatineau Hills to ships at sea."[23] Even a seasoned sailor such as Harold Beament constantly struggled with his art and his audience to get the lines of the ships "right":

> *during my actual service as a war artist it was kind of difficult to separate the naval officer from the war artist in thinking and resolving just how I would tackle certain problems. I used to work a lot at night in my studio in London … pleased with the canvas when I went to bed. I'd wake up in the morning and … I'd think, good God, I wouldn't put to sea in that vessel…. It's not seaworthy, and I'd start making it seaworthy from the naval officers point of view, and constipation would set it … that's spiritual constipation …*[24]

In many cases, Beament found his "original statement was qualified in the direction of possibly being reasonable to the eyes of some other Naval Officer but not so acceptable to somebody who was looking on art for art's sake." In this regard, when Vincent Massey saw *Passing?* (CWM 19710261–1042), he remarked: "Beament, why aren't you painting them all that way?" The artist was chuffed by this remark, coming especially from "someone like

Vincent Massey who had quite a definite eye … a sort of supervising uncle to all the war artists over in England…."[25]

Tom Wood found the business of war boring and the long weeks at sea tedious. The inactivity wore him down and he sympathized with the crew that had to remain with the

Alex Colville, *Painting Ship*.

ship while he went ashore for the comfort of his studio. "You really might say that you are in jail for 21 days" when making a crossing, he recalled:

> When there was action, it was pretty abstract ... a change in pitch in the asdic....
> When you are in a convoy with ships 25 miles across ... rarely did you see action
> in the Hollywood sense of the word, with tracers and guns and planes and that sort
> of things.... On a ship you don't see the enemy ... I would only see smoke off the
> horizon 15 miles away.[26]

Early in 1944 Wood had connected with Tony Law and sailed with him during a dangerous MTB mission off France, jumping at the opportunity that offered a respite from convoy duty (e.g., Law, *Windy Day in the British Assault Area*, CWM 19710261–4123, or *Motor Torpedo Boats Leaving for Night Patrol off Le Havre*, CWM 19710261–4107).

The three-week-long crossings in convoys were challenging for the artists used to the quiet and contemplative atmosphere of a shore-based studio. When the threat of U-boat attack diminished in May of 1943, the artists turned to genre painting and portraiture to fill their time. Even Alex Colville found life onboard challenging, pressed for suitable subject matter to satisfy the *Instructions*. It would be difficult to say that Colville had captured the war "vividly and veraciously" in *Painting Ship* (CWM 19710261–1683).

Like A. Y. Jackson and others in the First World War, the naval artists avoided confronting the ugliness and misery of war. Harold Beament skirted the issue in his *Burial at Sea* (CWM 19710261–0994) with a balanced composition: as the draped corpse slips quietly over the side, the viewer's attention is diverted through colour, line, and gesture to the padre saying final prayers. Beament was depicting a personal experience, as he later recalled the service for a merchant seaman killed during a U-boat attack in the Gulf of St. Lawrence: "I decided to give the chap a decent send off ... I didn't like [it] but stopped the engines as the body went over the side ... didn't want the Jerries to get a sight on you ... while you were sitting like a duck."[27]

Jack Nichols confronted the atrocities of war head-on. His penchant was people. Not a traditional portrait painter, Nichols instead captured the "inner spirit" of his subjects with an undercurrent of strong graphic design. Orphaned at 14, Nichols took odd jobs in Toronto to support himself and his craft. Self-taught, his style did not follow a specific school but his work was encouraged by the artists Frederick Varley and Louis Muhlstock.

Nichols was commissioned as a naval artist in 1944 after being contracted along with Michael Forster to document the Merchant Navy for the NGC. Arriving in England in time for the D-Day embarkation, the artist sailed across the Channel to record the invasion in "a small merchant vessel, overflowing with soldiers and sailors."[28] His *Normandy Scene, Gold Beach Area* (CWM 19710261–4306) is reminiscent of Rodin's *Burghers of Calais* both in subject matter and execution. Rodin portrays the Burghers, fourteenth-century French heroes, as vulnerable yet defiant at the moment they are being led out to what they believed was their execution. Similarly, Nichols' homeless French citizens, wrapped in blankets and comforted by soldiers, face their fate with the same determination as their forbearers in Calais. Interestingly, the central figure bears a strong resemblance to the artist.

Jack Nichols, *Atlantic Crossing*.

In his portrayal of life at sea Nichols delineates his figures with a heavy hand and uses a monochromatic colour scheme to emphasize the mundane existence of the crew. In *Atlantic Crossing* (CWM 19710261–4285) the sailors are animated with exaggerated expressions and the Mannerist-like staging within a shallow and oblique foreground. This placement draws attention to the cramped living quarters below deck. Like the Mannerists, motion is created with the strong use of gestures and contour. In other works, Nichols cleverly chooses graphite and charcoal to draw a parallel to the grime and squalor-like living conditions onboard some ships. In *Taking Survivors On Board* (CWM 19710261– 4312) Nichols' survivors are rendered in much the same way that Henry Moore treated his subjects taking shelter in the London Underground. Both use a dramatic and darkened palette, deliberate overdrawing and delicate shading to heighten the pathos of their subjects.

The *Instructions to Artists* recommended that the human figure appear prominently in paintings to embody "the spirit and experiences of the Canadian troops."[29] Even without the CWR's memorandum distributed with the *Instructions*, many of the naval artists chose to focus on people as subjects on their own. According to Leonard Brooks:

> *Our terms of reference were to interpret as we could or make sketches. We could wander around and do anything. Being on board a ship sometimes there's not that much to paint … I'd go down to where they were cooking.… I put my uniform on, went to sea and was part of the discipline and life of a ship. Then I would return to London, take off my uniform, tuck myself away, and try to put together some of the paintings which I did as an artist alone in my room.*[30]

Brooks felt that his focus on the day-to-day shipboard activities of the crew elevated the self-pride in his subjects and the job that they were tasked to do. In *Potato Peelers* (CWM 19710261–1147), Brooks illustrates the quieter side of war. The painting of two sailors, perhaps from the Prairies, sitting "next to a couple of cans of gasoline in their life jackets" making preparations for the next meal in the middle of the Battle of the Atlantic, typified to him metaphorically Canada's all-encompassing war effort: "They were busy all the time, between that kind of thing and action stations. There was never a dull moment, when they weren't on watch, or peeling potatoes or doing something." According to Brooks, his portrayal of the ordinary routine of the fighting sailor provided an element that the camera could not capture. His watercolour snapshots, "often made under great difficulty on a tossing deck, [in] a cold wind, and [in] on-going action, caught at the time some of the feelings, the mood of the moment …"[31]

While primarily tasked to record the war at sea, the naval war artists would invariably pitch in when needed. "I spent many a long watch on the freezing open bridge of a Corvette to relieve a tired, worn-out seaman," remarked Brooks.[32] When "action stations" sounded in HMCS *Saguenay*, Rowley Murphy "dropped his paint brushes in a hurry to man a machine gun."[33] D.C. Mackay captured just such an experience in his *Corvette Bridge* (CWM 19710261–4211).

Indeed, the Canadian War Record paintings were all the more poignant because of the experiences and development of the individual artists. To be sure, compared to the art produced for the Canadian War Memorials Fund in the First World War, the Second World War program lacked diversity. Missing were the avant-garde painters — the cubists, futurists, modernists, and vorticists — whose unique contribution defined the CWMF and creatively impacted the development of future generations of Canadian artists. Nevertheless, A.Y. Jackson credited the "fresh vision" of the CWR participants with injecting life back into Canadian art with their introspective approach to portraying Canada at war:

> *There is a feeling of honesty and sincerity in these records … and little that is sentimental or melodramatic. The real value of our War Records programme was*

Leonard Brooks, *Potato Peelers*.

Canadian War Museum 19710261-1147

*that our artists, through their experiences, gained a deeper understanding and a
fresher vision with which in later days they were to stir up the rather sluggish
stream of Canadian art.*[34]

While the "national" school of art predominated early selection, the war artists embossed
their work with a personal stamp that was not seen before in traditional Canadian painting. Their "eye-witness" reporting on canvas conveyed a sense of time and feeling that the
camera could not, contributing to our understanding of the human element of the war.

After the war, Vice-Admiral G.C. Jones, Chief of the Naval Staff, attested to the importance of the war art collection: "The cold realism of the camera and the vivid colours of the

painter have given the people of Canada in this war a far greater knowledge of the work and objectives of their Navy than they ever had before."[35] The naval artists captured life at sea as those who are sailors know it still today.

Editor's Note: The paintings referred to in this chapter, but not reproduced, can be viewed on the Canadian War Museum website, *www.warmuseum.ca/cwm/explore/collections*, by linking to the "Artifact Catalogue" and entering the image credit number as the keyword.

Notes

1. LAC, RG 24, Vol. 11749, Canadian War Artists Committee, *Instructions for War Artists*, 2 March 1943.
2. CWM Beament's Artist's file, Harold Beament to H.O. McCurry, 22 October 1939.
3. James W. Essex, *Victory in the St. Lawrence: Canada's Unknown War* (Erin, ON: Boston Mills, 1984), 15.
4. CWM Murphy's Artist's file, Joan Murphy interview with Donald Mackay, 31 August 1978.
5. *Ibid.*
6. CWM Murphy's Artist's file, Rowley Murphy to H.O. McCurry, 25 March 1941, and McCurry to Murphy, 4 April 1941.
7. NGC, Canadian War Art, 5.1, H.O. McCurry to W. B. Herbert, Bureau of Public Information, 6 December 1940.
8. LAC, *Instructions to Artists*, Annex B.
9. A.Y. Jackson, *A Painter's Country: The Autobiography of A.Y. Jackson* (Toronto: Clarke, Irwin, 1976), 163.
10. David J. Bercuson and J.L. Granatstein, *Dictionary of Canadian Military History* (Toronto: Oxford University Press, 1992), 114.
11. Bernard Riordan, *C. Anthony Law: A Retrospective* (Art Gallery of Nova Scotia Exhibition Catalogue, Halifax, NS, 12 May–25 June 1989), 7.
12. Jackson, 163.
13. NGC, A.Y. Jackson to H.O. McCurry, 27 January 1943.
14. CWM Brooks's Artist's file, Interview with Leonard Brooks, 25 October 1977.
15. CWM Murphy's Artist's file, Rowley Murphy to H.O. McCurry, 20 February 1943.
16. CWM Forster's Artist's file, Forster to H.O. McCurry, 16 June 1944.
17. CWM Forster's Artist's file, H.O. McCurry to Forster, 22 June 1944.
18. CWM Wood's Artist's file, *Ottawa Citizen* (circa 1945, article filed without a caption or date).
19. CWM Wood's Artist's file, Tom Wood to H.O. McCurry, 13 January 1945.
20. Rowley Murphy, "An Artist with the Royal Canadian Navy," *Maritime Art* (December 1942–January 1943), 45.
21. CWM Beament's Artist's file, Joan Murray interview with Donald Mackay, 13 August 1978.
22. Murphy, 45.
23. CWM Brooks's Artist's file, Cynthia Malkin, "A War Artist Remembers," *The Sunday Post*, 11 November 1979.
24. CWM Beament's Artist's files, Joan Murray interview with Harold Beament, 15 May 1979).
25. *Ibid.*

26. CWM Wood's Artist's file, Joan Murray interview with Tom Wood, 2 May 1979; and CWM Brooks's Artist's file, Cynthia Malkin, "A War Artist Remembers," *The Sunday Post*, 11 November 1979.

27. CWM Beament's Artist's files, Joan Murray interview with Harold Beament, 15 May 1979.

28. Dean F. Oliver and Laura Brandon, *Canvas of War* (Ottawa: Douglas & McIntyre, 2000), 137.

29. Maria Tippet, *Lest We Forget: Souvenons-Nous* (London [Ontario] Regional Art and Historical Museums, 1989), 34.

30. Joan Murray, *Permanent Collection: The Robert McLaughlin Gallery* (Oshawa: Herzig Somerville Ltd., 1978), 14.

31. CWM Beament's Artist's files, CBC Radio interview, Leonard Brooks, 26 September 1945 (transcript).

32. CWM Archives, Brooks's Artist's File, Joan Murray interview with Leonard Brooks, 25 Oct 1977 (CWM Archives, Brooks' Artist's File).

33. Rowley Murphy obituary, *Toronto Star*, 15 February 1975.

34. Jackson, 165.

35. Grant MacDonald, *Sailors* (Toronto: Macmillan, 1945), iii.

CHAPTER 7

A Brave New World, 1945–60

Isabel Campbell

What the R.C.N. wants to know is whether our present naval types are obsolete, not how to make an atomic bomb or even how to drop it.
— CAPTAIN H.N. LAY, DIRECTOR OF NAVAL PLANS
AND INTELLIGENCE ON OPERATION CROSSROADS
(1946 BIKINI ATOLL ATOMIC TESTS)

With the dropping of atomic bombs on Hiroshima and Nagasaki in August 1945, the Second World War came to an abrupt and unexpected end. The bombs marked the beginning of an era of nuclear deterrence that challenged conventional maritime warfare strategy and seemingly rendered the world's foremost navies, the USN and the RN, not to mention smaller navies like the RCN, almost irrelevant. Postwar threat assessments demonstrated the relative weakness of the Soviet Union (especially its navy), the unlikelihood of immediate combat, and the long-term need for greater air defence. Western governments, therefore, made a priority of establishing strong peacetime economies, while naval officers worried that the warships and weapons developed during the Second World War might prove redundant for future wars. Science and technology were the waves of the future. Officers in the Royal Canadian Navy already knew that their current anti-submarine warfare capabilities could not adequately handle the latest German submarine types, the true fast submarines, which appeared during the latter years of the war. While by August 1945 the allies had defeated Germany, Japan, and Italy, most of the RCN's 400 warships were small, slow and obsolete. The Canadian Naval Surplus Disposition Committee planned to keep only the most modern larger ships in service, and it had already

John Horton, *The Changing Fleet After World War 2*, with the carrier *Magnificent* conducting flight operations surrounded by her escort group of Tribal-class destroyers.

begun dismantling the "sheep dog" navy that had defended convoys under the dangerous and difficult conditions of the Battle of the Atlantic. Faced with a combination of the unparalleled pre-eminence of the United States, the decline of Britain, and the lack of a credible maritime threat, the RCN knew it had a tough battle ahead to defend its core components, cruisers and aircraft carriers, in particular. Only by judicious planning, by cooperation with the American and British navies, and by flexibility in the face of change, would the RCN be able to defend its resources in the peacetime era ahead.

As we have seen in chapter 4, careful wartime negotiations with the RN allowed the RCN to acquire two light fleet aircraft carriers (*Warrior* and *Magnificent*), two cruisers (*Uganda* and *Ontario*), and a flotilla of Crescent-class destroyers near the war's end. In mid-1945, the RCN's post-war defence plans envisioned building upon its 1939 pre-war plans for flotillas of Tribal-class destroyers on each of the Pacific and Atlantic coasts, anticipating a defensive striking force of one aircraft carrier, two cruisers, and nine destroyers on each coast. As in the previous interwar peacetime period, the RCN was to concentrate upon the defence of Canada first, having the capacity to repel all but heavy task forces from the adjacent oceans, but it now foresaw three additional post-war tasks that have remained the basis of Canadian defence white papers over the decades to come: the protection of sea lines of communication; "hemispheric" or continental defence with the Americans; and support for international security through the United Nations. The deepening of defence cooperation with the U.S. in place of Britain created a new geo-strategic context for the RCN, while the addition of aircraft carriers to the fleet created a formidable new challenge of a different sort. Even after the government, in October 1945, cut the numbers of vessels planned almost in half, the RCN emerged from the Second World War with a much more impressive fleet than it had before 1939. What Douglas Abbott, the minister of national defence for the Naval Service, styled as the future "good, workable little fleet," quoted by Alec Douglas in his introduction to this book, would consist of "probably" two light fleet carriers, two cruisers and 10 to 12 fleet destroyers, along with some frigates for training purposes and other vessels in reserve.[1] And so, the active fleet for 1946–47 had the carrier *Warrior;* the cruiser *Ontario;* the destroyers *Crescent, Micmac,* and *Nootka;* the frigate *Charlottetown;* the minesweepers *Middlesex, New Liskeard, Wallaceburg,* and *Revelstoke;* the training ship *Sans Peur;* the auxiliaries *Dundalk, Dundurn,* and *Laymore;* a stores carrier, *Eastmore;* and a few smaller coastal vessels and tugs, along with some ships listed in the reserve force.

The challenge, paradoxically, was that after training so many wartime personnel, a shortage of well-qualified officers and ratings became the gravest problem facing the Canadian Navy almost immediately at the war's end. On 28 September 1945, the Canadian Cabinet optimistically approved a permanent naval force ceiling of 10,000 and a reserve naval force ceiling of 18,000. In truth, even as the RCN began the unpleasant task of demobilizing its personnel from a high of 92,529 in April 1945, there were fewer than 4,600 all-ranks in the "permanent force" RCN. The first to leave the navy were the "hostilities only" personnel who had not committed to serve after the war's end. However, due to shortages of certain

The Bikini Atoll tests were conducted to assess the destructive power of atomic blasts on ships at sea.

trades needed to help manage demobilization, such as naval writers, administrative staff, and firefighters, some of these personnel were not permitted to leave even after Minister Abbott made his public promises in Parliament. As their more fortunate colleagues found better paying civilian jobs and returned to their families, resentment in this group grew. Others who had joined the RCN in 1940 and 1941 for seven years of service expecting the war to last at least that long and who now hoped to leave "early" also became restless. In the end, the RCN had to rely heavily upon a small "interim" force of naval reservists — not all of them willing — to beef up the numbers until March 1947. As has been seen in the wartime chapters, differing perspectives and poor communication between the pre-war professional navy and wartime naval reservists had resulted in deep-seated bitterness. While some talented reservists such as the controversial Jeffrey Brock joined the permanent navy, most left for more promising civilian careers. Brock believed that the pre-war permanent officers contained many mediocre individuals who clogged up the promotion process, while some permanent force officers believed the former reservists lacked proper training and did not enforce discipline.

Abbott recognized that the key to reducing these tensions, while establishing a larger and more effective permanent force, was the better peacetime integration of the reservists. For that reason, his October 1945 pronouncements also included the establishment of a single reserve service combining the wartime RCNRs and RCNVRs, as well as incorporating new groupings of naval air reservists and university naval training divisions, all serving under one set of regulations and wearing a uniform similar to the permanent force — the latter point underscored by ending the wartime practice of officers sporting different stripes to distinguish the three former "services."

Chief of the Naval Staff, Vice-Admiral Rollo Mainguy, shares a coffee in the seamen's mess of *Athabaskan* while visiting the ship in Korean waters, February 1953.

Department of National Defence PMR98-151

However, despite these and many other well-intentioned reforms, the post-war Canadian Navy was not a happy institution. Desertions, absence without leave, and a host of other personnel problems plagued the navy from 1945 to 1949, although the poor morale of 1947 had improved slightly in 1948 as modest reforms were implemented. The chronic troubles came to a head in a quick succession of "incidents" — sometimes referred to as "mutinies," but in reality only brief work stoppages — in February and March 1949 aboard *Athabaskan*, *Crescent*, and *Magnificent*.

The commission of inquiry charged to investigate the situation published its findings as *The Mainguy Report*. Admittedly an enlightened and visionary document setting out a process to avoid repetition of the mistakes of the past, it also perpetuated a stereotypical view criticizing the upper ranks of the RCN as dominated by pre-war permanent force officers with overly British attitudes, and concluded that the problem was an absence of Canadian traditions in the navy. *The Mainguy Report* spoke to a need to "Canadianize" the naval service, and clearly the navy's senior leadership failed to appreciate the importance of symbols to the new national consciousness being developed by post-war Liberal governments through measures such as the Citizenship Act of 1947. Yet, in the intervening decades, naval officers adopted it as an important reference, although more recently historians have come to question its assumptions and findings.

The consensus now is forming that, while stating many obvious truths in guiding officer-rating relationships, *The Mainguy Report* also misrepresented the actual condition of the RCN in 1949. Even as the chief of the naval staff (Vice-Admiral Harold Grant) gave short shrift to "Canadian symbols," he laboured to modernize the navy and improve conditions with the few resources at his disposal in a climate of severe government retrenchment. Recent studies credit Grant's reforms, but point out that the far-reaching rank and trade group re-organization he implemented exacerbated a pre-existing shortage of able-bodied seaman to perform heavy labour in the three affected ships. A more general underlying cause was the perhaps unavoidable intergenerational tension that arose among the pre-war force, veterans of the Second World War, and post-war recruits — the bulk of the junior ratings — who lacked wartime experience and seemed "soft" to the older personnel. Finally, brief stoppages were nothing new: the RCN, like the RN, had a tradition of work stoppages even during wartime. In the broader context of past experiences, ratings saw stoppages as a means of protest, and invariably authorities at the time recognized most of their complaints as legitimate. After 1949, the inconsistency inherent in such an *ad hoc* process finally was officially clarified through the institution of welfare committees and formal grievance procedures. Subsequent generations of Canadian sailors have proudly sported "Canada" flashes on their shoulders.

Despite the personnel issues, RCN formations on both coasts had busy schedules and the few operational warships undertook a surprising number of cruises and operations during these bleak years. The year 1947, in addition to being marred by widespread dissatisfaction in the fleet, also witnessed several embarrassing groundings and mishaps, and tragic air accidents. It was a low point in the RCN's post-war experience. The best moment was undoubtedly Trafalgar Day, 21 October 1947, when the Fairey Firefly aircraft of 826 Squadron made rocket attacks on the captured German submarine *U-190* in Operation Scuppered off the coast of Nova Scotia. Unintentionally proving the efficacy of naval air, the submarine sank more quickly than anticipated and Commander Hugh Pullen, captain of destroyers aboard *Nootka*, cancelled bombing runs by the Supermarine Seafires of 883 Squadron, while the planned attacks by the 4.7-inch guns of *Haida* and *Nootka* proved both unnecessary and unsuccessful. The operation signalled a renewed emphasis on anti-submarine warfare as the RCN began fitting Squid mortar bombs and other ASW equipment into its destroyer forces.

Naval air continued to develop an important role in anti-submarine warfare as well as in the air defence of North America at this crucial early stage of its development. However, northern defence also took a higher priority and in September 1948 the carrier *Magnificent* (which had replaced *Warrior* earlier that year) cruised up to the Ungava Peninsula accompanied by *Haida* and *Nootka*. The two Tribal-class destroyers remained in northern waters visiting Churchill, Manitoba and then returning to Halifax through the Strait of Belle Isle. After the cruise, Commodore G.R. Miles, the commanding officer of *Magnificent*, observed

Library and Archives Canada PA-138210

The Tribal-class destroyer *Nootka* earning her reputation as a "train buster," bombarding Package 1 on the North Korean "Windshield" patrol area, 28 May 1951.

that station-keeping and manoeuvring had improved, but "that the sloppy habits of the wartime years, will only be eradicated by steaming in company with as many ships as can be made available."[2] The RCN had already adopted the American tactical organization and communication system based upon a flexible task force concept and so by 1948 ships on both coasts formed small task groups to accomplish specific goals. For example, in October and November 1948, *Ontario*, *Cayuga*, *Athabaskan*, *Crescent*, and *Antigonish* formed Task Group 215 and sailed to Pearl Harbor for extensive anti-submarine warfare training along with shadowing, night encounter, and other exercises with American forces. After this cruise, Rear-Admiral E.R. Mainguy, Flag Officer Pacific Coast, agreed with his warship commanders on the "incontestable" need for a definite RCN tactical policy and a live submarine for practice; however he concluded that basic training remained a priority and that the few Pacific coast ships could not yet keep a submarine employed full time. The Atlantic fleet also relied upon borrowed American and British submarines for training purposes.

Nonetheless, in 1948 the Canadian government approved building the icebreaker HMCS *Labrador*, in addition to three new anti-submarine destroyer escorts (which eventually culminated in the commissioning of the St. Laurent class in the mid-to-late fifties), four minesweepers, and one gate vessel. The RCN's carrier and destroyers had taken part in deck landing training, convoy protection, gunnery, night encounter, search and strike, and other exercises throughout 1947 to 1950, nationally and in company with American and British ships in the Caribbean and Bermudian waters. Despite the meagre naval resources, the ships

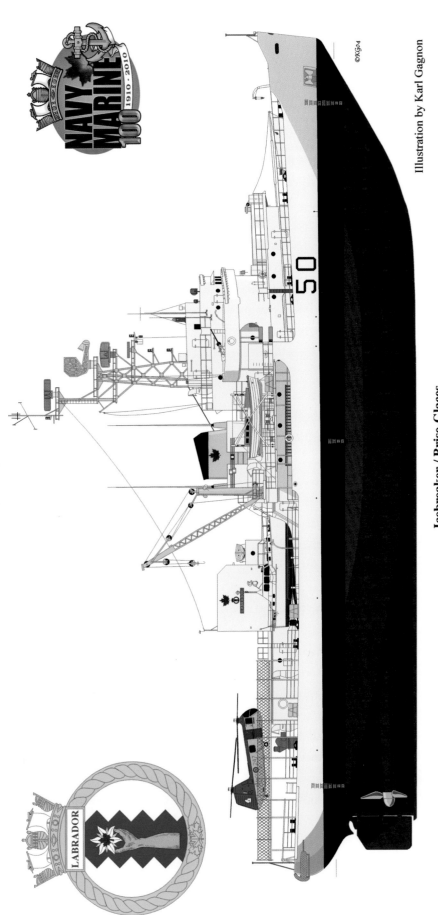

Illustration by Karl Gagnon

Icebreaker / Brise-Glaces
Classe LABRADOR Class

0 m   5 m   10 m

H.M.C.S. LABRADOR
1957

Launched 14 December 1951. Built by Marine Industries Ltd., Sorel.

08 July 1954 - 22 November 1957

Dimensions: 82 m x 19.2 m x 8.1 m   Crew: 228
Displacement: 6,490 tons   Speed: 16 knots
Armament: 2 x 1 - 40 mm.

N.C.S.M. LABRADOR
1957

Lancé le 14 décembre 1951. Construit par Marine Industries Ltd., Sorel.

08 juillet 1954 - 22 novembre 1957

Dimensions: 82 m x 19,2 m x 8,1 m   Équipage: 228
Déplacement: 6 490 tonnes   Vitesse: 16 noeuds
Armement: 2 x 1 - 40 mm.

of the Pacific coast at various times cruised through the Panama Canal to take part in large scale exercises with the Atlantic fleet. Naval air, still in its infancy, took over the air station at Shearwater in Dartmouth, Nova Scotia, from the RCAF, and maintained two carrier air groups of four squadrons equipped with Sea Fury and Firefly aircraft, along with No. 1 Air Training Group, Air Stores Depot, and a school of naval air maintenance. In the meantime, the Naval Research Establishment equipped all RCN warships with bathythermographs and began research on the oceanography of the Atlantic and Pacific Coasts along with innovative work in corrosion, allowing the RCN to contribute to the American and British naval research with significant accomplishments in their own right (see postscript at the end of the chapter for more details).

Continuing the close hemispheric defence relationship developed during the Second World War, the Joint Canada-United States Military Cooperation Committee (MCC) was formed with military planners from both countries to prepare a binational emergency defence plan along with longterm tentative plans. Although Canadians had difficulty acquiring American defence equipment because of security and exchange problems in the late 1940s, the RCN had already begun standardizing communications and other specific operating procedures and equipment during 1947, while still relying upon British procedures and equipment in other areas. Indeed, the British military also began some standardizing to American equipment and procedures. In the end, the three allies standardized much, trying to adopt the best equipment, but keeping national interests and industries in mind. Often the process was haphazard, but it permitted the RCN eventually to find its own footing on a rather slippery path.

In the wake of Soviet intransigence during the Berlin Crisis in 1948, many European nations began to negotiate with Canada and the U.S. to form NATO. On 4 April 1949, Belgium, Canada, Denmark, France, Iceland, Italy, Luxembourg, the Netherlands, Norway, Portugal, the United Kingdom, and the United States committed to collective mutual defence against aggression on their territories. While many of these European nations had distinguished naval histories, their immediate lack of resources and still devastated economies caused them to rely upon the USN, the RN, and the RCN for the defence of the North Atlantic. World tension increased when the Soviet Union exploded its first atomic bomb in September 1949, and soon the Canadian government had committed the bulk of the RCN's forces to the defence of the eastern Atlantic in the event of war. For nearly a decade to come, under NATO defence plans even the destroyers stationed on Canada's west coast were earmarked for "EASTLANT" and only a few small frigates, minesweepers, and local defence vessels were reserved for North American waters.

However, North American air defence had increased in significance and it received the lion's share of the defence dollar with the building of the early warning lines across Canada's north during the 1950s. Canadian responsibilities extended to the defence of Newfoundland and Labrador, even before it joined Confederation in April 1949, a burden shared with the United States, which had several bases scattered across the strategically located province, including a naval base at Argentia, and a large participation in air defence. Canada also committed resources to European defence. All the planning presupposed a war in Europe, and although Canada had sent the *Crescent* to Nanking in February 1949 during the course of the Chinese Civil War, no one anticipated a war in the Pacific — certainly not a war over Korea, an area of little interest to most western nations. Thus, when North Korea attacked the South on 25 June 1950, the Canadian government was ill-prepared and caught off guard. Under the auspices of the United Nations, the Canadian government joined the Americans and others in countering the attack.

By 5 July 1950, three destroyers from the Pacific fleet — HMC Ships *Sioux*, *Athabaskan*, and *Cayuga* — headed off to join the action on the far side of the ocean under the command of Captain Jeffry Brock. *Sioux*, despite its name, was a "V"-class destroyer with three 4.7-inch guns in single turrets, while *Athabaskan* and *Cayuga*, both proper Tribals, had six four-inch guns in three twin turrets. Command of the sea gave the United Nations an advantage, and although they were short on destroyers, the U.N. naval forces supported the land war very effectively. In general, RCN destroyers screened aircraft carriers, blockaded the occupied West Coast of Korea, and provided fire support against both North Korean maritime forces and land targets. They also took part in a number of other key missions.

Doug Bradford, *A Dangerous Threat*, pictures the "V"-class destroyer *Sioux* manoeuvring through local shipping while on patrol in Korean waters, not knowing if friend or foe manned them.

For example, during the Inchon landing of September 1950, Brock commanded RCN destroyers and several South Korean warships forming the Blockade Force, Southern Group. While they saw little action, these forces harassed North Korean forces and bombarded a variety of targets such as gun pits, look out points, trenches, and defensive positions on enemy held islands and coastal areas.

In October 1950, the American General Douglas MacArthur, the United Nations commander in Korea, pushed his forces north beyond the 38th parallel separating the Koreas to take the Northern capital of Pyongyang, and then continued north to the Yalu River forming the border with China. During this time, *Athabaskan* patrolled with American amphibious forces in the Sea of Japan off the East Coast of the Korean peninsula, while *Cayuga* and *Sioux* blockaded the West Coast, where Brock began a relief effort to assist island fishermen who were starving because they were unable to fish during wartime conditions. During these long periods at sea, the Canadian warships lacked afloat logistic support and relied upon American and British supply systems, receiving only sporadic mail service until the RCAF established regular flights to Korea. In November, they sailed to Hong Kong for a period of recreation and then joined a reduced United Nations West Coast naval squadron during what proved to be a lull before the Chinese People's Republic launched a massive counteroffensive across the Yalu River on 25 November. U.N. forces, caught off guard, retreated rapidly south.

As friendly forces attempted to withdraw from the port of Chinnampo (located about 35 kilometres inland along a narrow channel), Brock, in command of a task element of three Canadian, one American, and two Australian destroyers, responded to the desperate request for assistance. In the course of a difficult night passage on 4–5 December, HMAS (His Majesty's Australian Ship) *Warramunga* ran aground, freeing itself to return to the western entrance to the river. Shortly thereafter, *Sioux* touched bottom and in working free ran into a loose channel marker, damaging its starboard shaft, forcing its return to the western entrance. When the four other destroyers reached the port early in the morning, the Chinese had not yet arrived. Brock's force covered the departure of refugees and then began a concentrated bombardment to destroy rail lines, oil tanks, supply dumps, and factories along the waterfront. Meanwhile, *Athabaskan* proceeded some eight kilometres west of the city and destroyed three pillboxes to establish a safe anchorage for the small force's withdrawal the next night. Brock received a Distinguished Service Order for his leadership and service, while his navigator, Lieutenant A.L. Collier, received the Distinguished Service Cross for his success in navigating *Cayuga* as the lead ship on this hazardous duty.

By that time, a small Canadian army advance party had arrived in South Korea and the 2nd Battalion Princess Patricia's Canadian Light Infantry arrived in February 1951 to take part in the lengthy "war of patrols" that developed along the restabilized 38th parallel. Through this time, the RCN concentrated upon defending the West Coast or "friendly" islands, screening carrier forces, and taking part in "train-busting" — shooting up the trains and rail lines running along the East Coast. *Cayuga*, *Haida*, *Huron*, *Iroquois*, and *Nootka* (all Tribal-class destroyers), as well as *Crusader* (a Crescent-class destroyer) and *Sioux*, did subsequent tours in Korean waters, with *Athabaskan* completing three tours before the armistice of July 1953. *Crusader* earned accolades as the leading train buster in the predominantly

American Task Group 95, which destroyed 28 trains in total. The only enemy-inflicted RCN casualties came when *Iroquois* was bombarding an East Coast rail line: a shore battery hit the ship, killing an officer and two ratings, seriously wounding two others, and lightly wounding eight more on board.

Korean duty strained the RCN's limited resources, but shortly after the conflict began the Canadian government approved building the 14 St. Laurent-class destroyers (the second seven of these received improved armament and hull sonar and became the Restigouche class), along with 14 minesweepers and a number of gate vessels. They also approved the purchase of 75 TBM Avenger anti-submarine aircraft and 12 Hawker Sea Furies to replace the earlier Firefly and Seafire aircraft. At the same time, RCN commitments to NATO increased, and the RCN began to take part in Supreme Allied Commander Atlantic (SACLANT) exercises, including Mainbrace in 1952 and Mariner in 1953. The Avengers of 881 Squadron had trained in night fighting and they did especially well during Mainbrace,

The Halifax fleet enters the harbour on the occasion of its Golden Anniversary.

an exercise designed to test SACLANT's northern flank support for the European land battle. HMCS *Quebec* (formerly *Uganda*) and *Magnificent* took part along with over 170 NATO warships. As expected, such large-scale exercises highlighted American and British differences, problems of coordination and, as it turned out, the limitations of carrier task forces in bad weather. While the Atlantic fleet cruised to Europe, the Caribbean, and Northern waters, *Ontario* sailed from Esquimalt to Australia, New Zealand, Fiji, Samoa, and Pearl Harbor to exercise with units of the Royal Australian, Royal New Zealand, and Pakistani navies in 1951. By the autumn of 1952, *Ontario* carried out a full program of naval training while cruising around South America.

During that year, the RCN also initiated an intense naval reserve training program on the Great Lakes. Though the RCN was not a bilingual force, in 1952 they began to train French-speaking recruits at the basic training school HMCS *D'Iberville* in Quebec in professional naval subjects in both French and English to increase the representation of francophones and improve retention. Unfortunately, a 1955 study revealed that nearly 40 percent of French speaking recruits left the RCN in their first 10 months compared with 15 percent of English speaking recruits, and the RCN remained a predominantly Anglophone institution for several decades to come. Nevertheless, by 31 December 1956, the RCN had grown to just over 19,000 personnel and it had 55 fighting and mobile support ships in commission, including one carrier (*Magnificent*), one cruiser (*Quebec*), 15 destroyers, 10 frigates, six coastal escorts, 10 minesweepers, seven inshore patrol craft, an icebreaker, and a repair ship. The destroyers included the first two new destroyer escorts, *St. Laurent* and *Assiniboine*. In addition to the above, there were 16 other vessels under construction and 54 in reserve. Naval aviation also contributed two operational fighter squadrons, two operational anti-submarine squadrons, two training squadrons, along with pilot conversion training to helicopters and other functions. The first experimental anti-submarine helicopter squadron, HS-50, had commissioned on 4 July 1955 at Shearwater, near Dartmouth, Nova Scotia. Although a shortage of trained pilots made its critical work more difficult, nonetheless the idea of flying helicopters off destroyers gained ground as the squadron proved their utility in landing trials on the frigate *Buckingham*.

RCN ships took part in the NATO exercises New Broom V and VI in the spring and autumn 1956, which involved the use of Canadian ships and aircraft in the anti-submarine role and in the protection of merchant shipping. Concurrently, Canadian minesweepers took part in exercise Sweep Clear One. After *Bonaventure* commissioned on 17 January 1957, and *Magnificent* remained in service briefly to transport Canadian troops to the Suez, the RCN actually realized its "two carrier" dream for at least a few months. While the troop transport role did not arise often, the concept remained relevant in RCN plans. More regularly, *Bonaventure* carried Banshee jet fighter aircraft, Tracker anti-submarine aircraft and Sikorsky helicopters for its primary ASW role. By this time, the American SOSUS (Sound Surveillance System) network to locate and identify submarines through a system of deepwater "passive" hydrophones (that is, for "listening" as opposed to "active" pinging sonar) began operations, including newly built stations first at Shelburne, Nova Scotia, and later at Argentia, Newfoundland. The Naval Research Establishment, Dartmouth, Nova Scotia, was busy with the development of variable depth sonar, and work with helicopters progressed.

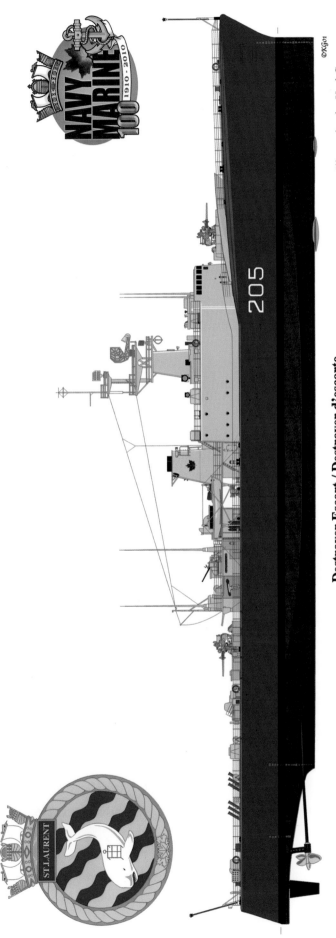

Destroyer Escort / Destroyer d'escorte
Classe ST-LAURENT Class

Illustration by Karl Gagnon

H.M.C.S. ST-LAURENT (II)
1955

Launched 30 November 1951. Built by Canadian Vickers Ltd, Montreal.

29 October 1955 - 14 June 1974

Dimensions: 111.6 m x 12.8 m x 4 m
Displacement: 2,263 tons   Speed: 28 knots   Crew: 249
Armament: 2 x II - 76-mm; 2 x I - 40 mm; 2 Limbo; torpedoes.

N.C.S.M. ST-LAURENT (II)
1955

Lancé le 30 novembre 1951. Construit par Canadian Vickers Ltd, Montréal.

29 octobre 1955 - 14 juin 1974

Dimensions: 111,6 m x 12,8 m x 4 m
Déplacement: 2 263 tonnes   Vitesse: 28 noeuds   Équipage: 249
Armement: 2 x II - 76 mm; 2 x I - 40 mm; 2 Limbo; torpilles.

0   5   10 m

Eventually, these developments helped the RCN face the extremely difficult challenge of dealing with the first nuclear submarines, though naval historian Marc Milner correctly concludes that the St. Laurents could hardly do so and even the newer Restigouche-class destroyers could not stop missile-firing submarines. In 1957, the RCN ordered four new "repeat Restigouche" class (which became the Mackenzie class) and two more for 1958 (the Annapolis class). By early 1959, Naval Board decided to rebuild the original seven St. Laurents into an "improved" class equipped with variable depth sonar and helicopters, enhanced by the development of the "Beartrap" haul-down system, which allowed helicopters to land on the destroyer decks under nearly all weather conditions.

In addition, the Canadian Cabinet had approved the building of two tanker-supply ships in 1958. The first of these, *Provider*, was still under construction when the decade ended, but the RCN entered 1960 with a modern capable fleet of much greater flexibility. The Canadian Navy had succeeded in pushing forward a new joint RCN-RCAF "Concept of Maritime Operations" in 1957, which resulted in revised mobilization plans with a greater emphasis upon North American defence rather than eastern Atlantic defence in the early days of all-out nuclear war. The concept of operations created three zones: an inner one extending 320 kilometres out from the coast where submarines might launch missiles at shore targets and from which they should be excluded; a middle combat zone where submarines should be destroyed before reaching the inner zone; and an outer zone for the early detection and harassing of submarines. By 1960, forces on the East Coast of Canada developed the "Beartrap" concept (not to be confused with the helicopter haul-down equipment of the same name) of patrolling likely missile launching locations for submarines, acting on "cueing" from the SOSUS system to support maritime forces, a process tested in "SLAMEX" exercises, just as reality caught up with theory. RCN monitoring of the Soviet fishing fleet, which appeared off the Atlantic coast of Canada in the mid-1950s, revealed several "unidentified" submarines close to shore. A real threat now existed.

During the Second World War, the RCN had learned the importance of "tame" submarines for anti-submarine warfare training. In the post-war period, the RCN relied upon a loaned American submarine on the West Coast and British submarines of the Sixth Submarine Squadron on the East Coast. Not surprisingly, they hoped to acquire Canadian submarines to improve anti-submarine training. Meanwhile, by 1957, the RCN became aware of the importance of nuclear powered submarines (SSNs) as an anti-submarine weapon and pursued the acquisition of this type for both training and operational purposes. Discovering eventually that the employment of SSNs would be beyond their means, the RCN decided instead to acquire conventional submarines, as will be seen in chapter 8. The useful operational life of the Banshee fighter aircraft also ended about this time, and the RCN retired them in 1962 without replacement. Air defence remained a thorny problem for the Canadian fleet, though naval staff carefully examined new anti-air and anti-missile missile systems and kept track of new technological developments to address this issue.

The naval world in 1960 was a difficult one for a smaller professional force like the RCN. American historian David Alan Rosenberg has described the massive proliferation of American nuclear weapons by 1960 in a seminal article aptly entitled "The Origins of Overkill."[3] Even the newly elected American president, John F. Kennedy, ran his campaign based upon fear of a "missile gap." We now know this was fictitious, but if Soviet forces were still well behind, they were working hard to catch up in an expensive arms race led by the American nuclear submarine force and the Polaris missile. The reality of mutually assured destruction (MAD) allowed the RCN to focus upon the actual use of naval power in peacetime and limited wars, as well as preparations for nuclear war. Unlike the RCAF and the Canadian Army, the RCN did not pursue access to nuclear weapons with any vigour. Rather, the RCN laboured to maintain its 20 percent of the small Canadian defence budget, with which it sought to specialize in anti-submarine warfare with the flexibility to undertake minesweeping, some troop transport, and maintain minimum standards of air defence and gunnery.

Captain Lay's statement at the beginning of this chapter, that "what the R.C.N. wants to know is whether our present naval types are obsolete, *not* how to make an atomic bomb or even how to drop it," had been confirmed correct by the verdict of history. The brave new world of atomic weapons had not spelled the end to conventional maritime forces, as the Korean Crisis, the Suez Crisis and the increasing importance of United Nations peace-keeping actions demonstrated. The RCN had a relevant and even significant role to play because Canadian naval units deployed quickly and effectively when their government needed them.

Notes

1. House of Commons *Debates,* 9 and 22 October 1945.
2. LAC, RG 24, Vol. 11529, Miles to Flag Officer Atlantic Coast, "Reports of Proceedings, *Magnificent,*" October 1948.
3. David Alan Rosenberg, "The Origins of Overkill: Nuclear Weapons and American Strategy, 1945–1960," in *International Security* (Spring 1983).

Maritime Research and Development, 1945–60

Harold Merklinger

The post-war restructuring of defence activities saw a defence research board (DRB) established to report directly to the minister of national defence. Formed on 28 March 1947, DRB absorbed 18 laboratories including NRE. In spite of this effort, the growing Soviet submarine threat demanded the re-invigoration of naval research and development. Consequently, an expanded Naval Research Establishment was planned for 200 personnel by 1955, while a new site, the Pacific Naval Laboratory (PNL), was established in Esquimalt in August 1948, initially with some 30 personnel. The Naval Engineering and Test Establishment (NETE) opened at LaSalle, Quebec, in 1952 to develop and prove systems for the navy's advanced-design destroyer escorts.

At NRE, scientist John Longard conducted the first full survey of water temperature as a function of depth (in HMCS *Sans Peur*) in the fall of 1946. His studies confirmed that sonar transmissions in East Coast waters were being refracted downwards, away from submarines near the ocean surface, meaning sonars needed to be placed deeper in the water. Consequently, NRE developed a variable depth sonar (VDS) for towing from the new ships. The Americans and British did not believe that the simple Canadian towed sonar concept could work. Side-by-side tests in 1958 of the U.S., U.K., and Canadian designs demonstrated nearly identical performance, and the RN thereafter adopted the Canadian design while the USN repackaged existing sonars in a similar configuration.

Meanwhile the mothballed wartime fleet was rusting away. Since 1823 it had been understood that a bronze propeller connected to a steel ship immersed in saltwater would act as a "battery" that accelerated corrosion. A painstaking five year science effort by Kenneth (Barney) Barnard of NRE resulted in effective corrosion protection methods that were adopted worldwide. Barney received the Order of Canada in 1978 for this work.

In 1949, the DATAR (Digital Automated Tracking and Resolving) project was begun by Lieutenant Jim Belyea and a man named Stan Knights (working with Ferranti-Packard Canada). The project aimed to integrate all radar, sonar and vehicle position data, and to transmit and share it within a task group. While the project was abandoned due to size (8,300 vacuum tubes per ship) and cost ($80 millions to fit the fleet), it became the model for nearly all subsequent command and tactical data systems, and its unusual data input device — the track ball — will be found on many ships today.

Renewed hydrofoil work begun independently by ex-RCN officer Duncan Hodgson was transferred to NRE in May 1951. Early prototypes were disappointing, but a breakthrough came by reversing the original Bell-Baldwin design, putting the main foils aft and the steerable foil forward. By January 1960 there was confidence that a 180-tonne craft capable of foil-borne operation in a high sea state could be built.

To support the research and development effort, the navy added research vessels to their post-war fleet. HMCS *Cedarwood* (AGSC 539), along with former warships like *New Liskeard*, *Sackville*, *Kapuskasing*, *Oshawa*, and *Fort Francis*, not only supported the acoustics and oceanographic survey program off the Canadian coasts, but also commenced probes into the Arctic. From this time on, the Canadian Navy has maintained its own fleet of research vessels.

Department of National Defence CN-5071

The prototype CAST 1/X variable depth sonar undergoing trials fitted in the destroyer *Crusader*.

The original "trackball" developed for the innovative DATAR datalink system was fashioned from a five-pin bowling ball.

Ferranti-Packard, courtesy John Vardalas

CHAPTER 8

Years of Crisis: The Canadian Navy in the 1960s

Richard Oliver Mayne

There are no absolute solutions to the questions posed and it is obvious that we can argue ourselves in or out of any problem. Therefore, since we cannot with certainty forecast the future, it becomes important to shape our forces on the known with sufficient flexibility to react to the unknown.
— FALLS REPORT, 31 JANUARY 1967

Nine days after he had become chief of the naval staff on 1 August 1960, Vice-Admiral Herbert Sharples Rayner suggested to his Naval Board that little was going to change on his watch. Since his predecessor, Vice-Admiral Harry DeWolf, was "turning over the 'ship' in good shape and on the proper course," Rayner told his officers that they merely had to press on and the navy would continue to weather relatively fair seas.[1] Those reassuring words were short lived. Soon after Rayner took over, the navy would be flooded by technical, strategic, tactical, financial, political, and organizational changes that would leave it sailing rudderless into an uncertain future. These events made the 1960s one of the most tumultuous periods in the Canadian Navy's history.

If the navy truly experienced a "Halcyon Age" in the 1950s, as a number of scholars have claimed, it was the product of Harry DeWolf's firm leadership. His political masters were offering limited funding for future construction, and as a result DeWolf realized that the

David Landry, *HMCS* Chaudière —
1962 Fisheries Patrol, investigating
Soviet trawlers on the Grand Banks.

RCN had no other choice but to specialize in anti-submarine warfare. Yet the root causes that would trigger so much uncertainty in the 1960s were starting to blossom in the final years of his tenure. A new American strategy, known as "flexible response," placed greater emphasis on conventional rather than potential nuclear responses to deter aggression and crises in the Third World. This caused some Canadian naval officers to question whether DeWolf's decision to specialize in ASW was the right one. Without general-purpose ships the RCN could easily find itself in the embarrassing position where it would be unable to participate in important alliance missions involving the use of conventional forces in limited war situations. A crisis in the Congo quickly drove the point home to the new Vice-Admiral Rayner. Although there was no need for the RCN to assist in this particular mission, the government suggested that the likelihood of naval involvement in a future United Nations operations was high.

Technical developments and alliance commitments also served to suggest that the RCN needed to incorporate some flexibility into its force structure plans. With an explosion of innovative technologies changing the nature of naval warfare, the post-war naval revolution ushered in a new era in ship construction. Due to the emergence of Soviet supersonic aircraft, guided missiles, and fast nuclear-powered submarines, naval designers were left with few options but to build bigger and more expensive ships packed with highly technical detection, weapons and propulsion systems. To complicate matters further, another new NATO strategic doctrine, known as "MC 70," told the alliance that in the event of war the supreme allied commander Atlantic (SACLANT) would take the fight to the Soviets by destroying submarines in the eastern Atlantic. This, however, would put allied naval forces well within the range of Soviet aircraft. The problem for the RCN, some argued, was that a specialized ASW fleet without medium range anti-aircraft missiles, or replacements for either the Banshee fighter or the aircraft carrier *Bonaventure*, would be left out of NATO's advanced operations and instead would be relegated to secondary duties in the western Atlantic.

The question of how much versatility the Canadian Navy should possess was not an easy one to answer. Rayner's solution was to build "a balanced anti-submarine force" that would be "three-fifths anti-submarine surface vessels, one-fifth anti-submarine submarines and one-fifth general purpose ships."[2] Based on its NATO commitments, the RCN was expected to provide a fleet of 43 ships, and applying the formula to this total produced a force of nine submarines, eight general purpose frigates (GPFs), and six "heliporter" frigates, which would complement the seven St. Laurent-, seven Restigouche-, and six Mackenzie-class destroyer-escorts (DDE) that would still be in service by the early 1970s. While Rayner felt that this program was realistic, he nevertheless knew it would be a hard

The fleet that wasn't: this June 1961 view of a combined USN-RCN Task Force has much of the navy's ambition on display, including in the right foreground a nuclear attack submarine (USS *Triton*) and, in the second line to left of *Bonaventure*, the carrier USS *Essex*.

sell to a cost-conscious government. As a result, he turned to his vice-chief-in-waiting, Jeffrey "Brimstone" Brock, to help him make the pitch to the other service chiefs as well as the government.

Brock's report was the centrepiece of Rayner's campaign to get final approval for the GPFs, submarines, and heliporters. On 31 July 1961, Brock and his committee delivered with a program of eight GPFs, 12 conventional and nuclear submarines, 12 heliporter frigates, two Arctic patrol vessels, and two tankers, as well as various upgrades and modernization programs that represented a totally unrealistic and impossibly expensive fleet. *The Brock Report* has often been interpreted as the most blatant manifestation of the RCN's long-standing desire to acquire a large, multi-purpose navy. This represents a misreading of the report's purpose: third-party opinions offered at the time actually suggest it was successful in achieving its primary aim. As Rayner would later explain, Brock's paper fleet was simply a guide that was never meant to sail. Instead, by allowing it to identify the ideal force structure, Rayner would use Brock's report as a tool to acquire the more realistic ASW fleet with a relatively small measure of versatility that he was really pursuing. Although Brock did not realize it, his report was, therefore, the "smoke and mirrors" that suddenly made Rayner's preferred program (eight GPF, six ASW heliporter frigates, and six USN Barbel-class submarines) look much smaller, and earned it a ringing endorsement from the distinguished defence research scientist Dr. R.J. Sutherland, who applauded Rayner for his attempt to make "a slight alteration" to the navy's "super-specialized" ASW nature.[3]

Rayner was willing to make considerable sacrifices to get what the Canadian Navy needed to be an effective force at sea. This was particularly true when it came to establishing a submarine service. When acquiring the American Barbel-class subs proved problematic, since Diefenbaker's government was concerned about the high cost of these submarines, Rayner listened carefully to the suggestion by defence minister Douglas Harkness to take a close look at the British Oberon class instead. If accepting the less capable Oberon was the price for establishing a submarine service, it was one that Rayner was more than willing to pay.

The navy had good reason to focus on the acquisition of the Oberons and GPFs. A large portion of the existing fleet consisted of Tribal- and Crescent-class destroyers as well as Prestonian-class frigates, all Second World War era ships that would be coming to the end of their useful operational lives by the mid and late 1960s. Block obsolescence was one of the greatest problems facing the RCN at this time, which made it essential to get a replacement program in the shipyards as soon as possible. Indeed, the GPFs were intended to spend the majority of their career not only supporting the anti-submarine fleet, but also answering Rayner's versatility requirement, with shore bombardment guns, guided missiles, and a small trooplift capability, should the RCN ever need it.

The Cuban Missile Crisis in October 1962 went a long way toward showing that Rayner's anti-submarine focus was the right one operationally. The American mid-month discovery of a Soviet attempt to establish ballistic missile bases on the Caribbean island sparked a political and military showdown that brought the world to the edge of nuclear annihilation until a naval "quarantine" (effectively a blockade) of the approaches to Cuba forced Moscow on 28 October to agree to dismantle the sites. Operations at sea as such were

intense, and the RCN played a major role in the ASW aspects. It is generally accepted that the anti-submarine portion of the crisis began when a Zulu-class submarine was sighted alongside a Soviet fleet auxiliary ship on 22 October 1962. Although it cannot be confirmed without access to Soviet naval archives, this submarine was likely the one that RCAF Argus aircraft later detected and then tracked over the period 26–29 October on its way to the northeastern seaboard. In any event, the probability that other Soviet submarines (nuclear-armed with either torpedoes "for self-defence" or offensive missiles) were off the coast of North America made the task of detecting them critical, the more so since by 27 October American and Canadian officers believed they had made contact on various occasions with seven submarines in the Atlantic (two of which were reported to be in the Canadian area of operations) as well as at least one in the Pacific.

To avoid public panic sailors were not recalled from leave and the fleet was sent to sea under the guise of national "exercises." The reality, however, was that the RCN was doing as much as it could to prepare for war. The operational commander in Halifax, Rear-Admiral Kenneth Dyer, was not prepared to take any chances in the nuclear age, and the scope of the Canadian Navy's actions capture the seriousness of the crisis: ships and aircraft were dispersed with wartime payloads and provisions; secondary headquarters and bases were prepared; vessels in maintenance were rushed to sea; and *Bonaventure* and its escorts were ordered home from a NATO exercise in the eastern Atlantic. Of the 136 "contact-events" made in or near Canada's WESTLANT (western Atlantic) zone — without Soviet archival corroboration the number that were actual submarines remains a mystery— there is little doubt that HMCS *Kootenay* was firmly tracking a Foxtrot off Georges Bank in early November (though the crisis had passed, monitoring of Soviet activity continued, to ensure compliance with the Kennedy-Khrushchev agreement). Despite close encounters with Soviet trawlers that steered aggressively toward the Canadian destroyer in an active attempt to break its contact with the submarine, *Kootenay* nevertheless stuck with the target until relieved by USN forces. In the end, it appeared that there were at least two Soviet submarines in the 160-kilometre deep Canadian patrol area straddling across the Atlantic from Cape Race to a point roughly 500 kilometres to the west of the Azores, and either RCN or RCAF forces detected both of them. It was an impressive display and an important contribution.

Department of National Defence DNS-24685

The sea-based fighter air defence of the fleet, as provided by these Banshees flying over *Bonaventure*, would prove too costly to maintain, and both aircraft and carrier would be scrapped by the end of the decade.

The RCN's response to the crisis nevertheless spawned a controversial legacy. It is generally accepted that Dyer placed the RCN on a war footing and kept its ships at sea — effectively mobilizing the RCN's East Coast fleet — without explicit direction, because senior political and naval leaders in Ottawa were paralysed by the crisis. However, some analysts then and since have argued that the decision was not Dyer's to make, and in consequence his behaviour constituted a serious breach of the democratic ideal that elected officials control the military. Other scholars, however, are quick to counter such claims by observing that Dyer simply did what the CANUS (Canada-United States) alliance for the defence of North America required him to do: long before the current crisis, Canada had promised under the Basic Security Agreement that it would send its ships to sea in the event of a sudden emergency, and according to historian Wilf Lund, "[Dyer] recalled that it was a very intense situation and remembers thinking to himself, 'This could be the end' and he acted accordingly within the authority that had been delegated to him."[4] When viewed through this prism, Dyer's actions are much easier to justify. Indeed, no matter what one's opinion about its mobilization, the seagoing fleet emerged from the crisis confident that it could protect North America. Not only did its ability to patrol an area ranging from the Grand Banks to the approaches of New York City free USN ships for the actual blockade of Cuba, but also Canadian naval forces had successfully tracked a number of Soviet submarines.

That confidence, however, was soon challenged by certain operational realities suggesting that, while the RCN was capable of tracking Soviet submarines, it did not have the equipment to destroy them. The combination of the hull-mounted AN/SQS-503 search, 502 attack, and 501 bottom search sonars, along with the eventual introduction of the variable depth AN/SQS-504 sonar, gave the RCN destroyer-escorts an effective detection range of approximately 6,400 metres. Relying on ship-launched torpedoes and Mk 10 Limbo mortars (a direct descendant of Second World War technology) with a range of a mere 900 metres, the gap between the detection and weapon ranges in the destroyer-escort was so great that enemy submarines could attack the Canadian warships with virtual impunity. The marriage of the Sea King helicopter (that could operate some nine to 18 kilometres from the parent ship) to the destroyer-escort was intended to close this gap.

While the mock-up flight decks on *Buckingham* and *Ottawa* helped to ascertain the idea of flying helicopters off destroyers was technically feasible, it was not until the first Sea King helicopter was delivered in May 1963 and trials began on *Assiniboine* in November that the Canadian Navy truly learned the "DDH" helicopter-carrying destroyer concept had its limitations. Although the vast majority of observers agreed the Sea King was one of the best ASW platforms, extensive study suggested that the RCN was placing too much faith in its ability to restore the destroyer's tactical advantage over the nuclear submarine. The most serious of these issues was the important question of "dead time" — the period between the aircraft's launch and the point it reached the target — as it was determined that the aircraft had to be airborne and within nine kilometres of the contact to be effective. To some extent the same logic applied to *Bonaventure*'s fixed-wing Tracker aircraft, and as a result the solution to dead time was to add the "ASROC" anti-submarine rocket-thrown torpedo system (that could deliver a torpedo out to a range of 11 kilometres in a matter of minutes) to the Restigouche-class destroyer-escorts (DDE).

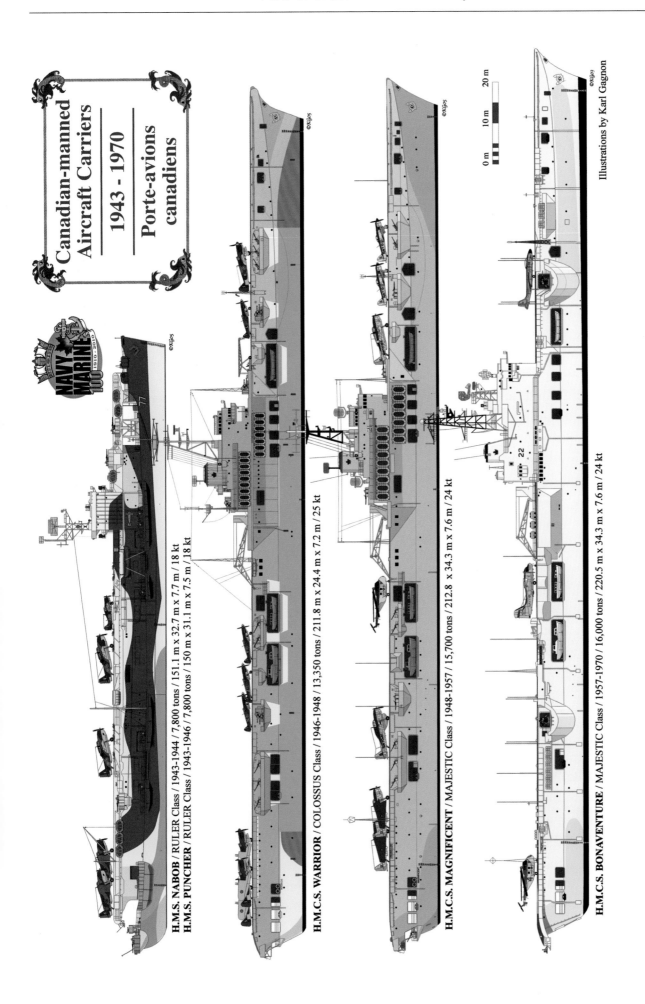

Canadian-manned Aircraft Carriers

1943 - 1970

Porte-avions canadiens

H.M.S. NABOB / RULER Class / 1943-1944 / 7,800 tons / 151.1 m x 32.7 m x 7.7 m / 18 kt
H.M.S. PUNCHER / RULER Class / 1943-1946 / 7,800 tons / 150 m x 31.1 m x 7.5 m / 18 kt

H.M.C.S. WARRIOR / COLOSSUS Class / 1946-1948 / 13,350 tons / 211.8 m x 24.4 m x 7.2 m / 25 kt

H.M.C.S. MAGNIFICENT / MAJESTIC Class / 1948-1957 / 15,700 tons / 212.8 x 34.3 m x 7.6 m / 24 kt

H.M.C.S. BONAVENTURE / MAJESTIC Class / 1957-1970 / 16,000 tons / 220.5 m x 34.3 m x 7.6 m / 24 kt

0 m   10 m   20 m

Illustrations by Karl Gagnon

Tactics within the RCN were also facing a larger revolution that would change the way officers thought about the concept of ASW operations. For much of the late 1950s and early 1960s the RCN had been leaning toward the idea that anti-submarine warfare could be left in the hands of friendly submarines working in concert with shore-based maritime patrol aircraft. Important operational exercises now identified a serious flaw in this concept: there were too many incidents where aircraft attacked friendly submarines in error. The best use of the anti-submarine submarine, therefore, was to treat it as a scout or lone hunter. New technologies and tactics were coming together to form a Canadian concept of operations based around destroyer groups of DDHs and DDEs protected by general purpose frigates. This would give each group the capability to defend itself from air threats, while combining the detection ranges of hull and variable depth sonars with the attack capability of the helicopter and ASROC. The fact that aircraft carriers were not included in this long term planning was no accident. In Rayner's navy the aircraft carrier's days were numbered, particularly since naval aviation was expensive, accounting for almost one-quarter of the navy's annual budget. This was particularly relevant with the election in April 1963 of a Liberal government set upon introducing costly new social programs.

Prime Minister Lester Pearson and his Cabinet were out to reform government as well as Canadian society. In that spirit of change, the new defence minister Paul Hellyer was determined to leave his mark on the Canadian military by making it more fiscally efficient and operationally relevant. Pointing to the sweeping conclusions of the Glassco Royal Commission on Government Organization, Hellyer also wanted to achieve economies for new equipment through the integration and eventual unification of the navy, army, and air force into one service.

The creation of the Sauvé Committee mandated to conduct a general review of Canada's defence policy was seen in many circles as a means to use a bipartisan parliamentary committee to justify heavy cuts to the department. Whether or not there was any truth to this claim can be questioned, but there was no doubt that the Canadian Navy was facing severe cutbacks. Not long after he had taken over as minister of defence, Hellyer instructed all the services that they would have to operate on a fixed budget of $282 million each year for three years. The sacrifices the navy had to make to meet these targets were considerable. Stations were closed, equipment upgrades were slashed, and plans were made to decommission the remaining Tribals earlier than intended, but it was the potentially deep cuts to the ship replacement program that hurt most of all.

Rayner had an almost fanatical devotion to the RCN's alliance obligations. Consequently, he was concerned that the minister's budgetary exercise, euphemistically known as "Operation CUTBACK," would, by 1970, leave the navy well short of its 43-ship commitment to NATO. In fairness to the minister, the force goals so firmly obsessing Rayner were arbitrary figures negotiated between Canadian naval officers and their alliance counterparts. In consequence, the final decision as to what naval forces Canada would contribute indeed rested with the nation's elected officials and not the Naval Board or SACLANT.

Force goals aside, the fact the General Purpose Frigate program was a Conservative initiative that was well over its estimated cost (having soared from $264 million in 1962 to just over $428 million within the year) made it a ripe target for a minister who was looking

Selected Canadian Naval Aircraft

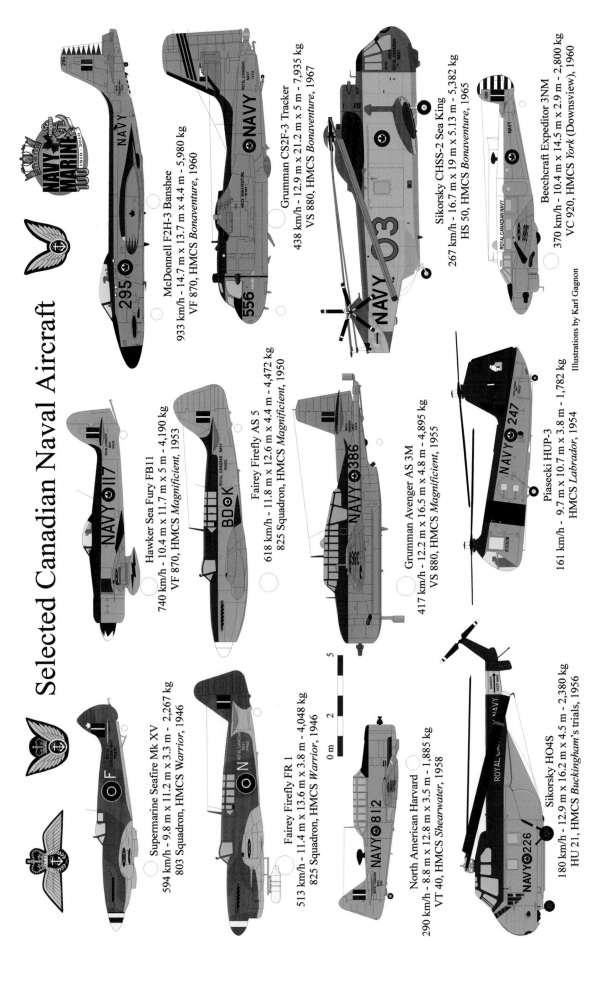

McDonnell F2H-3 Banshee
933 km/h - 14.7 m x 13.7 m x 4.4 m - 5,980 kg
VF 870, HMCS *Bonaventure*, 1960

Grumman CS2F-3 Tracker
438 km/h - 12.9 m x 21.2 m x 5 m - 7,935 kg
VS 880, HMCS *Bonaventure*, 1967

Sikorsky CHSS-2 Sea King
267 km/h - 16.7 m x 19 m x 5.13 m - 5,382 kg
HS 50, HMCS *Bonaventure*, 1965

Beechcraft Expeditor 3NM
370 km/h - 10.4 m x 14.5 m x 2.9 m - 2,800 kg
VC 920, HMCS *York* (Downsview), 1960

Illustrations by Karl Gagnon

Hawker Sea Fury FB11
740 km/h - 10.4 m x 11.7 m x 5 m - 4,190 kg
VF 870, HMCS *Magnificent*, 1953

Fairey Firefly AS 5
618 km/h - 11.8 m x 12.6 m x 4.4 m - 4,472 kg
825 Squadron, HMCS *Magnificent*, 1950

Grumman Avenger AS 3M
417 km/h - 12.2 m x 16.5 m x 4.8 m - 4,895 kg
VS 880, HMCS *Magnificient*, 1955

Piasecki HUP-3
161 km/h - 9.7 m x 10.7 m x 3.8 m - 1,782 kg
HMCS *Labrador*, 1954

Supermarine Seafire Mk XV
594 km/h - 9.8 m x 11.2 m x 3.3 m - 2,267 kg
803 Squadron, HMCS *Warrior*, 1946

Fairey Firefly FR 1
513 km/h - 11.4 m x 13.6 m x 3.8 m - 4,048 kg
825 Squadron, HMCS *Warrior*, 1946

North American Harvard
290 km/h - 8.8 m x 12.8 m x 3.5 m - 1,885 kg
VT 40, HMCS *Shearwater*, 1958

Sikorsky HO4S
180 km/h - 12.9 m x 16.2 m x 4.5 m - 2,380 kg
HU 21, HMCS *Buckingham*'s trials, 1956

for savings and was about to reorganize the military in fundamental ways. Yet Rayner's desire for the RCN to meet its alliance force goal commitment placed a strain on the navy even before Hellyer had become minister. Essential training often was sacrificed just to keep ships at sea, and by the end of 1962 there were signs that morale was starting to suffer. While many sailors complained about excessive sea time and the obvious over-extension of the Navy, a series of reports also suggested that the RCN was failing to satisfy the expectations of new recruits. The feeling that men were being employed in menial tasks and sent on dull cruises did little to convince individuals to re-engage. There was more. A lack of standardized on-the-job training and dissatisfaction with housing and the high cost of living did little to arrest the Canadian Navy's low re-engagement rates. In the end, most of these reports came to the same conclusion that "there is no evidence to say that morale is dangerously low. There is evidence that it is not as it could be."[5]

Excessive commitments and decreasing morale may not have had a direct impact on the fleet's efficiency, but the navy's declining re-engagement rate in conjunction with an inability to attract new recruits was creating a serious manning problem. In fact, while serving as Flag Officer Atlantic Coast in July 1963, Rear-Admiral Brock had warned that the personnel situation in his command was deteriorating so badly that the only safe way he could send *Bonaventure* and its escorts on an exercise was to pilfer sailors from ships in refit and maintenance periods. For Brock this was a real and worsening crisis, and he grew increasingly frustrated that naval headquarters was not taking decisive action. As serious as this growing manpower crisis was, however, naval headquarters was preoccupied with its own problems.

Reducing alliance force goal commitments would have allowed the navy to free up crews by paying off ships (taking them out of service) without the need to replace them. The problem, however, was that such a move would undercut Rayner's key argument that the navy needed its balanced ASW fleet replacement program to maintain its current alliance commitments. Adding to the confusion was the new vision that Hellyer had for the Canadian military, which he called "Mobile Force." As the minister later would explain, Mobile Force basically involved "an air transportable fighting unit which could be airlifted with its equipment for quick deployment anywhere in the world."[6] This concept, however, being rather amorphous, offered encouragement to certain naval officers to press the case for their preferred ship class over other types. For example, giving Mobile Force a sealift capability would require aircraft carriers, and as a result the minister's vision could be used as a means to give naval aviation a second chance. While this challenged Rayner's notion of working a small measure of versatility into a specialized anti-submarine force, the idea of giving the Canadian Navy an increased capability to respond to United Nations and limited war situations was something that Hellyer was willing to explore. According to one observer, however, the internal debate over versatility left the navy's senior staff "seething" and "dangerously fragmented" throughout 1963 and early 1964.[7]

The GPF was the first casualty of this growing internal debate over force structure. Although Hellyer was moving toward cancellation, it appears he had been considering a proposal from Rayner that would see the RCN acquire a smaller program of four GPFs. This moment of pause from the minister was the product of advice from one of his key advisers (defence scientist R.J. Sutherland) who suggested that the GPF was the ideal ship-type to meet the RCN's current needs. Whether or not the minister would have actually followed this advice is uncertain; however, Hellyer certainly was not going to advance a program that a number of senior officers were quietly hoping would get axed and thereby clear the way for their desired platform. On 10 October 1963 he announced the cancellation of the General Purpose Frigate.

It was actually a bitter former senior officer named James Plomer who helped Hellyer justify his decision to cancel the GPF. Having taken early retirement because he had been passed over for a promotion, Commodore Plomer was anxious to settle the score from his self-imposed exile. In a highly critical article in *Maclean's*, Plomer charged that the navy had morale, maintenance, and readiness problems, all due to the navy's senior staff being a "self-perpetuating, self-selecting group of admirals." Raking the Canadian Navy over the coals for a general purpose ship that was too slow and costly, Plomer told Canadians that the GPF was trying to do so many tasks that it could not perform any one of them particularly well. The notion that the RCN's senior leadership was filled with officers who were holding onto the outdated and class-based traditions of the Royal Navy resonated with Hellyer. In time Hellyer would tackle the issue of naval traditions with his plan to unify the three services into a single "Canadian Armed Forces," but at the time of Plomer's charges it was his conclusions on the navy's force structure that garnered the most attention.

Plomer had claimed that Rayner's force structure was a grave mistake and the cancellation of the GPF only served to reinforce that perception. Left without a cohesive procurement strategy, the RCN's fleet planning was thrown into a state of chaos and confusion for well over a year, with various groups within the navy divided between a destroyer force specializing in anti-submarine warfare, an amphibious fleet centred on the Iwo Jima and Essex-class carriers, or one that could accommodate both. It was a fruitless debate. Shopping for expensive carriers or nuclear submarines did not make sense given that Hellyer was slashing the military's budget. Put another way, the navy should have realized that there was only enough money to build either a fleet for anti-submarine warfare or one for limited war situations, but not both.

Firm direction was required to help the navy navigate these troubled waters and that was something the beleaguered Rayner could no longer provide. He had little strength left, going so far as to tell the minister in November 1963 that he would only stay on as chief of naval staff for another eight months, at which time it was his intention to retire. This effectively left the navy with a lame duck at a time when it needed a tiger. In fairness to Rayner, Mobile Force had put him in a difficult situation. Ignoring the minister's sudden interest in limited wars risked the possibility that the navy would be left behind if Canadian defence policy somehow shifted in this direction. The same was true for the minister's interest in the possible acquisition of nuclear submarines — a development that was predicated by evidence that two Soviet nuclear submarines had recently violated Canadian sovereignty in the Arctic. There was no crystal ball at naval headquarters to say that the current incarnation of Mobile Force would stall at the planning phase or that nuclear submarines would prove too rich for the government's blood (as we now know happened in both cases), and therefore Rayner had little choice but to hedge his bets. Moreover, challenging

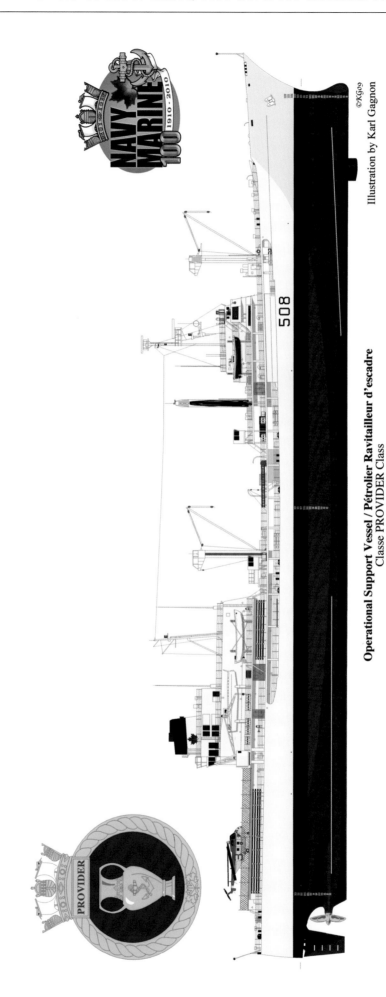

©AG09

Operational Support Vessel / **Pétrolier Ravitailleur d'escadre**
Classe PROVIDER Class

Illustration by Karl Gagnon

H.M.C.S. PROVIDER (II)
1967

Launched 05 July 1962. Built by Davie Shipbuilding and Repairing Co. Ltd., Lauzon.

28 September 1963 - 24 June 1998

Dimensions: 168 m x 23.2 m x 9.1 m
Displacement: 22,700 tons   Speed: 20 knots   Crew: 142
Armament: none.

N.C.S.M. PROVIDER (II)
1967

Lancé le 05 juillet 1962. Construit par Davie Shipbuilding and Repairing Co. Ltd., Lauzon.

28 septembre 1963 - 24 juin 1998

Dimensions: 168 m x 23,2 m x 9,1 m
Déplacement: 22 700 tonnes   Vitesse: 20 noeuds   Équipage: 142
Armement: aucun.

0   5   10 m

ministerial directives at a time when the government was in the process of cutting budgets was not smart politics. From that perspective, therefore, Rayner did the right thing by forming yet another *ad hoc* study group to look into force structure, with Commodore H.G. Burchell as chair.

Tasked with studying alternative naval programs, Burchell was fair and understood the dangers that the building factionalism in the RCN posed, but his report did little to bring any stability. Advancing a three-module concept built around *Bonaventure* and two Iwo Jima-class amphibious assault ships, Burchell's committee designed a flexible force that — while keeping anti-submarine warfare as its primary function — placed the greatest emphasis yet on multi-role operations. The Burchell Report claimed that the three-module force could be sustained with a yearly budget of $252 million, but this was just the annual operating cost — questionable in its own right — and the fact that a price tag on building this fleet was not being properly debated at the staff level led to much circumspection.

Part of the problem for the Canadian Navy was that the minister was not providing clear direction on where the government was planning to take Canadian defence policy. The Liberals were uncertain how to deal with the growing instability in the Third World and, wanting to keep their defence options open for as long as possible, they were keen to avoid binding "the government to a particular formula which might prove an embarrassment in the future."[8] When the *White Paper on Defence* appeared in March 1964, it was vague on the subject of naval force structure. Other than recognizing that the RCN's primary role was to make an effective "Alliance contribution" through a modest anti-submarine warfare fleet, the white paper's only clear message for the navy was that it was to deliver "the maximum intensity of surveillance and maximum defence potential for the least cost."[9]

The white paper's message on cost had other important implications for the service. Economies would also be made through the integration and eventual unification of the Canadian military, and rather than having chiefs and individual staffs representing the navy, army, and air force, the new Canadian Forces headquarters would be organized along functional lines under the authority of a single chief of the defence staff. Integration meant that the Naval Board and Staff would cease to exist on 1 August 1964.

Operational experience at sea was certainly showing why it was so important that the navy get an immediate replacement program for more anti-submarine destroyers. In particular, operational commanders were happy that the DDH was making tremendous strides to becoming a reality. The completion of helicopter trials on the converted destroyer *Assiniboine*, the anticipated commissioning of the purpose-built *Nipigon* in May 1964 and *Annapolis* in December, along with the completion of two of *Assiniboine*'s converted sisters — *St. Laurent* (4 October 1963) and *Ottawa* (21 October 1964) — would give the Canadian Navy a total of five DDHs by the end of the year. There were other reasons to celebrate. The original four Sea King trial helicopters had given the RCN much-needed experience with the type but the arrival of the first Canadian-built aircraft in September 1964 meant there would be a steady supply until the production line was complete. Moreover, the impending trials between the fleet's first operational support ship, HMCS *Provider*, and the destroyer *Yukon* in May would give the navy a considerable logistical support capability to operate well beyond

Canada's littoral waters. And finally, the navy could also rejoice from the fact that the first of the Oberon submarines (*Ojibwa*) was launched in February.

These additions, however, did not make up for the RCN's losses. Getting rid of three of the last four Tribal class destroyers (*Nootka*, *Cayuga*, *and Micmac*), as well as placing the escort maintenance ship *Cape Breton* and all 10 RCN minesweepers into reserve helped generate funds for new equipment. Although the Tribals were far too old to make any real contribution to the RCN's anti-submarine warfare effectiveness, their early decommissioning had an impact on East Coast force structure: without replacements, the Third Destroyer Squadron was disbanded, while the First was below strength, making it difficult for it to carry out its mission.

The real issue to the operational commanders was not that the Tribals were being decommissioned; rather, it was the fact that these destroyers were being taken out of service without replacement, meaning that the navy would soon fall short of its 43-ship alliance commitment. Reducing the number of ships assigned to SACLANT brought further disruption to both coasts, as it necessitated a reorganization that saw three Atlantic destroyers head west while five Pacific destroyers went to the East Coast command. Such reorganization and consolidation made it next to impossible to maintain cohesion, with ships constantly joining or leaving the commands. In the words of one squadron commander, the situation made "it difficult to advance the overall efficiency of the Squadron as a unit."

By the time these transfers were complete in 1965, the five West Coast St. Laurents would join their Atlantic sisters in exchange for two Mackenzies and a Restigouche. Every single DDH was going to serve on the East Coast, leaving the West with a mixture of destroyer-escorts and frigates. While the Flag Officer Pacific Coast observed that the net loss of two destroyers "was a serious blow to our effectiveness," he was further disappointed when the RCAF reduced its Neptune patrol aircraft strength by four.[10] The lack of air support to the Pacific command was a particularly thorny issue. Earlier pleas to reassign either RCN Tracker aircraft or RCAF Argus to help deal with the Soviet cruise missile submarine threat were met with sympathy, but resulted in little action because the East Coast barely had enough aircraft to meet its own requirements.

As disturbing as these sacrifices were, however, an important exercise off the East Coast of North America forced the Canadian Navy to become even more introspective regarding its anti-submarine warfare commitment. SLAMEX 2/64, conducted between 16 and 23 September 1964, was billed as one of the most realistic attempts to test the "Atlantic system" by simulating a Soviet submarine missile attack on North America. Only the Cuban Missile Crisis of 1962 had come closer to the real thing, and the findings from SLAMEX were staggering. Ten of the 14 submarines — the vast majority — made it to their launch points, and the damage to North America had they been real Soviet submarines would have been catastrophic. For the previous two years the Canadian Navy had been obsessing over Soviet nuclear-powered submarines, only to have SLAMEX prove that the alliance could not even deal with the much slower diesel ones. There was only one conclusion: the Canadian Navy needed to take whatever it could get from the limited resources being offered by the government to invest in anti-submarine platforms.

Even before SLAMEX, however, senior officers were finally starting to accept the fact that the government would never provide the funds to build either multiple-purpose aircraft

The RCN's revolutionary ability to land a big helicopter onto a small heaving deck is demonstrated by this Sea King approaching *Assiniboine*.

carriers for limited war operations or expensive nuclear submarines. Vice-Admiral Dyer, who had taken over from Rayner as chief of the naval staff and was now the chief of personnel in the newly integrated Canadian Forces headquarters, gathered the remnants of the old Naval Board together and began a process that would finally develop a coherent force structure. Dyer had come to see the paradox that Rayner could never reconcile: how the navy was expected to acquire expensive platforms for an improved anti-submarine capability as well as an expanded limited war function, at the same time that the government was drastically slashing the defence budget. Reluctantly, Dyer came to accept the fact that only the destroyer could give the navy the widest range of capabilities with the funds being made available for new equipment.

The Canadian Navy's manpower problem was another key factor making Dyer's decision to build new destroyers a relatively easy one. Personnel shortages were having a terrible impact on the fleet's cohesion, operational effectiveness, training, and maintenance, as it was not uncommon for ships to experience a full crew turnover within any given year. The solution to this instability, according to a pivotal report written by Rear-Admiral W.M. Landymore, was to create a "cyclic system" in which ships were manned in such a way that a crew's training and individual needs would be "in phase" with the ship's operational and maintenance requirements. Although a clever idea, it did require an unusual and disruptive reorganization in which "on the designated day, a myriad of sailors with kit bags over their shoulders changing ships was the prevailing sight in the dockyards at Halifax and Esquimalt."[11]

While the cyclic system did eventually bring stability to the personnel situation, it was not designed to deal with the basic problem that the navy needed more recruits. And without sufficient personnel the system finally crashed on the East Coast in October 1964. Just as Brock had warned during the manning crisis of July 1963, the navy now found itself in a position where a lack of manpower resources was preventing it from sending ships to sea. The simple reality for the officers who wanted a construction program based around larger aircraft carriers, therefore, was that there were not even sufficient personnel to man the navy's current ASW fleet let alone a future one designed for multiple roles. Realizing that Hellyer was now anxious to give Canadian shipbuilders some naval contracts, Dyer and his ad hoc staff put their differences aside. The fleet that emerged was a realistic and specialized program consisting of a new class of four DDHs (the DDH-280s, which were also called "Tribals," because they were named after Native tribes, like their Second World War-vintage predecessors, or "Iroquois class," [which will be used henceforth] because *Iroquois* was the name given to the first one built), two additional fleet replenishment ("auxiliary oil replenishment" or AOR) ships, and two more Oberons, as well as an upgrade for *Bonaventure* and the conversion of the seven ships of the Restigouche class into ASROC carriers.

Unfortunately, the announcement of a new naval program did little to solve the navy's larger problems. The integration of Canadian Forces headquarters, supposedly designed to bring efficiency and economy, instead was producing much confusion, at least in the short term. So, too, did the creation of the minister's seven new functional commands — one of them being Maritime Command (MARCOM) — that effectively carved up the many functions formerly handled by the Canadian Navy. It led to some strange arrangements, and the subsequent chaos made it difficult for the navy to resolve many of its key issues.

This was certainly true for MARCOM's attempt to deal with its manning crisis. There was continued difficulty in producing enough sailors to keep ships at sea. A shortfall of over 500 men on the East Coast meant that the navy was lacking crews for three destroyers and one frigate, and to make matters worse it was clear that further reductions would be required once *Bonaventure* was recommissioned after its refit. Things were not much better on the Pacific coast where a predicted shortage of over 300 tradesmen in early 1966 resulted in a call to place three frigates into "hot reserve." The easiest solution, of course, would have been to reduce MARCOM's NATO force goals, but even Hellyer seemed to disagree, telling his officers "that a more judicious use of manpower would permit continued operations of ships."[12] If this was sending MARCOM a strange message, it certainly was not the first time nor would it be the last, as Hellyer's pattern of cutting the navy's budget while

getting his senior naval leadership to explore ways to maintain or even expand operational commitments would continue.

In late 1966 Hellyer announced that even though MARCOM's primary role would remain ASW he wanted once again to investigate the possibility of giving the Canadian Navy some general-purpose capabilities. Chief of Defence Staff (CDS), General J.V. Allard, wanting to avoid being caught in the "ring of 'Ad Hockery'" that had existed in 1963–64, gave MARCOM explicit instructions to conduct a study on the navy's current effectiveness as well as the type of flexibility that would be required in the future. Led by Captain R.H. Falls, the Maritime Systems Flexibility Report found that the ballistic missile-firing submarine (SSBN) threat was by far the greatest to North America. This conclusion, of course, was not new. What had changed was that the Soviets were developing the Yankee and Delta classes that would finally give them SSBNs with a comparable degree of firepower to the Americans. As bad as that was, the estimate that 40 percent of the Soviet submarine force

Rear-Admiral W.M. Landymore, Flag Officer Pacific Coast, presents the White Ensign for safekeeping to the Dean of Christ Church Cathedral, Victoria, British Columbia.

would be nuclear by 1977 (including 45 SSBNs) only made things worse. And that led Falls and his group to the sobering conclusion that the U.S. would feel compelled for its own protection to patrol Canadian areas if MARCOM was unable to do so. A strong Canadian ASW force was the only way to prevent such a scenario, making "our contribution to this defence a relatively easy, and at the same time essential, way of maintaining our sovereignty as a nation with pride and dignity."[13] As far as flexibility was concerned, Falls felt not only that the current maritime forces possessed a significant sealift capability, but also that any increase in flexibility would come at the expense of the ASW force unless more money was forthcoming.

Fall's instincts proved correct. Discussion around a Defence Planning Guidance document, intended to produce a five-year program out to 1972, revealed how unanticipated inflation rates would lead to a reduced DND budget of $1.725 billion. Although this meant that the Canadian Forces would not be maintaining the force levels approved in 1964, MARCOM was nevertheless given a hefty list of roles to perform. Rather than preparing for the coming cuts, the commander of MARCOM, now Rear-Admiral J.C. O'Brien, did as he was told and observed that he would need "a balance of forces" to create the type of flexibility that Hellyer wanted. It was a large fleet that would cost a considerable sum. For instance, part one of his plan (1967–77) called for the immediate acquisition of two amphibious fleet support vessels and two large destroyer command ships, the conversion of the Fundy-class minesweepers into mine hunters and the four Mackenzies into general purpose destroyers; and the eventual acquisition of 30 maritime patrol aircraft and a new training sub. The options for part two (1977–87) were even more costly and included calls for various mixtures of large attack carriers, helicopter carriers, general-purpose destroyers, and nuclear submarines. This fleet never stood a chance. Instead, the new defence minister, Leo Cadieux, told MARCOM what it should have already known: that the reduced budget would require major cuts (in the order of $234 million). Rather than exploring new acquisitions, MARCOM spent much of 1968 looking for ways to reduce its current program. Even such painful reductions as the prized DDH-280 (Iroquois class) and Operational Support Ship programs were investigated, but in the end MARCOM settled on cutting the Improved Restigouche program from seven to four ships.

As difficult as this debate over force structure was for MARCOM's senior leadership, the changes brought on by the follow-on to integration — full-blown "unification" — were worse. A significant number of flag officers elected early retirement rather than face the prospect of having to put on the new green tri-service uniforms to serve in the "Sea Element of the Canadian Forces." Only Rear-Admiral Landymore fought a spirited defence against unification. It achieved little and only a short time passed before Hellyer more-or-less showed him the door. Most accounts of this emotional time focus on Hellyer's reasons for unifying the forces (to produce a 25-percent saving in administrative costs that could be applied to capital equipment purchases), and the impact that the loss of the naval uniform and the demise of traditions had on the navy. But it is the question of morale that remains to be properly explored. While it is clear that unification had a demoralizing effect on many senior officers and non-commissioned officers when it came into effect on 1 February 1968, there is some doubt about its impact on junior officers and ranks. Indeed, reports from this period suggest that the morale of newer members was more likely to be affected by issues that impacted their home life. The key to preventing a mass exodus of personnel from the navy was not the fight against unification, but rather a series of initiatives designed to increase incomes, reduce sea-time, and improve shore conditions. The average sailor's ability to provide for his family's well-being was what truly mattered, and as a result most would wear the new uniform as long as it came with improved naval housing, better pay that eased the pain of being at sea, and an increased marriage allowance.

The 1960s were clearly a turbulent decade for the Canadian Navy. Key changes — ranging from technical to organizational — resulted in an unstable operating environment and the navy did not respond well to them. Calls to explore a potential limited war capability led to unnecessary friction among the senior staff as budget cutbacks and operational factors both conspired to ensure that the navy had little choice but to focus all its resources on ASW. But even in this regard the navy was over-committed, as was evident by its ongoing manning crisis and decreasing morale. Perhaps the only way the navy could have avoided this hardship would have been to admit its limitations, prepare for reductions and consolidate around its strengths. In some measure that is what occurred, but as with other times in its history such actions were more the product of happenstance rather than careful planning.

Notes

1. DHH, 81/520/1000–100/2, Box 25, File 5, Naval Board Meeting, 10 August 1960.
2. DHH, 79/246, File 100, Rayner to Minister of National Defence (Douglas Harkness), 8 May 1961.
3. LAC, RG 24, acc 1983–84/167, Box 151, File 1279–162, R.J. Sutherland, "Comments on Report of the Ad Hoc Committee on Naval Objectives," 16 November 1961.
4. W.G.D. Lund, "The Rise and Fall of the Royal Canadian Navy, 1945–1964" (doctoral dissertation, University of Victoria, 1999), 489.
5. DHH, 122.069 D1, "Morale in the fleet" [no date, 1963].
6. LAC, RG 24, Vol. 21811, Minister to Chiefs of Staff Committee, 27 August 1963, and "Mobile Force Study of Composition and Cost, Terms of Reference."
7. DHH, 99/36, Box 84, File 2, W.A.B. Douglas to S. Mathwyn Davis, 28 August 1986.
8. LAC, RG 2, Vol. 6264, Cabinet Minutes, 25 March 1964.
9. DHH, 80/225, Folder 11, *White Paper on Defence*, March 1964.
10. DHH, 76/51, Folder 4C, Aide memoir, CANUS North Atlantic Strategy, June 1966.
11. Lund, 518.
12. DHH, CDS to Minister, 18 August 1965.
13. Maritime Systems Flexibility [Falls] Report, 31 January 1967.

Maritime Research and Development, 1960–68

Harold Merklinger

The advent of the nuclear submarine followed by the transit of the USS *Nautilus* under the Arctic Ocean added new dimensions to the ASW problem. The RCN realized not only that it had a third ocean to defend, but also against a threat demanding a faster response from defending systems. Consequently, naval research and development investigated a variety of responses.

Having successfully tested the concept of a big ASW helicopter operating from a frigate in calm waters, subsequent research led to development of the innovative "Beartrap" — a "helicopter hauldown and rapid securing device," devised in conjunction with Fairey Aviation and Dowty, which enabled operations in rough weather. In December 1963 the first Sea King was hauled down aboard the modernized HMCS *Assiniboine*, revolutionizing ASW operations.

The goal for hydrofoil design was to develop a fast 180-tonne ASW warship capable of operating in heavy seas in the open ocean. NRE conducted extensive work on a one-quarter scale foil system while de Havilland Canada developed the overall design and structure. HMCS *Bras d'Or* (FHE-400) was finally delivered — not without incident — in July 1968, and briefly held the record for the world's fastest warship. The ship was also intended to include the first digital combat control system, the AIS 240, which was never fitted. However renamed "MARTADS" (Maritime Tactical Data System), it was used to develop the combat control system for the upcoming DDH-280, Iroquois-class destroyers.

With the bulk of Canadian oceanographic work now taken up by civilian agencies, scientists at NRE and PNL began studies into means to improve sonar performance and optimize future designs. PNL undertook minor oceanographic work such as examination of the microstructure and wave patterns created by a submarine wake, and also began research to look at acoustic and electromagnetic systems for the under-ice detection of submarines. More generally, the acoustic program included research into types of "noise" affecting sonar performance: own-ship noise; noise from flow over the sonar dome; background ocean noise; and sound back-scattered from the sea surface, the ocean bottom, and from sea life. One of the future design concepts was an extension of the VDS concept to provide reliable long-range performance by towing as deep as 3,650 metres. Although the concept appeared feasible, Canada was unlikely to possess ships large enough to tow

such a length of cable. Canadian researchers and sailors also participated in USN-led work to perfect passive listening systems that would monitor submarine activity within whole ocean basins, essential to the Cold War SOSUS network.

Maritime engineers also were busy developing improved methods for at-sea replenishment and advancing the state of the art in sonar. Equipment permitting side-by-side, near-full-speed, liquid fuel and solid stores replenishment at sea was proven in 1964 when HMCS *Provider* successfully replenished *Yukon*. The Canadian quick-engage/disengage hoses and "tensioned-span-wire system" became a NATO standard and the model for medium navies around the world. The AN/SQS-505 sonar (in hull-mounted and VDS variants) was designed in conjunction with NRC and Westinghouse, giving the fleet an improved all-around capability; it is still in service.

With the construction of two purpose-built research vessels (CF Auxiliary Vessels *Endeavour* and *Quest*), this period saw a partial renewal of the research fleet.

This 1964 drawing from a Fairey Aviation brochure depicts the elements of the Canadian-developed "Beartrap" helicopter haul-down system.

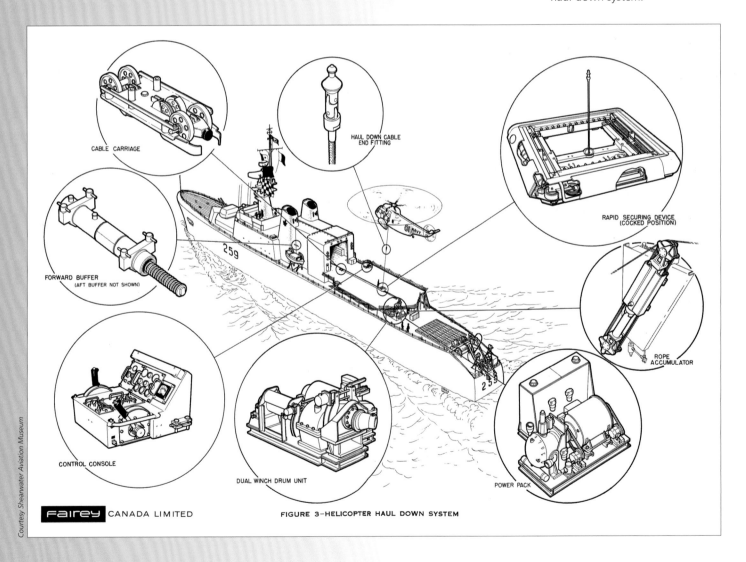

CABLE CARRIAGE

HAUL DOWN CABLE END FITTING

RAPID SECURING DEVICE (COCKED POSITION)

FORWARD BUFFER (AFT BUFFER NOT SHOWN)

ROPE ACCUMULATOR

CONTROL CONSOLE

DUAL WINCH DRUM UNIT

POWER PACK

Courtesy Shearwater Aviation Museum

Fairey CANADA LIMITED

FIGURE 3—HELICOPTER HAUL DOWN SYSTEM

On 16 July 1969, HMCS *Bras d'Or* (FHE-400) set a speed record for an ocean-going vessel of 61 knots.

CHAPTER 9

From Uncertainty to Maturity, 1968–89

Peter T. Haydon

*The Government believes Canada's maritime forces must be
reoriented with the long term objective of providing a more versatile
general purpose capability ... [T]his policy will take a long time
to implement fully because of the life of current equipment, but it
will govern both the acquisition of new equipment and, where
applicable, modifications to existing equipment.*
— DEFENCE IN THE 70S

At the time nobody believed that it would take two decades to implement the new policy, but it did. In June 1968, Pierre Elliott Trudeau became Canada's fifteenth prime minister, swept in on a wave of public optimism that heralded his rise to power as the dawn of a new era. A need to "do things differently" was a frequent theme of his early speeches, and Canadians seemed to embrace that view. However, the Canadian Navy (now known officially as Maritime Command), was less enthusiastic about some aspects of the new direction, particularly as expressed in Trudeau's April 1969 speech on defence and foreign policy quoted above, which also contained the seeds of a new era at sea that threatened to undermine its entrenched trans-Atlantic roots:

*We're beginning to realize now that we're not a one-ocean country, not an Atlantic
country, not even a two-ocean country, an Atlantic and a Pacific. We're a three-*

Richard Rudnicki, *Persian Gulf War — Enroute*, shows HMC Ships *Athabaskan*, *Terra Nova*, and *Protecteur* in a formation scene little changed from 1975.

ocean country. We're beginning to realize that this Pacific seaboard is more important to Canadians than we realized in the past.[1]

Feeling politically vulnerable and recently stripped of its individuality on being pressed into the newly unified armed forces, the navy was understandably suspicious of suggestions to change its focus. The Hellyer reforms of the mid-1960s had left it much smaller, through personnel cuts and by not replacing the wartime destroyers and frigates, with the result that Canada's naval commitment to NATO had been cut in half since 1963. Trudeau's vision threatened to disrupt the strategic comfort zone provided by NATO. Facing further budget cuts and with no plans for new ships beyond the four Iroquois-class destroyers and two more replenishment support ships, the Canadian Navy was not overly optimistic about its future. This gloomy outlook was not helped by a widely held view within National Defence Head-quarters (NDHQ) that the navy was the "bad boy in the corner" for opposing some concepts of unification, the loss of the distinct naval identity in particular. Misnamed the "Admirals' Revolt" by the media, the independent actions of a handful of senior officers were wrongly seen as symbolic of naval attitudes. Not surprisingly, the navy entered the Trudeau era with some trepidation. It would take another 15 years before it fully regained its self-confidence.

The story of the navy's fortunes from 1968 to the end of the Cold War in 1989, winds its way through a series of political twists and turns in which money, or more precisely the lack of it, plays a major role. Technology also plays its part, particularly so as the navy tried to remain proficient in anti-submarine warfare in a time of fiscal constraint during which new technologies were changing the nature of naval operations around the world. It is a remarkable story of perseverance and faith, particularly faith in a political process that everyone hoped would provide the funds for the much-needed fleet modernization. It took leadership to sustain that faith and give the navy hope that there was actually light at the end of the tunnel. But the politicians did not provide that light immediately; rather, they laboriously studied and restudied defence policy in search of cheaper options.

An "in-house" review of defence policy, that was as much about money as policy, started in the spring of 1968 and brought out all the internal divisions within Cabinet. Although many of the discussions focused on a "non-alignment versus alignment" philosophy for Canadian defence and foreign policy, the debate was really about the cost of NATO and whether Canada should remain part of the Allied military structure. The Department of External Affairs (DEA) was the champion of NATO, not just because of the Canadian role in its birth but because membership in the Alliance was seen as prudent security policy. That view eventually prevailed. Similarly, bilateral continental defence was seen as a fundamental requirement in preserving political and territorial sovereignty.

The need to make further cuts in the defence budget became more pressing as the defence review ran its course even as the economy slowed-down. Cabinet's decision to hold the defence budget at the 1968 level of $1.72 billion put DND in an impossible position: there was not enough money to meet the established commitments. In September 1969, the defence minister, Leo Cadieux, announced the department's plans for operating within the frozen budget. For the navy, these held no surprises, as the adjustments had all been negotiated beforehand. The carrier HMCS *Bonaventure* would go, a decision accepted reluctantly by the admirals but in the final analysis it was better to give up the aging carrier with little remaining tactical value to NATO than to surrender a squadron of ASW destroyers that NATO needed badly. The four new Iroquois-class destroyers would still be built and the two replenishment ships, the AORs, would be completed. Three Restigouche-class destroyers would be placed in reserve to provide people for the new destroyers. But the navy had to fight hard to hold the cuts at that level. Further cuts in force levels were seen as an abrogation of defence responsibilities within NATO and in the Pacific that could lead to American forces assuming part or all of the responsibility for those waters.

After much political wrangling, the *1971 Defence White Paper* emerged in August and with it came some enlightenment about the future of the operational navy (Maritime Command): the Argus long-range patrol aircraft (LRPA) would be replaced; there would be a modest fleet modernization program; fleet size was set at 24 destroyers (some would be in reserve); and the fleet would become "general purpose" in nature rather than specialized for ASW. As the department and the admirals agreed, the problem lay in making the new model work within the meagre budget, and although the navy's future still seemed bleak, the NATO and bilateral commitments still had to be met, which meant that the ships had to be kept operationally effective.

Despite the loss of its traditional identity, the navy quickly focused on operations instead of politics. The rationale was twofold: first, the majority of young officers in the fleet did not abandon the navy during the unification crisis — they had too much invested in their naval careers, had acquired family responsibilities, and did not have enough invested in the stock market to contemplate career changes; also, because the navy had been "culled" at the higher ranks through forced manpower reductions and by the early retirements of those who opposed the Hellyer reforms, prospects of better pay for all ranks and better promotion opportunities made conditions of service look much better. Second, the dynamic leadership of Vice-Admiral J.C. "Scruffy" O'Brien, commander of Maritime Command, made people turn their attentions back to the job to be done at sea. O'Brien's message, delivered in his usual colourful language, was to "Go find the bloody Russian submarines and leave the politics to me!" Wisely, the navy did both.

"Sisters of the Space Age" — a rare shot of the entire Iroquois class at sea in the mid-1970s.

Department of National Defence EKS-9

With O'Brien's unequivocal encouragement, the Canadian Navy threw itself into ASW operations at a time when the Soviet Navy was expanding its capability and global reach, and in response NATO desperately needed to show competence at sea as a deterrent to Soviet adventurism. The Canadian Navy's contribution was the commitment of as many ships as possible to NATO exercises and keeping one destroyer in the newly established Standing Naval Force Atlantic (STANAVFORLANT). At the same time, the Americans were asking for greater Canadian naval and maritime air presence in the North American littoral, especially in the Pacific, to offset the U.S. Navy's commitments to Southeast Asia. In addition, there was Trudeau's push to assert Canadian sovereignty, especially in the Arctic, which saw ships deploy into northern waters and generally spend more time visiting remote communities on both coasts.

Because of the navy's focus on operations, its reputation as a first-rate ASW force was maintained, albeit with some technical difficulty. Learning to function without the aircraft carrier in the early 1970s was a challenge but was soon overcome. Sea King ASW helicopters operating from the converted St. Laurent-class destroyers provided close and distant support and increased the fleet's operational flexibility. The arrival in the early 1970s of the two new replenishment support ships, *Protecteur* and *Preserver*, and the four Iroquois-class destroyers, improved the situation enormously. By the end of the 1970s the fleet had evolved into a series of self-contained ASW task groups (still called squadrons at the time) able to function almost anywhere in the world.

Significantly, the navy had started to become uniquely Canadian rather being a quasi-clone of the Royal Navy. The "unified" green uniform, a source of ridicule in NATO where all other navies still wore traditional black or dark blue uniforms, was universally disliked but did not become an obstacle to professional competence. A more traditional uniform eventually returned in the mid-1980s and was sufficiently different from the British uniform to be easily recognizable as distinctly Canadian, and was worn with pride. That the navy was able to transform itself into an independent "national" navy and side-step the potentially self-destructive politics of identity was Scruffy O'Brien's legacy — a legacy that has not been given adequate credit as one of the Canadian Navy's more important transformational moments. Without O'Brien's leadership the navy would not be what it is today and it would not be able to carry out the important role assigned to it in the post–Cold War era.

When O'Brien told the fleet to "go find the bloody Russian submarines" he wasn't really doing anything more than telling the ships to focus on their primary job. That was what they did in NATO, that was what they did within the bilateral continental defence structure, and that was what they did in home waters when the occasional Soviet submarine ventured in a little close. On paper though, the Canadian Navy had four main functions:

- *conduct surveillance in Canadian and adjoining waters and respond to threatening situations, with priority on foreign submarine and warship activities, which was usually done in conjunction with U.S. forces under the Canada–United States continental defence plans;*
- *maintain a visible presence in Canadian waters as a deterrent to criminal and other unfriendly acts and as an expression of sovereignty over those waters;*

> • *contribute ships to NATO deterrence, including STANAVFORLANT, to contingency operations before an outbreak of hostilities, and to war plans; and*
>
> • *support Canadian foreign policy in many ways including making port visits and taking part in United Nations' peacekeeping operations.*

Those tasks were carried out under two assumptions. First, that ships designed and trained for complex NATO tasks could easily carry out domestic and continental tasks. Second, that other than by a surprise attack any future war would be preceded by a period of tension during which it would be essential to conduct ASW operations in North American waters while implementing contingency plans for the reinforcement of Europe.

Canada's operational commitment to NATO's supreme allied commander, Atlantic, (SACLANT) was 16 destroyers in varying degrees of readiness (some immediately, some after 15 days notice, and some after 30 days), three submarines, and an assortment of maritime aircraft. The three replenishment ships were retained under national control, and four destroyers remained under national control in the Pacific for CANUS operations. The Canadian Navy's "war" tasking thus started long before any formal declaration of a state of emergency or war, and this reality ran contrary to the initial concept for "unified" war planning adopted by NDHQ, where many non-naval staff officers seemed unable to grasp the fundamental principles of Cold War maritime strategy. Senior naval officers frequently had to explain that navies fought a different war initially in serving as "enabling" forces to the roles played later by land and air forces. This lack of understanding was one of the reasons why the navy was seen as an obstacle to the concept of unification.

The Canadian fleet was organized into ASW destroyer squadrons, but because of their lack of adequate air defence the ships were usually integrated individually into larger multinational formations or were joined by a U.S. Navy guided missile destroyer to provide that capability. Their task was the protection of shipping, especially the trans-Atlantic reinforcement shipping, which established training requirements within a logical progression of individual, team, ship, and formation exercises. The latter were part of the series of NATO maritime exercises culminating every year in a major "war game" such as Ocean Safari, Teamwork, or Northern Wedding.

On average, the STANAVFORLANT commitment was filled permanently with one destroyer, there were two or three formation-level NATO exercises a year with ships operating in either squadrons or task groups, and there was one major fleet exercise every two years. The submarines generally supported two NATO exercises a year. With refits, trials,

Department of National Defence SL79-19

STANAVFORLANT ships in formation off the Rock of Gibraltar, with the flagship destroyer *Iroquois* in the centre, February 1979; just to the right (her port side) is the British destroyer HMS *Sheffield*, which would be lost three years later in the Falklands War.

and work-up training requirements, as well as at least one national and one joint Canada–United States or CANUS exercise a year, the Atlantic fleet was at its maximum activity level. The wartime tasks of the Pacific fleet were part of bilateral continental defence plans under which Canada had ASW responsibility for the Strait of Juan de Fuca and much of the Gulf of Alaska. The Pacific fleet exercise schedule was conducted almost entirely within the Canada-United States defence structure with the high point being the biennial Pacific Rim (RIMPAC) exercise. During the Vietnam War, the U.S. Navy had to rely on reserve-manned ships to maintain the long-standing sequence of bilateral naval exercises. This placed an additional burden of the Canadian ships, but one they bore with pride and efficiency.

Catching O'Brien's "bloody Russian submarines" was a lot easier said than done. Not only were they elusive but the navy also had to hone its ASW skills to give it an even chance. The Soviet Navy was in a period of growth in which their exploitation of new technologies started to erode NATO's tactical advantage at sea.

In the early 1970s, the combination of declining U.S. naval fleet capability as a result of the Vietnam War and a case of strategic blindness in some European capitals led to the troubling view that NATO could lose control of the Atlantic. The important lesson from the Second World War that you cannot reinforce or recapture Europe without first having control of the Atlantic was temporarily forgotten. This was frightening and so NATO took a series of actions that included a revamping of naval war and contingency plans and a new approach to collective force development.

In the late 1970s and 1980s, as American naval capability in the Atlantic was restored after Vietnam, the Soviet naval role expanded from flank protection to include a defence in depth along the likely U.S. Navy attack routes especially through the Norwegian Sea. The result was a massive Soviet building program of large and very capable ships, several types of submarine, and some highly effective missile-armed fighter bombers. Although the Soviets may have planned to attack NATO reinforcement shipping, that task didn't have the same strategic priority as defeating the Americans — and thus NATO — in the Norwegian Sea, or, better, stopping them from getting there. As one analyst explained much later, "the Soviet Navy was intended for brief, intense clashes where it could do as much damage as possible, then retreat at flank speed. The Soviet fleet's main purpose thus was seen as primarily sea denial rather than sea control."[2] Curiously, it took the West quite a long time to figure out the Soviet strategy and to realize that control of the Norwegian Sea was the key to the whole thing. The NATO initiatives required some reorganization of the Canadian fleet in the 1980s and also influenced modernization and ship replacement programs. But until that happened, the Canadian Navy had to make do with the existing fleet.

In 1968 the Canadian fleet was still relatively modern but was reaching the point where new technologies, including those being integrated into the Soviet fleet, were beginning to add urgency to the need for modernization. Keeping pace with new technologies was a constant Canadian naval problem because of political reluctance to commit the necessary funds to fleet modernization, especially as building new ships was an increasingly expensive undertaking. As a result, the existing ships had to be kept effective by a stream of modernization programs. Continuing the process begun in 1962, when the St. Laurent-class destroyers were converted to carry and support the Sea King ASW helicopter, the fleet was

Department of National Defence HSC72-910

One of O'Brien's bloody Russian submarines, a Hotel-class SSBN sitting disabled on the surface northeast of Newfoundland, found by an air force Argus, 15 March 1972.

in a near-constant state of modernization under a series of programs such as the DEstroyer Life EXtension Plan (DELEX) and Submarine Operational Update Program (SOUP). Although the four new Iroquois-class destroyers held the promise of remaining technologically current at sea, on their own they were not enough. They lacked an area air defence weapons system to protect a group of ships, though they did have the latest ASW detection, command and control, and propulsion technologies. Despite being designed as flotilla leaders, the destroyers were used initially in much the same piecemeal way that escorts had been used since the Second World War. This was not a Canadian problem; in the 1970s NATO had not yet developed its concepts of operations sufficiently to respond to new Soviet submarine and aircraft tactics, and long-range weapons; as a result, NATO adopted a rather *ad hoc* response to the Soviet threat. This would change.

The loss of *Bonaventure* resulted in one technical and two tactical problems. Lack of long-range ASW surveillance formerly provided by the CS2F Trackers was partly solved in the short-term by using "Jezebel" low-frequency acoustic ranging (LOFAR) sonobuoys and fitting the associated AQA-5 signal analysis equipment in the destroyers. Sea Kings were used to drop the buoys but could not monitor them. Long-range maritime patrol aircraft (LRPA) provided distant support in North American waters, invariably in response to contacts gained by the undersea passive SOSUS arrays operated jointly by Canada and the United States. Towed passive sonar arrays in ships and submarines were a better solution, but that technology was still in its infancy in the 1970s. Tactical coordination, another important function of the carrier, was handled reasonably well by the destroyers but there was a shortage of experienced "direction" specialists to deal with complex sea-air tactical situations. This was eventually resolved in the 1980s as the autonomous task group concept evolved with a shift to tactical rather than administrative formation staffs. Providing adequate support for deployed Sea Kings proved more difficult. The St. Laurent-class destroyers had a basic first-line maintenance capability but the hanger was too small to do much work and they carried few spare parts. The Iroquois-class destroyers and the new replenishment ships had better facilities but were still short of spares and test equipment. There was no alternative to the carrier for operational flexibility and technical support, but that capability was unaffordable and politically unacceptable. Canadian ingenuity and determination was able to keep the fleet reasonably effective, but it was obvious that the ships were losing the technology race and soon would not be able to keep pace with the NATO allies or the Soviets. New, modern ships were essential if Canada was to remain a credible member of the naval alliance.

The *1971 White Paper* called for a comprehensive review of Canada's future maritime security requirements as a precursor to getting new equipment. This review was started in November 1971 and the results submitted to Cabinet in May 1972 with the recommendation that the Argus LRPA be replaced and that a new shipbuilding program be started. Plans to replace the Argus went ahead relatively quickly while the ship program went through a series of further studies on design options. The first study, completed in late January 1974, looked at four notional designs: a 9,100-tonne surveillance control ship with up to nine helicopters embarked; a 2,275-tonne destroyer in both the general-purpose and ASW roles; a 1,350-tonne corvette/frigate also in general-purpose and ASW roles; and a 360-tonne hydrofoil. A follow-on study done in February and March 1974 looked at the feasibility of undertaking a major capability upgrade on the Mackenzie-class destroyers and considered options for acquiring four more submarines. Neither study made firm recommendations; they merely offered observations about the degree of difficulty and cost-effectiveness of those ideas. A third study, done during August and September 1974, responded to the naval planning staff's request to look at three specific design options refined from the earlier studies through a series of departmental meetings and workshops. At that stage it was obvious that a 2,700- to 3,600-tonne vessel alone met Canadian requirements and it soon became clear that a Canadian-designed and built patrol frigate (CPF) based on the operational characteristics and capabilities of the U.S. Navy's FFG-7 frigate was the best solution.

The final design and the names of the building yards naturally required political decisions, and not for the first time the political expedient of linking shipyard work to electoral ridings became a factor. Yet, the political decision took longer than expected or desired, and the delay had serious implications on fleet effectiveness. Some of the delay was due to the convoluted bureaucratic process associated with major spending programs, but Canada also faced a financial crisis in the mid-1970s when interest rates rose to frighteningly high levels and all capital spending was put on hold. Managing the defence budget during that period was a nightmare and resulted in a separate series of studies to find ways of meeting the various commitments on a fixed budget.

By early 1974, inflation had turned the country's financial situation into a crisis from which DND was not exempt. In August 1974 the minister of national defence went to Cabinet to seek advice: the military did not have enough money to maintain the existing level of activity which meant that the new defence policy (issued in 1971) was already out of date. That November, Cabinet directed a Defence Structure Review to look at all possible options for addressing DND's problem, including changing the NATO commitment, reviewing North American Aerospace Defense Command (NORAD), and re-examining Canadian involvement in strategic ASW. DND's initial reaction was to search for cost-savings in the usual places — personnel, operations, and maintenance; and capital programs. For the Canadian Navy, this "rationalization" meant a one-third reduction in days at sea which curtailed training cruises and scheduled exercises. Modernization programs were deferred and, in some cases, cancelled. As these and other reductions began to take effect, senior military planners began to vent their frustration over what they now perceived as a systemic problem of chronic under-funding in relation to assigned tasks and commitments. Chief

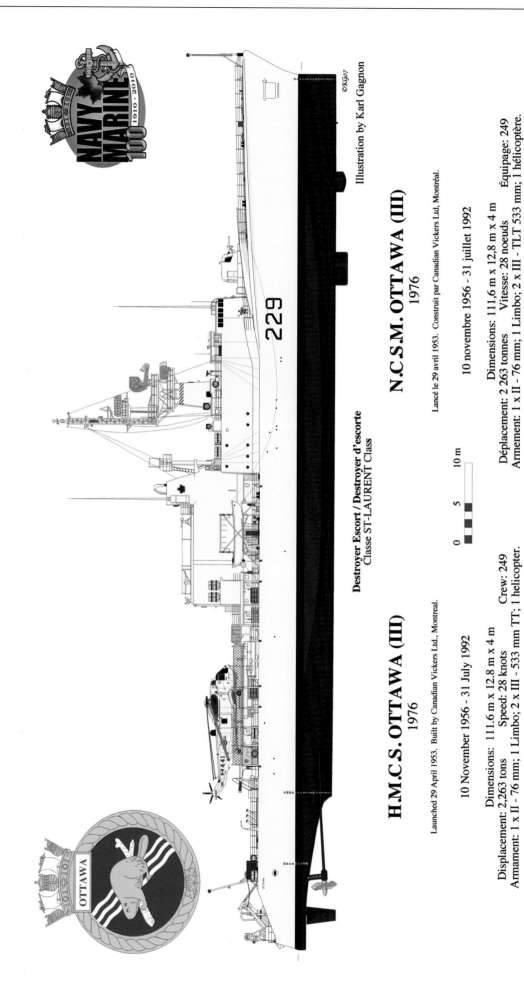

©KG07

Illustration by Karl Gagnon

Destroyer Escort / Destroyer d'escorte
Classe ST-LAURENT Class

H.M.C.S. OTTAWA (III)
1976

Launched 29 April 1953. Built by Canadian Vickers Ltd., Montreal.

10 November 1956 - 31 July 1992

Dimensions: 111.6 m x 12.8 m x 4 m
Displacement: 2,263 tons   Speed: 28 knots   Crew: 249
Armament: 1 x II - 76 mm; 1 Limbo; 2 x III - 533 mm TT; 1 helicopter.

N.C.S.M. OTTAWA (III)
1976

Lancé le 29 avril 1953. Construit par Canadian Vickers Ltd, Montréal.

10 novembre 1956 - 31 juillet 1992

Dimensions: 111,6 m x 12,8 m x 4 m
Déplacement: 2 263 tonnes   Vitesse: 28 noeuds   Équipage: 249
Armement: 1 x II - 76 mm; 1 Limbo; 2 x III - TLT 533 mm; 1 hélicoptère.

0   5   10 m

of the Defence Staff, General J.A. Dextraze, dug in his heels and demanded that if the military was to be forced to live within the current unrealistic funding arrangement, then certain capabilities, facilities, and commitments would have to be abandoned. This caught the attention of the politicians, particularly because some believed they had resolved the matter of defence priorities once and for all during the 1969 defence review process and in the *1971 White Paper*. The result was a three-phase comprehensive study of the defence situation. The first report, submitted in February 1975, re-examined the various tasks and directed political attention on the issues that determined force structure and related infrastructure. Three of the five foreseen "core" DND tasks concerned the navy and its three-phase tasking of national sovereignty, continental security, and supporting the reinforcement of Europe. One of the side effects of the review was that the navy's unique role was finally understood and the navy started to gain support around the Cabinet table.

The report on force structure, the second phase, was sent to Cabinet on 10 November 1975 and contained a section on "Maritime Combat Capabilities" that convinced the politicians to move ahead quickly with plans to replace the older destroyers. The problem was that the ship replacement program was trapped in the third phase of the Defence Structure Review process that attempted to develop a costed model for modernizing the forces. The program was also delayed by political wrangling and the never-ending questioning of the basic requirements that allowed for icebreakers and ocean surveillance as well as a couple of personal preferences for ship designs. The idea of a single, unified, government fleet emerged. As a result, the navy was directed to look at the possible advantages of ships more suitable and economical for use as back-up for fisheries enforcement in the longer term.

Eventually, in September 1977, the new ship program began to make political progress when one of the seemingly continual reviews concluded that warships can fulfill all aspects of sovereignty as in present practice but armed patrol vessels cannot fulfill the collective defence role, and to operate efficiently in Canadian waters this vessel would need to be in the 2,700-tonne range. In many respects, this was the breakthrough the navy had been looking for and paved the way for Cabinet approval of the shipbuilding program that December. But because of the political delays and the financial crisis, no progress had been made on routine fleet modernization and replacement, and some of the options already on the table (such as up-grading the Mackenzies) were no longer cost-effective. It was getting to the point where the future combat effectiveness of the fleet depended on getting new frigates, and that until they arrived operational readiness would suffer.

After two years of drafting, a formal Memorandum to Cabinet to replace the six remaining St. Laurent-class destroyers was presented on 3 November 1977. In a comprehensive annex, the earlier Cabinet direction to look at the advantages of smaller ships for domestic tasks was carefully and fully addressed. The conclusion took account of domestic, NATO, and Canada-United States defence commitments in establishing performance requirements:

> *The restrictions of sea keeping qualities, and speed preclude the employment of*
> *small patrol vessels in the open ocean to meet the full requirement of the protection*

A classic Cold War image: the helicopter-carrying destroyer *Nipigon* ploughs through North Atlantic waters, February 1981, with a Sea King helicopter and one of the tankers in the background.

of sovereignty. While lightly armed patrol vessels can perform in peace the tasks associated with protection of sovereignty and enforcement of regulations, the provisions of ships would be in addition to the requirement for 24 combat capable ships and would not provide a cost effective option.[3]

On 22 December 1977, Cabinet agreed to a basic fleet size of 24 destroyer-type ships. They also agreed that a 3,600-tonne general-purpose, frigate-type ship best met Canada's maritime security requirements. But approval was only given for six ships, and so the problem facing the naval staff was to replace the remaining 14 destroyers and the rest of the fleet in due course. Over the next couple of years a complete ship replacement program (SRP) emerged with some very optimistic planning dates.

Program	Ship Classes to be Replaced	Start Planning	Contract Definition Awarded	Building Contract	Delivery Date
CPF/(SRP I)	St. Laurent (6)	1976	1979–80	1981–82	1985–86
SRP II	Restigouche (3) and Mackenzie (4)	1980	1983	1985	1989–90
SRP III	Improved Restigouche (4), Annapolis (2), and St. Laurent (1)	1983	1986	1988	1992–96
CASAP	Oberon submarines (3)	1985	1988	1990	1995
OSS	Provider and Preserver (2)	1989	1992	1994	1998–2002
SRP IV	Iroquois (4)	1993	1996	1998	2002–04

Although the Liberal government stated its intention to build six frigates in December 1977 a contract to build them was not approved until June 1983. The initial concept called for the ships to be built in the 1985–90 timeframe, but the length of time taken up by the bureaucratic process did not allow a ship to be built for delivery in 1985. The situation wasn't helped by the fact that the contract got off to a bad start because of the fragile nature of the Canadian shipbuilding industry at the time and the 10-year hiatus in navy ship-building programs. Consequently, there were few yards capable of building warships and some of those were in financial difficulty. There had also been a revolution in naval technology in the last 20 years that saw not only the introduction of new systems and weapons but also extensive changes in the way ships were built. But a core of experience existed, much of it in the Quebec yards that had built the four Iroquois-class destroyers. The frigate program was thus an opportunity for the shipyards to modernize, but it would take a considerable start-up effort to get the program going. This added to the overall cost and gave rise to the notion that Canada would do better by buying warships offshore.

Predictably, the process by which the contract was awarded was complex and intensely political. In wanting to split the contract in an attempt to keep as much of the industry alive as possible, especially in Quebec, the government put itself between the proverbial "rock and a hard place" where the politics of major crown projects were brought into conflict with the business aims of a highly competitive industry. Work was farmed out to get the maximum regional economic benefits and this resulted in a near-disastrous mix of Quebec shipyards trying to work with Saint John Shipbuilding (SJSL), which initially lacked the expertise to manage the overall program. A subsequent consolidation of the Quebec yards helped, but left a polarized dispute between the main players, SJSL as the prime contractor and Marine Industries Limited (MIL) as a sub-contractor for three of the ships. Even the company that was awarded the initial design contract, Versatile Systems Engineering (VSEI), was caught-up in the reorganizations. The program was behind schedule before it even started.

Although SJSL had difficulty getting the program started, they were eventually able to solve the problems with the help of a U.S. shipyard, Bath Iron Works. But a formidable range of obstacles combined to affect an already technically complex program: the economic collapse of the original main sub-contractor (Versatile); the rivalry between shipyards within the frigate program and over other potential government contracts, including the ill-fated SSN project; and political requirements for regional benefits. Under the circumstances it

Department of National Defence ETC85-3601

Canadian and allied ships tied up at Canada Place Pier in Vancouver harbour for the navy's 75th anniversary assembly, 23 August 1985.

is doubtful if any Canadian yard could have started the project on time.

With the incentive of getting the contract to build the second batch of six frigates and with its own house in order, SJSL naturally wanted to get the program back on track. When SJSL was awarded the second contract in December 1987 without binding requirements for sub-contracting, the way was clear to start addressing construction problems but the relationship between SJSL and MIL had to be resolved first. The matter was eventually taken to court, yet despite the legal action work continued in both yards. As the program continued to slip, SJSL assumed full responsibility for the design, hull construction, and assembly of the frigates and eventually was able to complete the whole 12-ship program on time. Three hulls were built in MIL and nine in SJSL with Paramax supervising the systems integration. Unfortunately, the program's rough initial start and the subsequent shipyard disputes dampened public enthusiasm for the new ships when, in reality, the program should have been universally seen as a masterpiece of Canadian design and innovation. The new ships would not enter service until the early 1990s and in the meantime, the old ships had to bear the burden of Canada's naval commitments to NATO and continental defence.

By the early 1980s the Canadian Navy's role had evolved into a series of largely inter-related and more clearly defined "home" and "away" tasks that, although still NATO-centric, began to acknowledge the emerging importance of the Pacific, foreseen by Trudeau. Fleet operations were largely driven by the need to train to undertake three main tasks:

- *Provide a destroyer continuously with the Standing Naval Force Atlantic and provide a commodore to serve as the STANAVFORLANT commander within a rotation with other Alliance navies, which happened about every five years.*
- *Provide three or four destroyers and a logistics support vessel to the family of SACLANT Maritime Contingency Force (Atlantic) plans that ranged from conducting deterrence operations, to protecting reinforcement shipping, to supporting amphibious operations, to keeping Soviet naval units under surveillance.*
- *Conduct ASW operations in North American waters with U.S. naval forces to seek out Soviet ballistic missile submarines and other submarines deployed into those waters ahead of an aggressive political move; in this the naval response to the 1962 Cuban Missile Crisis remained an entirely credible scenario.*

An additional task of protecting the Canadian Air-Sea Transportable (CAST) Brigade Group was included, but this was controversial within NATO and was dropped from the national contingency tasks in the late 1980s. While not greatly different to the roles of a decade earlier, there was a more precise operational requirement that made force planning and exercise scheduling much easier.

In 1979 SACLANT started a study to develop a new concept of maritime operations, CONMAROPS. That document provided the link between the largely symbolic Standing Naval Force, the family of maritime contingency plans that were intended to be activated in the early phases of a deepening crisis, and actual war fighting. One of the study objectives was to achieve a better integration of national forces into a multinational concept. This was difficult; the NATO naval family had a tendency to be a community of communities rather than a single community with single purpose. The framework for the new concept was influenced by studies recently conducted by the Americans, particularly *Sea War 85*. CONMAROPS became the means whereby the NATO navies could be integrated into a single and effective force.

In 1984, Commander SACLANT, Admiral Wesley MacDonald, came to Ottawa and briefed Canadian parliamentarians on the new concepts for the NATO war at sea, including the requirement for Canadian area air defence systems and the need for a Canadian task group system. To some this might seem an outrageous attempt by an American to influence Canadian politics; in reality, there was nothing odd about a NATO supreme commander, regardless of nationality, briefing politicians of any member state of the alliance on the roles their forces would play in wartime. More to the point, Canadian officers serving on the SACLANT staff had developed the new concept in large part. The concept itself was complex in calling for a mixture of ships formed as a task group with its own combined command and control capability, local area air defence, and sophisticated ASW systems with a lot of integral air support in the form of embarked helicopters and its own underway logistic support. The model of the Dutch Task Group was used as the NATO standard and it was on this that the Canadian model was structured with only minor changes. Variant one was for the western Atlantic (WESTLANT) with a lower requirement for air defence than the eastern Atlantic (EASTLANT) variant. What this meant for Canada was that the time had come to "fish or cut bait" and initiate the various programs needed to make the task group an operational reality.

Indeed, shortly after the SACLANT briefing, the minister of national defence introduced the 1984–85 defence estimate to Parliament with a pertinent statement on force structure: "the Maritime Force Structure is being developed around the operational concept of balanced, self-supporting national task groups, each with an appropriate mix of vehicles for the tasks assigned." NATO force goals for 1987–92 called for three Canadian task groups to be available by 1987 and a fourth by 1992. From that point it was up to the Canadian Navy to produce that capability; initially using the existing ships but with obvious reliance on the new frigates in the longer-term.

The new Canadian fleet model of autonomous task groups with blended warfighting capabilities required a major change in the way ships were assigned to tasks and exercises. Even though the new task group model of a modernized Iroquois-class destroyer with two to four frigates and an AOR would not be operational until at least the mid-1990s, the navy started making organizational changes some 10 years ahead of that date. Besides the equipment changes, plans were made to reorganize the fleet structure and end the long-standing

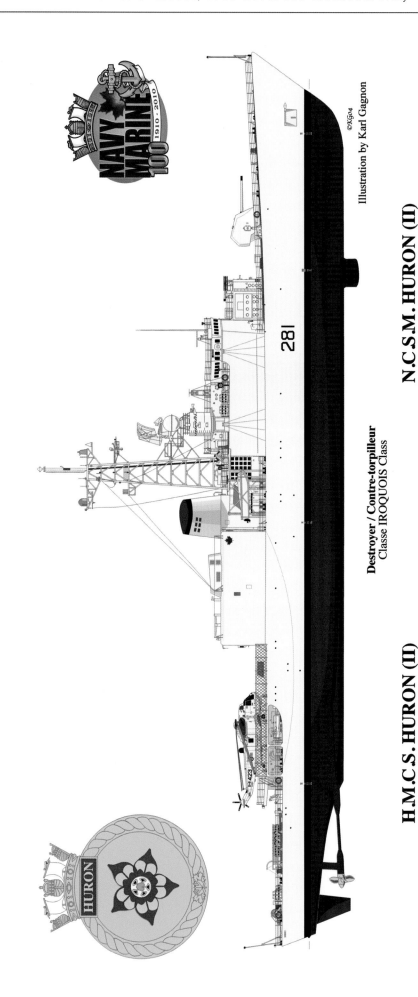

Illustration by Karl Gagnon

Destroyer / Contre-torpilleur
Classe IROQUOIS Class

H.M.C.S. HURON (II)
1977

Launched 09 April 1971. Built by Marine Industries Ltd., Sorel.

16 December 1972 - 30 March 2005

Dimensions: 129,8 m x 15,2 m x 6,6 m
Displacement: 4,200 tons   Speed: 29 knots   Crew: 245
Armament: 1 x I - 127 mm; Sea Sparrow missiles; torpedoes;
1 Limbo; 2 helicopters.

N.C.S.M. HURON (II)
1977

Lancé le 09 avril 1971. Construit par Marine Industries Ltd., Sorel.

16 décembre 1972 - 30 mars 2005

Dimensions: 129,8 m x 15,2 m x 6,6 m
Déplacement: 4 200 tonnes   Vitesse: 29 noeuds   Équipage: 245
Armement: 1 x I - 127 mm; missiles Sea Sparrow; torpilles;
1 Limbo; 2 hélicoptères.

concept of keeping ships in squadrons on the basis of equipment type. Changes were announced in July 1986 with the establishment of an operational task group on each coast and a parallel support group responsible for all refits, trials, and work-up training needed to prepare ships for duty in the task group. One year later, HMCS *Huron* went to the West Coast in exchange for *Gatineau*, and a helicopter support facility was established on the Pacific. *Annapolis* and *Terra Nova* subsequently exchanged coasts in late 1989 to complete the reorganization.

Bridging the technology gap between the aging fleet of the 1970s and the modernized CPF/Tribal (Iroquois class) task group was done systematically. Under DELEX, the existing "steam" destroyers were given new radars and sonars along with new electronic-warfare and communications equipment; more important, they were given the ADLIPS automated datalink and plotting system. These upgrades allowed the ships to integrate into NATO formations and carry out a useful ASW role, although still with a greater vulnerability to air attack than ideal. What the program did was to restore faith in a reasonable search and intercept capability for the helicopter-destroyer ASW team. Towed array systems were still under trial, but would be operational before much more time passed. The submarine operational upgrade program (SOUP), comprising new sonars, periscopes, communications, and fire-control systems, and fitting of tubes for the Mk 48 torpedo, converted the three aging *Oberons* back into operational submarines and allowed them to be assigned to NATO for use in the GIUK (Greenland, Iceland, U.K.) gap barrier, intended to stop Soviet submarines from threatening Atlantic shipping routes. These improvements were, in fact, very necessary appeasements to SACLANT to convince him that the Canadian Navy was not about to default on its commitments to collective defence by not having combat capable ships and submarines.

Some work still had to be done. For instance: the Iroquois-class destroyers had to be modernized to undertake the task group leader role and provide the local area air defence capability. The replenishment ships were getting older and would need replacement, *Provider* especially, and the Sea King helicopters also needed replacing. The new frigates were designed as multi-purpose vessels but they had yet to prove themselves operationally. Overall, it was a very sound plan that would provide Canada with a modern, combat-capable, general-purpose navy.

However, there would be a couple more political hurdles to clear. The Trudeau government had been defeated in June 1984 by Brian Mulroney's conservatives who came to power promising yet another defence review. The Canadian Navy saw no need for another review as increased capital spending would have solved most of the immediate problems, but the new government decided to make it a little more complex. While they took their time writing a new white paper, which was largely a public relations exercise, two maritime issues dominated the discussions: sovereignty and submarines. The former largely was triggered by the summer 1985 Arctic cruise of the U.S. Coast Guard icebreaker *Polar Sea* and the latter by suggestions that the replacements for the aging Oberons should be nuclear-powered to provide greater endurance.

The *1987 Defence White Paper* linked the two issues and proposed that Canada acquire a fleet of 10 to 12 nuclear-powered submarines to protect Canadian sovereignty, especially

Mike Stevens

Although obsolete for operational purposes, the Mackenzie class found a new lease on life as the West Coast training squadron, enjoying deployments far and wide, such as this to Glacier Bay, Alaska.

in the Arctic. This was much easier said than done. To begin, there was the enormous problem of whether to build them in Canada or to buy them offshore, which engaged both the British and the French in making proposals for the necessary technology transfers; predictably, Canada-Europe engineering consortia quickly emerged. But there was considerable opposition to the plan from a variety of sources. The Americans saw absolutely no need for such a capability and were quite prepared to address the political issue of the right of transit through the Northwest Passage. Political and public opposition to the nuclear-powered submarines was intense, with many fearing that Canada was making a great mistake and sliding down the path to becoming a nuclear power — confusing, conveniently, nuclear propulsion with nuclear weapons. The navy signed on to the new idea and naively exchanged eight frigates from the long-term plan for the 10 to 12 nuclear-powered submarines.

Strategically and tactically the concept made sense, but throughout the public and private discussions to refine the project, program costs were not developed accurately, especially those to create the necessary infrastructure. It was no surprise when the program was cancelled in the April 1989 budget; the financial costs of backing off were small, and a potentially destructive political confrontation was avoided. The impact on the navy, however, was considerable: the loss of eight frigates from the overall modernization program, not to mention the additional delay in seeking a conventional submarine replacement, meant that the ability to deploy three autonomous task groups, let alone a fourth, had just vanished. The navy would have to be a two task group fleet with the possibility of providing a third group only on mobilization for a major crisis.

The fall of the Berlin Wall on 9 November 1989 symbolically ended the 40-year Cold War. O'Brien's "bloody Russian submarines" no longer presented a threat to North American or European security. Almost coincidentally, by that time the Canadian Navy had largely made the transition from a specialized ASW force that would have been assigned piece-meal to NATO in various formations, to a concept of national task groups assigned specific tasks. The very complex period from the uncertainty of 1968, when politics threatened to tear the navy apart, to the dawn of a new era of international uncertainty in November 1989 was one in which the Canadian Navy matured into a truly national entity. In view of the almost continual political opposition to naval modernization through those two decades, the transformation is the more remarkable. Had O'Brien not encouraged the fleet to "Go find the bloody Russian submarines and leave the politics to me!," that maturing process might have been very much more difficult.

Notes

1. P.E. Trudeau, "The Relation of Defence Policy to Foreign Policy," *Statements and Speeches*, 12 April 1969 (69/8).
2. Marshall Lee Miller, "Soviet Military Development," *Armed Forces Journal International* (April 1987), 36.
3. Memorandum to Cabinet, *Maritime Surface Ship Requirements*, 3 November 1977 (PCO).

Maritime Research and Development, 1968–89

Harold Merklinger

Integration of the defence department was accompanied by rationalization of the management of military research and development. In 1974 the former DRB laboratories were grouped under a newly appointed chief of research and development (CRAD) reporting to the associate deputy minister (materiel), and a research and development "Program Review Committee" now advised CRAD on appropriate priorities and funding levels. The intent was to ensure that research activities responded to CF imperatives and that there should be a smooth transition from research to equipment selection, development, and in-service support.

Spending reductions limited the implementation of past research initiatives. The FHE-400 hydrofoil program, for example, although a technical success — the vessel met or exceeded specifications — was deemed unaffordable and cancelled. The hydrodynamics research effort was redirected toward conventional ships (structures, hydrodynamic stability, propeller design, noise reduction, and the like), as well as other new concepts such as a SWATH design. Nevertheless, the hydrofoil program had introduced the Canadian Navy to gas turbine propulsion and modern digital command and tactical data management and communications systems, and these technologies were further developed for the DDH-280, Iroquois-class ships. In the case of data management the technology was retrofitted with compatible modifications to earlier classes (as the "ADLIPS" Automated DataLink and Plotting System). During this period DND's maritime engineers reached a peak in their capacity to design and develop complete warship systems, as exemplified by the Iroquois class.

In the mid-1970s Canada learned from the U.S. and U.K. about progress being made toward a passive acoustic submarine detection capability for naval vessels. "Towed arrays" (a long, linked series of hydrophones) had been tried during the First World War and they were later adopted by mineral exploration organizations looking for seabed resources. The former PNL and NRE, now renamed respectively DREP (Defence Research Establishment Pacific) and DREA (Defence Research Establishment Atlantic), conducted a study of these arrays in naval applications using research vessels participating in navy exercises on both coasts. The Experimental Towed Array Sonar System (ETASS) evolved from adaptions of commercial arrays into a test-bed system using a half-length USN array in HMCS *Fraser*,

with excellent results. The subsequent Canadian Towed Array Sonar System (CANTASS) project, combining the Canadian-developed "dry end" shipboard processing and display with the "wet end" USN AN/SQR-19 sensor array, delivered a groundbreaking system for the Halifax class. Related projects provided towed arrays for Canada's Oberon submarines and a potential replacement design for the AN/SQR-19. The signal processing hardware developed for CANTASS was also applied to active sonars, leading to the AN/SQS-510 hull-mounted active sonar fitted in Canadian, Belgian, and Portuguese warships.

Many other research and development projects addressed different requirements, including technology for surveillance in the Arctic, mine countermeasures, the control of the infrared and radar signatures of ships, satellite communications systems, diver support, electronic warfare, ship machinery control, fire-safe materials, and ASW helicopter systems. Scientists also assisted Canadian and NATO studies on fleet compositions for the future. Toward the end of this period, quick studies were undertaken to assist in selection of a nuclear submarine for Canada.

The demise of the hydrofoil program was erroneously linked to renewed emphasis on the Arctic.

183

Defence Research and Development Canada Atlantic

Following the mothballing of *Bras d'Or*, the DREA hydrodynamics program broadened to include other non-conventional hull forms, such as this radio-controlled model of a SWATH vessel — a concept first proposed by Frederick G. Creed in 1938.

CHAPTER 10

The Transformation Era, 1990 to the Present

Richard H. Gimblett

Standing here on the deck of HMCS Halifax, *we can see the past, the present and the future of the Canadian Navy. Originally [ordered] during the Cold War, some questioned the need for these frigates after the collapse of the Soviet Union, but times changed, the world changed and through it all, there remained a need for a strong, modern and adaptable navy. During the last decade and a half, these frigates have been to the four corners of the world, performing every conceivable mission. And like the workhorses they are, they rarely get the praise they deserve.*

PRIME MINISTER STEPHEN HARPER, HALIFAX,
NOVA SCOTIA, 5 JULY 2007[1]

The fall of the Berlin Wall would not appear to have been a monumental event for the Canadian Navy, as the summer of 1990 found the East Coast task group preparing as usual for the annual NATO fall exercise in north European waters. For all the outward nonchalance, however, behind the scenes, the collapse of the Soviet Union as the nominal Cold War opponent presented senior naval commanders cause for concern. The Canadian Navy's *raison d'être* for the previous 40 years was gone, just as the service was at its post–Second World War nadir; increasingly derided in the media as "rusted-out" and irrelevant, the Canadian fleet was essentially unchanged from that of 1975.

Department of National Defence SU2007-0281-02

John Horton, *Operation Apollo*, shows a Canadian boarding party approaching a merchant tanker to search for material or activity indicating the presence of terrorists onboard.

Plans existed for the mainstay of the fleet, the venerable steam-powered frigates commissioned in the 1950s, to be withdrawn for sequential replacement by a new class, the Canadian patrol frigates, or CPFs. Like the ships they were replacing, the patrol frigates were designed for north Atlantic ASW. The program also coincided with the planned withdrawal of the 20-year-old Iroquois-class destroyers (DDH-280s) for a mid-life upgrade (the TRUMP or Tribal Update and Modernization Program). These plans meant the fleet's capacity for operations would be severely diminished for the next half-decade, and already there were calls to scale back both programs as part of the anticipated "peace dividend."

Like the rest of the world, Canada was kicked out of the summer doldrums by Saddam Hussein's early-August invasion of Kuwait. Most observers were caught further off guard when it was announced that Canada's military response to the American-led Operations Desert Shield and Desert Storm was the dispatch of a naval task group to the Persian Gulf, contrary to speculation that participation would be limited to a post-hostilities army peace-keeping force. If anything demonstrated how badly prepared the Canadian fleet had been to take on the presumed Soviet adversary, it was the deep anxiety now felt at going to war against an Iraq equipped largely with Soviet-style forces buttressed by the deadly French

Mirage fighter and Exocet missile combination that had severely damaged the USS *Stark* only a few years earlier.

But the aging destroyer *Athabaskan*, the steam frigate *Terra Nova*, and the supply ship *Protecteur* did sail, hastily upgraded with new command and control (C2) systems and strapped-on modular weapons such as the Phalanx CIWS (Close-in Weapon System) anti-missile Gatling gun and Harpoon anti-ship missiles obtained from the CPF and TRUMP projects. Nor would their deployment prove to be a "one-off" crisis response. Over the ensuing two decades, the southwest Asia theatre of operations was to become a "home away from home" for the Canadian Navy, with every major surface warship in the fleet seeing service in the region at least once, and several on three or more deployments. To be sure, as will be seen over the next few pages, the fleet has been busily engaged elsewhere around the globe, but the southwest Asia deployments have provided a completely unanticipated boost to the fortunes of the modern Canadian Navy. The two decades spanning the arrival of the twenty-first century have witnessed an unprecedented introduction of modern technologies and changing concepts of operations in navies and militaries around the world, such that the period has been styled variously as "the revolution in military affairs (RMA)" or "the age

Visibly worn from her seven-month deployment to the Persian Gulf, which included 49 straight days at sea, *Athabaskan* returns to Halifax, April 1991.

Department of National Defence SWC-91-156-26

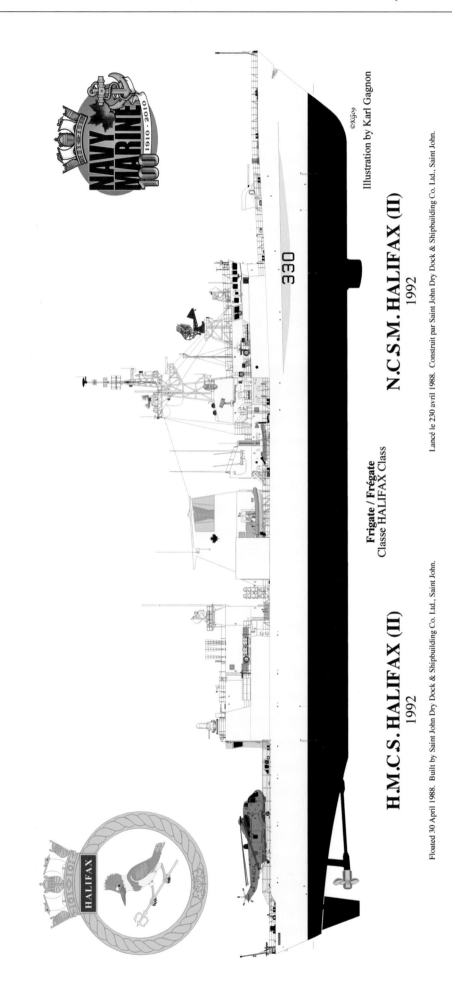

Illustration by Karl Gagnon

Frigate / Frégate
Classe HALIFAX Class

H.M.C.S. HALIFAX (II)
1992

Floated 30 April 1988. Built by Saint John Dry Dock & Shipbuilding Co. Ltd., Saint John.

29 June 1992 - Still in service

Dimensions: 134,1 m x 16,4 m x 4,9 m
Displacement: 5 235 tons   Speed: 28 knots Crew: 225
Armament: 1 x I - 57 mm; Harpoon missiles; Sea Sparrow missiles;
torpedoes; 1 x I - 20 mm Phalanx; 6 x I - 12.7 mm; 1 helicopter.

N.C.S.M. HALIFAX (II)
1992

Lancé le 230 avril 1988. Construit par Saint John Dry Dock & Shipbuilding Co. Ltd., Saint John.

29 juin 1992 - Toujours en service

Dimensions: 134,1 m x 16,4 m x 4,9 m
Déplacement: 5 235 tonnes Vitesse: 28 noeuds   Équipage: 225
Armement: 1 x I - 57 mm; missiles Harpoon; missiles Sea Sparrow;
torpilles; 1 x I - 20 mm Phalanx; 6 x I - 12,7 mm; 1 hélicoptère.

of transformation." The Canadian naval experience of many of these new technologies and operational concepts has been a direct result of the Gulf deployments, so it is no small claim that those have been a catalyst for the transformation of the Canadian fleet from a Cold War relic to one of the world's leading medium power navies.

That first Gulf war deployment in the summer of 1990 marked a dramatic break from many of the presumptions guiding employment of the Canadian Forces. For the first time in Canadian military history, participation in a major conflict was to be defined not in terms of the land force contribution, but by the exclusion of it and the inclusion of the contributions of the other services. It turned the Canadian Navy's world upside down — optimized for open-ocean anti-submarine warfare in the sub-Arctic waters of the north Atlantic and Pacific oceans, it suddenly found itself facing a primarily airborne threat in confined tropical waters.

But the sudden deployment also confirmed many basics were sound — such as the immense flexibility of general-purpose ship designs; the basic competence of well-trained sailors and practiced staff officers; and the immense benefits of investing in standardizing major systems, especially communications, with the United States Navy.

Indeed, these had all come together in the last few years of the Cold War, the real key being the fitting of Canadian flagships with American satellite communications and computerized command and control tools, so that by the late 1980s Canadian task group commanders were regularly exercising the ASW commander function in major NATO exercises. The job of Canadian ships in the gulf, therefore, was not a great leap. Even though their poor anti-air defences prevented them from holding a place in the forward operating areas of the northern Gulf, when USN commanders needed someone to coordinate the activities of the many other smaller navies in the southern Gulf, they delegated tactical control of the Coalition Logistics Force to the Canadian task group commander, which resulted in Navy Captain "Dusty" Miller becoming the only non-U.S. Navy officer assigned a subordinate warfare commander role in that conflict. Communications compatibility with the USN allowed Miller to pass information and orders up and down, between American commanders preoccupied with managing the very active war against Iraq, and the bulk of the coalition members whose ships did not enjoy communication equipments compatible with the USN. In a parallel development, Miller noted that the nature of the higher direction of warfare — associated now with coalition as opposed to alliance partners — was changing, leading him to suggest a re-definition of C2 from "command and control" to "cooperation and coordination."[2]

That first Gulf war sparked other significant shifts in Canadian military thinking. For one, the bold tactical decision by the original task group commander, Commodore Ken Summers, to station his ships in the central Gulf, well within Iraqi air attack range and notwithstanding the limited self-defence capabilities of the ships, was an inspired declaration that ours was a fighting navy not afraid to go in harm's way. For another, one of the factors that gave Summers the confidence to take that step was the commitment of a squadron (and eventually a wing) of CF-18 Hornet fighters to fly top cover for the naval forces in the Gulf — the first expeditionary combat deployment in modern air force history, which was also notable as it was conducted in concert with the U.S. Navy, instead of its traditional partner, the U.S.

United States Navy 020520-N-9312L-025

Through the late 1990s, the Halifax-class frigates operated as fully integrated elements of United States Navy (USN) carrier battle groups in the Persian Gulf region, such as *Vancouver* here with the USS *John C. Stennis*.

Air Force. And then, when Summers was shifted ashore to take command of all the Canadian Forces gathering in the Middle East, the establishment of his Bahrain base as the first true deployed joint headquarters (JHQ) in Canadian military history — and with a sailor in charge at that — heralded a true revolution in Canadian military affairs.

After the March 1991 ceasefire, the Canadian government wished to maintain a presence in the region, but the state of the fleet transition limited the effort, as had been expected. However, the introduction to the fleet in the mid-1990s of the highly capable Halifax-class frigates suggested opportunities to renew deployments, and 1995 saw two ships dispatched on separate missions. The first, HMCS *Fredericton* early in the year, was purely an effort to assist in the promotion of Canadian technology at various locations in the Gulf States. But the second saw *Calgary* operating not simply "attached" but as a fully "integrated" unit of the USS *Abraham Lincoln* carrier battle group, because of special access to high-level communications codes and equipment that would allow full utilization of the new Canadian frigate. *Calgary*'s deployment was a great success — among other things, having a shallower draft than most USN vessels, it spent much of August and September patrolling the northern Gulf off the mouth of the Shatt-al-Arab just outside the Iraqi 12-mile (19 kilometre) territorial limit — and became the model for future deployments. With the ongoing transition of the fleet, the momentary quiescence of Saddam, and the higher priority to provide frigates

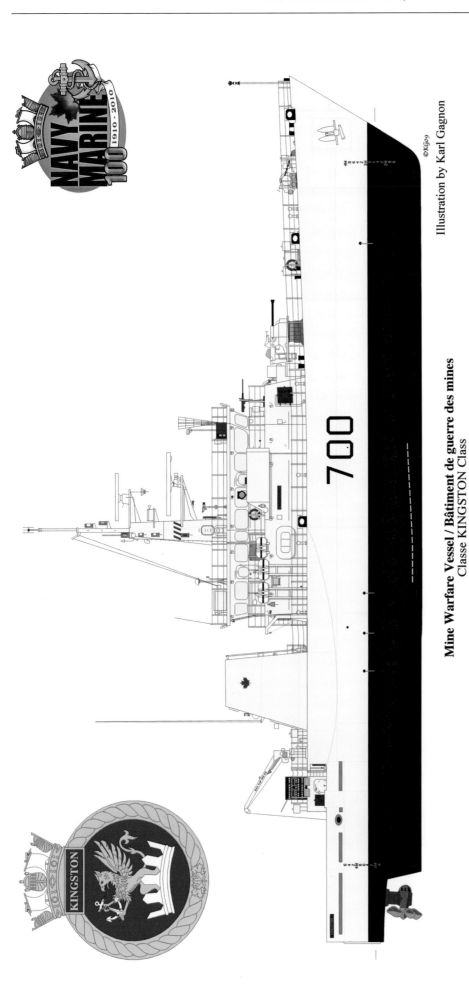

©XG09

Illustration by Karl Gagnon

Mine Warfare Vessel / Bâtiment de guerre des mines
Classe KINGSTON Class

0 m   5 m   10 m

H.M.C.S. KINGSTON
1995

Launched 12 August 1995. Built by Halifax Shipyards Ltd., Halifax.

21 September 1996 - Still in service

Dimensions: 55.3 m x 11.3 m x 3.1 m
Displacement: 934 tons   Speed: 15 knots   Crew: 35
Armament: 1 x 1 - 40 mm; 2 x 1 - 12.7 mm machine-guns.

N.C.S.M. KINGSTON
1995

Lancé le 12 août 1995. Construit par Halifax Shipyard Ltd., Halifax.

21 septembre 1996 - Toujours en service

Dimensions: 55,3 m x 11,3 m x 3,1 m
Déplacement: 934 tonnes   Vitesse: 15 noeuds   Équipage: 35
Armement: 1 x 1 - 40 mm; 2 x 1 - mitrailleuses de 12,7 mm.

to the Adriatic for the NATO embargo of the Former-Yugoslavia, however, it would be two more years before another frigate could participate with the Multinational Interception Force.

Before continuing that story, it is necessary to go back in time to pick up another thread in the "catalyst for transformation" theme. In the fall of 1992, in response to the slide of Somalia into failed-state status, HMCS *Preserver* was dispatched to support the deployment of the Canadian Airborne Regiment in the distribution of humanitarian aid. The deteriorating situation on the ground resulted in a constantly changing mission, one aspect of which was the inability to find a safe initial location ashore for the mission commander's headquarters. The solution was to reconfigure the ship's operations room as a floating JHQ — a measure fairly obvious to any navy that operates amphibious forces, but to the supposedly unified Canadian Forces (which in truth had never operated together as a tri-service "joint" force in actual combat) this was a radical departure. The success of at least this aspect of the ill-starred Somalia mission would be recalled a decade later when Chief of the Defence Staff, General Rick Hillier embarked upon his so-called transformation of CF command and control. More immediately, it led, within the Canadian Navy, to internalization of the idea that the long-overdue replacement of the replenishment ships should include the requirement that they be able to act as an afloat JHQ. Ironically, rather than speeding acceptance of the new tanker acquisition, an argument can be made that trying to define the level of jointness desired by the various services has delayed the acquisition of what is now called the JSS (joint support ship). Nonetheless, the concept has been a powerful catalyst for the transformation of not only the Navy but also the entire Canadian Forces.

With the "new world order" proving to be rather disorderly and in need of occasional Canadian naval intervention, modernization of the fleet had not been substantially delayed and proceeded largely as anticipated in the 1987 fleet plan. Even as the task group sailed for the Gulf in August 1990, the lead ship of the CPFs, *Halifax* (FFH-330), was undergoing acceptance trials. The remaining steam frigates were decommissioned in succession so that their crews could undertake conversion to the new types; the last to go was *Nipigon* (DDH-266) in 1998. Over the course of the last decade of the twentieth century, the Navy accepted the four rebuilt ships of the Iroquois class, as well as 24 new ships — besides the 12 patrol frigates, there were 12 Kingston-class (PB-700) maritime coastal defence vessels (MCDVs), replacing the 1950s vintage Bay-class minesweepers for use primarily with the Naval Reserve for the renewal of a mine countermeasures (MCM) capability and basic naval officer training. By the end of the decade, the three Oberon-class submarines were gone as well, being replaced by the Victoria (ex-Upholder) class of four diesel submarines acquired from the Royal Navy. In the year 2010, only the AORs *Protecteur* and *Preserver* remain of the Cold War fleet. If for no reason beyond the physical composition of the fleet, the last two decades has witnessed the transformation of the Canadian Navy. At the cusp of the Navy's Centennial, Canada has in its service arguably the best-balanced and most capable fleet in its history.

But the transformation extends to other levels as well. Throughout the latter stages of the Cold War, as the American and Soviet superpowers settled into their nuclear stand-off and Canadian fleet operational capability increasingly diminished, crisis response actions were a rarity and it was possible for sailors to predict their annual sailing schedules in accordance with the major NATO exercises.

Department of National Defence ET2006-0148-20

Maritime Operations Group 4, including all six of its assigned Kingston-class coastal patrol vessels, does a formation steam through the Gulf Islands, British Columbia.

Through the 1990s, the change in composition of the fleet was paralleled by a change in the longstanding relationship with NATO. Canada continued the practice of consistently contributing a ship to the Standing Naval Force Atlantic (STANAVFORLANT), but the availability of hulls and the press of other commitments precipitated a subtle but noticeable shift in the priority previously extended to what had almost come to be presumed an obligation. The first indication came in the immediate wake of the 1991 Gulf War when *Restigouche*, originally intended to replace one of the ships in the Gulf, was given the NATO assignment — the first West Coast ship to do so, and indeed the first Canadian ship to join STANAVFORLANT without a helicopter since its inception in the 1960s. Later in the decade, occasionally a tanker would come to pick up the duty (one had frequently been part of the group, but never as a replacement for a destroyer or frigate). The role was still an important one, as witnessed by Canada continuing to fill a turn in the rotating command of the NATO group, which came about twice in the course of the decade, and each time with one of the modernized ("TRUMP'd") Iroquois-class destroyers as the flagship, a role for which it was now truly fitted. As fate would have it, both those year-long assignments — in 1993–94 and 1999–2000 — coincided with the two occasions when STANAVFORLANT was deployed out-of-area to the Adriatic Sea for operations against the Former-Yugoslav Republic, and again the higher quality of command and control suite fitted in the Canadian destroyers was critical to successful coordination of the mission. However, a truer harbinger came in 1998, when the NATO-assigned frigate *Toronto* was detached from the NATO squadron to proceed to the Gulf as an immediate response to the United Nations call for additional forces to pressure Saddam Hussein to comply with U.N. weapons-inspection access. That type of re-assignment — and the gapping of the NATO commitment until the next scheduled deployment — would become an habitual response to the Canadian

Department of National Defence IS2002-1615

Leading Seaman Tara Watts, a member of *Montréal*'s boarding team, documents the crew of a dhow in the Gulf of Oman in the fall of 2002.

government's need for a forward-deployed frigate. Canada's naval commitment to NATO remains of continuing value to the Alliance. Indeed, when a change in the Alliance's concept of operations meant the reconstitution of STANAVFORLANT in 2006 in favour of a "Standing NATO Maritime Group" (SNMG-1), it was Canadian Commodore Denis Rouleau who was assigned to oversee the new force's year-long workup to fully operational status, a command he conducted from a succession of Iroquois-class destroyers. As NATO itself changes, Canadian warships have been part of the action, with the frigate *Toronto* participating in the circumnavigation of Africa in 2007 (an incredible expedition when one stops to think of it), and *Winnipeg* found itself at the front of the force's fight against Somali pirates in 2009.

The decreasing emphasis on NATO reflects an expansion of Canadian horizons beyond Europe, and as the country looks farther afield, the global reach of the fleet has positioned the Navy perfectly to contribute. If the "Persian Excursion" was the last war cry of the Cold War fleet, Canada's "New World Order Navy" very quickly found itself engaged at a higher operational tempo, as real-world brush-fire crises replaced the routine of peacetime exercises. The fisheries crisis on the Atlantic Grand Banks, illegal Chinese immigration on the Pacific coast, challenges to our Arctic sovereignty, and continued instability in the Caribbean basin all ensured gainful employment in home and hemispheric waters. Further abroad, the new frigates and modernized destroyers have proven to be showcases of Canadian technological know-how, and even the two supply ships have been dispatched for humanitarian assistance operations to places as diverse as hurricane-ravaged Florida and civil war-torn East Timor, in addition to their customary fleet replenishment role. The planned annual cycle of exercises promulgated in the fleet OPSKED (operations schedule) with traditional names like Ocean Safari, Teamwork, MARCOT, and RIMPAC, invariably has been overtaken with real-world operations with often only too-appropriate designations such as Friction (Persian Gulf, 1990–91), Deliverance (Somalia, 1992–93), Sharp Guard (the Adriatic Sea, 1992–95), Forward Action (Haiti, 1993–94), Ocean Vigilance (the Grand Banks "Turbot War," 1995), Persistence (the Swissair crash recovery in St. Margaret's Bay, 1998), Toucan (East Timor, 1999–2000), Megaphone (the boarding and recovery of the GTS *Katie* in the Gulf of St. Lawrence, 2000), Unison (the relief effort in the wake of Hurricane Katrina, 2005), Chabanel (support to the Royal Canadian Mounted Police [RCMP] for a drug bust in West Africa's Gulf of Guinea, 2006), and Horatio (Haiti again, but for hurricane relief, 2008). Significant for their listing as operations (even though they are in fact domestic exercises by the standard definition of the terms) have been the increasingly bold forays of the Navy into the high Arctic, culminating in Operation Nanook, which

Leading Seaman Tammy Comeau pipes the "still" as Commander Maritime Forces Atlantic Rear-Admiral Dean McFadden returns the salute of the submarines *Corner Brook* and *Windsor*, 21 December 2006.

saw the frigate *Fredericton*. coastal defence vessel *Summerside*, and submarine *Corner Brook* operating with other Canadian Forces and the Coast Guard into the Northwest Passage in August 2007.

And sailors found their skills in high demand also in diverse inland employment: as observers in Cambodia (Op Marquis, 1992), the Former-Yugoslavia (Op Bolster, 1991–94), and Darfur (Op Augural, 2005–08); as key members of the Strategic Advisory Team to the Afghan government in Kabul (Op Argus, 2005–08); and in general support of broader operations in Afghanistan (Op Athena, 2005 to date), where the unique skills of the Navy's clearance divers at disposing of improvised explosive devices (IEDs) have earned special recognition, including the award of the Star of Courage to Petty Officer 2nd Class Jim Leith for his "act of conspicuous courage in circumstances of great peril" in the fall of 2006. Leith portrayed the nonchalance typical of sailors just going about their professional business in these various activities, dismissing his dismantling of the explosive device with a simple, "These IEDs are technically not very sophisticated. I felt I was competent enough to disable it. A good dose of fear keeps you sharp."[3]

But returning to the main thread of the story, it is the Gulf deployments that really have come to define the modern Canadian naval experience. After a break from the initial forays in 1995 to allow completion of the fleet transition, by 1997 the Navy was ready to resume frigate deployments to the Gulf region. As had been established previously by *Calgary's* mission, the next ship to take on the task (the *Regina*, another from the West Coast) was also fitted with the full communications suite needed for high-level access, but by now it was recognized that the level of Canadian technical and communications interoperability with the USN was sufficient that Canadian ships could replace American vessels one-for-one in the order of battle. As such, a new twist on this mission was that *Regina* undertook the full regime of training and workups and made the transit to the Gulf as part of the San Diego-based USN surface action group with which it was designated to operate. The success of that effort led to the practice being regularized.

Although only one ship was to be sent each year, for a six-month period away from home port (meaning a gapping of the Canadian presence in the Gulf), the continuing non-compliance of Saddam Hussein with U.N. inspection requirements soon led to a more forceful and sustained Canadian presence. A flurry of United Nations Security Council Resolutions in 1997–98 culminated in the coalition (primarily U.S.-U.K.) Operation Desert Thunder, for which, as we have seen, the Canadian frigate assigned to STANAVFORLANT was diverted to the Gulf in support of the Multinational Interception Force (MIF). Even after that coalition drubbing, Saddam's compliance was short-lived, so the Chrétien government undertook to bolster its commitment to the MIF. What eventually became known in Canada as Operation Augmentation saw the deployments of a further succession of five frigates integrated in USN carrier battle groups and surface action groups in the three-year 1998–2001 period. Saddam's intransigence toward the U.N. increased such that HMCS *Winnipeg* (the last frigate so deployed) had to perform several non-compliant boardings through the spring and summer of 2001. Significantly, for its last patrol in July 2001, *Winnipeg's* captain, Commander Kelly Williams, was designated the on-scene commander for the northern Gulf, a first time for a coalition warship — again, full "connectivity" on

Department of National Defence Combat Camera 100_2249

A LAV-III crew of the Royal 22^e Regiment makes an amphibious landing during an exercise proving the Standing Contingency Force concept of operations, November 2006.

a form of classified internet known as the Coalition Wide Area Network or COWAN, was the key to performing this major warfare responsibility.

Another factor was the increasing persistence of the Canadian presence. The deployments through the 1990s did work to increase the familiarity of Canadian crews with the radical new satellite and computer-based communications technologies. But the Gulf deployments, for all of their individual effectiveness, being of such an irregular nature had failed to make a lasting impression on USN regional commanders — until, that is by 2000–01, when the steady succession of ships in-theatre made our presence an expected and accepted feature, resulting in the recognition accorded *Winnipeg*.

The decade of Gulf deployments had a deeper effect on the Navy's psyche than just technical competence. The Canadian Navy embarked also upon an intellectual revolution through the 1990s, seeking a better understanding of the meaning of sea power to medium power nations such as Canada, as distinct from the global force projection capabilities particular to the U.S. Navy. The articulation of a strategic vision for its purpose in the post–Cold War world was shaped in large measure by a thorough exploration of the meaning of the Gulf deployments. June 2001 saw the publication of *Leadmark: The Navy's Strategy for 2020*, which pointed variously to the utility of working in combination with alliances or coalitions,

SUBMARINES of the CANADIAN NAVY

HMCS/M CC1 (1914)
313/421 tons - 43.9 m x 4.7 m x 3.3 m - 13/10 knots

HMCS/M CC2 (1914)
313/421 tons - 46.3 m x 4.7 m x 3.3 m - 13.5/10.5 knots

HMCS/M CH14 (1921) - HMCS/M CH15 (1921)
364/434 tons - 45.7 m x 4.8 m x 3.7 m - 13/11 knots

HMCS U-190 (1945)
1,144/1,257 tons - 76.8 m x 6.8 m x 4.7 m - 18/7.5 knots

HMCS U-889 (1945)
1,144/1,257 tons - 76.8 m x 6.8 m x 4.7 m - 18/7.5 knots

HMCS GRILSE (II) (1961)
1,800/2,425 tons - 94.9 m x 8.3 m x 5.1 m - 20/9 knots

HMCS RAINBOW (II) (1968)
1,526/2,391 tons - 95 m x 8.3 m x 5.1 m - 20/10 knots

HMCS OJIBWA (1965) - HMCS ONONDAGA (1967) - HMCS OKANAGAN (1968)
2,007/2,406 tons - 90 m x 8.1 m x 5.4 m - 12/17 knots

HMCS VICTORIA (2000) - HMCS WINDSOR (2001) - HMCS CORNER BROOK (2002) - HMCS CHICOUTIMI (II) (2012)
2,221/2,475 tons - 70.3 m x 7.6 m x 5.5 m - 12/20 knots

Illustrations by Karl Gagnon

to the merit of interoperability with the U.S. Navy, and to the shift of naval operations into the littorals as an enabler of air and land operations. The struggle to articulate a vision for the Navy in a constantly changing global military environment has been re-engaged, with the intent to promulgate an updated strategic approach in 2010.

But in 2001, the Navy hardly had time to digest *Leadmark*, when in the aftermath of the 9/11 Al-Qaeda attacks, NATO invoked Article 5 of its Charter and the United Nations Security Council passed a series of resolutions authorizing collective action against terrorists, and Canada promptly began to implement its "new" naval strategy. As has been our nation's practice in the past, the Navy, once again, was the first responder to a major crisis overseas. Within hours of the Chrétien government committing Canadian Forces to join in the U.S.-led Operation Enduring Freedom (OEF), the frigate with STANAVFORLANT was detached to join a USN carrier battle group in the Arabian Sea, and within the month the West Coast frigate that had been preparing to deploy under the latest iteration of Op Augmentation sailed to join another carrier group. The main Canadian OEF effort fell under the national Operation Apollo, initially with the dispatch of a three-ship task group from Halifax with an embarked commodore, just as had transpired in 1990. The operations in this second Gulf War lasted a full two years and evolved through what can be seen in hindsight as four distinct phases. Each was an impressive achievement in its own right, demonstrating the amazing flexibility Canada has in its modern general-purpose fleet.

This time, contrary to the earlier experience, the modernized destroyers and frigates constituted a truly imposing force, and immediately upon arrival of *Iroquois* and *Charlottetown* in the Arabian Sea in November 2001 — after a 13,000 kilometre voyage and without need to put into port to replenish or re-equip — the Canadian task group was assigned the close escort of the U.S. Navy amphibious ready groups operating close inshore off Pakistan, including the direct "TACON" (tactical control) of U.S. Navy Aegis destroyers, a rare signal of USN trust in an ally. By January 2002, at the height of this first phase, there were six Canadian warships in the region (one-third of the entire surface fleet). As U.S. Marine operations in Afghanistan wound down (incidentally, replaced in Kandahar by the Canadian Princess Patricia's Light Infantry brigade group), the second phase went into full swing with attention shifting to the search for escaping leadership of Taliban and Al-Qaeda terrorists. The shortest path to their Horn of Africa bases, after making their way through Iran, was by sea across the Gulf of Oman (this area became known by its acronym as the "GOO," which also described the hot and humid conditions). Coinciding with the arrival of naval forces from other coalition partners into the area, the Canadians quickly took charge of this effort, closing off the GOO through the spring and summer of 2002 as an escape route. The third phase began with the buildup in the fall of 2002 of coalition forces for operations against Iraq, and continued through the war there. Although Canada opted not to participate directly in that conflict, it was recognized that the stream of coalition shipping through the Strait of Hormuz would be a "honey-pot" — an attractive target sure to lure terrorist attacks. The task group organized hundreds of close escorts through the Strait, which went off without major incident.

All of this effort was coordinated under the USN as part of Operation Enduring Freedom, but in the winter of 2002–03 the shifting of U.S. attention onto Iraq left many coalition

Department of National Defence HS2007-G026-011

Left to right: HMC Ships *Fredericton*, *Summerside*, and *Corner Brook* sail in formation past an iceberg during Operation Nanook, August 2007.

partners — including Canada — uneasy. The fluid nature of operations at sea, unlike the way those on land tend to evolve, means they cannot be separated by simple demarcations on a map, and the subtle distinction was lost on many Canadian observers then and since. U.S. naval commanders at the time were aware of the national sensitivities, and developed a solution to provide some arms-length separation of Operation Enduring Freedom from Operation Iraqi Freedom (OIF). Key to this was the creation of a new task organization command structure, which among other things elevated the Canadian-led task group in the Gulf of Oman to full task force status (the distinction between "group" and "force" indicating a potent increase in power), with a separate reporting chain direct to the coalition naval commander in Bahrain, rather than through an American admiral embarked in a USN carrier. Although the Canadian command of Coalition Task Force 151 has been misinterpreted by politicians and academics who sometimes seem wilfully inclined not to understand national command and control structures, the government of the day fully understood the distinctions and was comfortable with the navy's actions. Indeed, the case can be made that Commodore Roger Girouard's command of CTF 151 not only provided the government of Canada a much-fuller range of political options in managing its response to the crisis, but also it quite probably was instrumental in keeping the Enduring Freedom coalition together at a politically delicate time. U.S. Ambassador Paul Cellucci said it best when he observed that, "Canadian naval vessels, aircraft and personnel … provide more support indirectly to this war in Iraq than most of the 46 countries that are fully supporting our efforts there."[4]

The final phase began as operations in Iraq wound down, for even with "active" operations over, the value of regular merchant shipping through the Strait of Hormuz, as well as the ongoing hunt for Al-Qaeda, pointed to the need to maintain a Canadian naval presence in the Arabian Sea region. By the summer of that year, only the frigate *Calgary* remained in-theatre, and its return to Esquimalt in December 2003 marked the end of the largest sustained Canadian naval operation since the Korean War. Operation Apollo had required the effective mobilization of the Canadian Navy — the deployment of practically the entire major surface fleet (except for the one destroyer and the one frigate in extended refits), and nearly every one of the 4,200 sailors of all ranks and trades in sea-going billets. With a contribution typically constituting less than 20 percent of coalition naval resources, Canadian sailors accomplished some 50 percent of the measurable achievement: altogether they completed some 600 of the nearly 1,300 boardings, an average of nearly two a day for the duration of the operation; *Calgary* alone conducted 92 escorts through the Strait of Hormuz. But the real Canadian naval success was in leading the coalition effort at sea. Our navy was the first major fleet to arrive after the U.S. Navy. Many of the 49 other participating nations dispatched a frigate or supply ship to establish a presence, but most had little experience operating with the other fleets. Our ships' unique communications "interoperability" with the USN, plus our national experience of multilateralism, made it natural for the USN to delegate command of this fleet to the Canadian commodore. Coalition building is perhaps the most under-appreciated of the naval roles in the war against terrorism, and yet it is the most quintessentially Canadian. Command of Task Force 151 was the first operational-level command — the largest area of responsibility and span of control — exercised by a senior Canadian officer in an active theatre since the Second World War, and it was a singular national achievement that was lost sight of in the false debate over participation in the war against Iraq.

The Navy was supposed to take an "operational pause" to recover from the effort, but almost immediately, in January 2004, the frigate *Toronto* deployed back to the region, integrated with the USS *George Washington* carrier battle group. Operation Altair, the Canadian codename for the continuing naval presence in the region, continues to this day. It was envisioned as a return to the Op Augmentation single-ship deployments; however, the capabilities of the ships and the prowess of the crews quickly re-established their reputation, and opportunities have frequently arisen for the ship captains to exercise what are known as "Pulse Group Command" of small formations of multinational warships on focused operations. One of the most successful of these resulted in the captain of HMCS *Ottawa* being awarded the U.S. Meritorious Service Medal for that ship's tour in 2007, the citation reading in part, "Commander [Darren] Hawco's brilliant operational acumen included a high visibility boarding operation against a vessel suspected of trafficking international terrorists, and crucial escort duties for a damaged United States submarine transiting the treacherous Straits of Hormuz. His exhaustive efforts greatly improved maritime security and raised the bar for coalition operations."[5] The increasing success of those single-ship

Department of National Defence HS2009-E001-074

A night vision scope view from the frigate *Winnipeg* of her boarding party intercepting a boat of Somali pirates, April 2009.

deployments suggested a number of opportunities that could be exploited by the return of a full Canadian task group to the region, and so it came to pass that Commodore Bob Davidson exercised command of CTF 150 for the three months of June-September 2008, from his flagship *Iroquois*, with the frigate *Calgary* and supply ship *Protecteur* joining the other coalition forces just in time to anticipate the sudden increase in pirate activity off Somalia. In the fall of 2008, the only Halifax-class frigate to have not yet deployed to the southwest Asia theatre finally did so, when HMCS *Ville de Québec* was detached from duties with NATO's standing maritime group in the Mediterranean to provide escort for World Food Programme emergency aid shipments into Mogadishu, Somalia.

The successful transformation of the 1990s evidently delivered just the navy Canada needed to respond decisively to a range of domestic and international crises. But the aging of the fleet speaks to the urgency of getting on with renewal. The Halifax-class frigates were laid down in the early 1990s (nearly two full decades ago); the Victoria-class submarines first entered British service in the early 1980s (the better part of three decades ago); the destroyers and supply ships were commissioned in the early 1970s (coming on four decades ago). The Canadianization refit of the submarines is progressing well, with *Victoria* and *Corner Brook* due to re-enter service during 2010. A contract to perform the Halifax-class modernization has been signed, which will see the 12 frigates sequentially withdrawn from service over the next decade for their mid-life refit. But uncertainty lingers over the scope and timing of the Joint Support Ship tanker replacement project, and a new class of vessels designed for duty in the high north (the Arctic offshore patrol vessel, or AOPV) is still in the project definition stage. More critically, the government has yet to agree to replace the Iroquois-class destroyers, which are reaching the natural end of their hull service lives. Their looming retirement, coincident with withdrawal of the Halifax class for upgrade, means that for a critical few years in the middle of the next decade, Canada could have only four major surface warships available for deployment on a contingency operation.

This chapter in the history of the Canadian Navy looks to be ending much as it began — with the naval service facing a diminished capacity for operations for at least the next half-decade. But if history is any guide, as new challenges come along from unexpected quarters, the Canadian Navy is sure somehow to rise to the occasion.

Notes

1. "Prime Minister Stephen Harper Announces New Upgrades to the Navy's Halifax-Class Frigates," 5 July 2007, accessed at: *www.pm.gc.ca/eng/media.asp?id=1735.*
2. Jean Morin and Richard H. Gimblett, *Operation FRICTION: The Canadian Forces in the Persian Gulf, 1990–1991* (Toronto: Dundurn Press, 1997), 88.
3. Darlene Blakeley, "Navy Diver Awarded Star of Courage," navy website, 01 April 2009, accessed at: *www.navy.forces.gc.ca/cms/3/3-a_eng.asp?id=719.*
4. Quoted in Richard H. Gimblett, *Operation Apollo: The Golden Age of the Canadian Navy in the War Against Terrorism* (Ottawa: Magic Light, 2004), 125.
5. Darlene Blakeley, "U.S. Meritorious Service Medal Awarded to Ship's Captain," *The Maple Leaf*, 11:41 (3 December 2008), accessed at: *www.forces.gc.ca/site/Commun/ml-fe/article-eng. asp?id=4936.*

Maritime Research and Development, Since 1990

Harold Merklinger and Ross Graham

The end of the Cold War led to major cuts in all defence spending. Although the research arm initially adjusted through cutbacks in the amount of research contracted out, eventually the organization had to cut staff and facilities. DREP was officially closed in 1995, although the dockyard lab on the West Coast was retained as part of a smaller DREA, and in 2000 the research and development branch became an agency called Defence Research and Development Canada (DRDC).

Meanwhile, naval operations shifted from a focus on blue water ASW to the more diverse demands of littoral operations. This meant increased concern about anti-ship missiles launched from shore or minor warships, mines, diesel-electric submarines, and fast inshore attack craft, as well as developing and maintaining a "recognized maritime picture" (RMP) that included both merchant and military vessels.

Bringing the new generation of ships into service required scientific support in other respects. For example, when HMCS *Halifax* encountered an early diesel engine failure, DREA's East Coast dockyard lab demonstrated convincingly that the problem was class-wide, and that the engine connecting rods had been under-designed and therefore "under warranty."

DRDC responses to a renewed interest in mine countermeasures included an interim remote minehunting and disposal system (IRMDS), and a remotely operated, semi-submersible vehicle towing a variable depth, side-scan sonar to map and identify bottom targets (the developmental prototype continues in use as an interim operational system for the navy, pending a planned acquisition project). Quieter submarines also forced a renewed interest in active sonar. An experimental towed integrated active-passive sonar (TIAPS) project demonstrated the ability of active sonar to detect quiet submarines in both mono-static (source and receiver co-located) and bi-static (source and receiver located on different platforms) modes of operation, pointing the way for potential future sonar concepts. Signal processing expertise developed in this era also facilitated cooperative work with the Netherlands on development of a shipboard infrared (IR) search and tracking system for missile and air defence. The resulting "SIRIUS" system is part of the Halifax-class modernization package.

Exploiting the ever-increasing capabilities of commercial computers, DRDC upgraded model generation and visualization tools to enable advanced structural analysis for surface ships and submarines, for use in design and repair and to investigate motion and stability before putting a design to sea. It is probable that future systems will be able to simulate complete naval engagements incorporating both simulated sensor and weapons performance, as well as real or simulated human decisions in real time — or faster than real time.

Today's research program includes a wide range of activities: task group anti-ship missile and torpedo defence; command and control concepts and systems; combat and surveillance data fusion and interpretation, including automated decision aids; naval fire support; fixed and mobile autonomous systems; multi-platform cooperative ASW; mine and harbour defence; novel materials for weight reduction and signature control; ship damage control and maintenance; systems for long-range surveillance of Canada's maritime approaches; and operations research into current and future fleet operations. Many of the questions that are being addressed by these programs are the same as those posed by the navy of 100 years ago. The answers, however, are very different today!

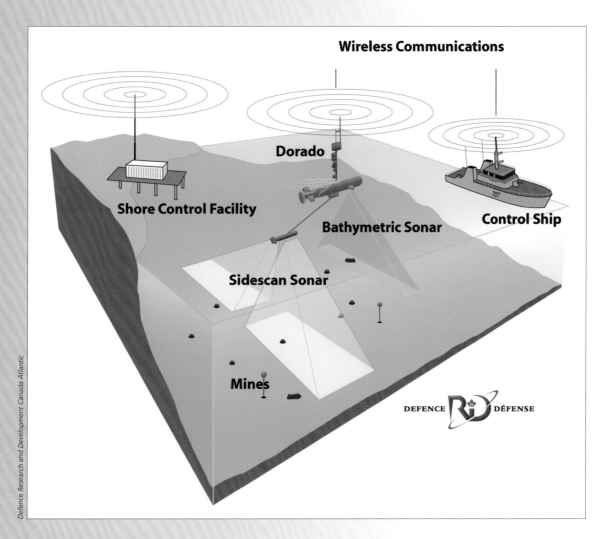

Defence Research and Development Canada Atlantic

This depiction of the interim remote mine-hunting and disposal system demonstrates the use of the "Dorado" semi-submersible vehicle to tow a side-scan sonar to map mine-like objects.

Dorado, with only mast showing, proceeds ahead of the mine warfare vessel *Whitehorse*.

Defence Research and Development Canada Atlantic

CHAPTER 11

The Problematic World of the Navy's Second Century

James Boutilier

I t is widely recognized that predictive analyses are fraught with difficulties. As one commentator observed, "we know a great deal but we understand very little."[1] Can we project trends into the future in a linear manner? At what stage are feedback loops triggered? And how are we to account for human agents whose decisions may be rational or not? Certainly, we have come to recognize that causation is increasingly multivariate and synergistic. The challenges to be examined are twofold: what will the world be like in the foreseeable future (say, out to 2025); and what will changed global circumstances mean for the Canadian Navy in terms of its character and operations?

Accordingly, this chapter is divided into two parts. The first part analyzes the major factors that are likely to shape our world almost two decades hence. Those factors include demography, resources, environmental trends, and geo-strategic developments. The second part analyzes the Canadian domestic scene in terms of defence policy and the ways in which the Canadian Navy will develop and be employed in 2025.

The forecast is sobering, even bleak. The twentieth century was an exponential century. Its great icons were the atomic bomb, the birth control pill, the space shuttle, and the internet. During the century, mankind's ability to kill became global and instantaneous for the first time in history. At the same time humans were able to tinker with demography as never before. We looked back on earth from outer space and realized that the philosophical

Defence Research and Development Canada Atlantic

Future warships in the Canadian fleet may yet come to include designs such as artist Geoff Bennett's 1984 interpretation of a large helicopter-carrying SWATH ship.

underpinnings of the Western concept of progress, of moving onward and upward endlessly, no longer applied. The world, in the largest sense of the word, was finite, not infinite. There was a stern corollary associated with this realization; that we were being driven inexorably from cultures of consumption to cultures of conservation. And news of that phenomenon could now be communicated anywhere on the face of the planet in the blink of an eye. All of these disparate realities were captured by the term "globalization." Globalization was predicated, in large part, on neo-liberal expectations of the primacy of democracy and free market forces, phenomena telegraphed with dramatic speed and power to every corner of the earth.

Mankind is on the cusp at the beginning of the twenty-first century. While the denizens of Western Europe in the late 1340s no doubt concluded that the Black Death heralded the end of the known world, their travails were, in retrospect, less existential than the ones facing their descendents over six centuries later. The catalogue of challenges facing mankind in this century is daunting and those challenges are, in many ways, truly existential.

The first and, arguably, dominant concern relates to demography. It took from time immemorial till 1830 for the population of the world to reach one billion. In the next 180 years it rose to over six billion and in the next 20 years it will rise by almost two billion. Put another way, we will be adding three Canada's per year for the next 20 years. What is particularly worrisome is the fact that 98 percent of that growth will be in those parts of the world least able to cope with the burden. The overall planetary increase in population will bring almost unimaginable pressures to bear on increasingly scarce natural resources — food, fuel, fish — and on the environment. What, we might ask ourselves, will be the impact on global warming of increasing the world's population by 25 percent in two decades? If the impact is profound, how will stocks of food and supplies of water be affected? In broad terms, globalization has resulted in more and more people being drawn out of poverty (although the gap between the rich and the poor continues to widen), but as Paul Collier has noted in *The Bottom Billion* (Oxford University Press, 2007), there are almost a billion people on the planet who are becoming worse off. If we look at Haiti, for example, Haitians have grown poorer every year for the past 40 years. Are the ranks of the "Bottom Billion"

The severe drought conditions being experienced in many regions of the world may lead to competition for fresh water resources.

Reuters

now to be further swelled? And, despite expending over two trillion dollars in foreign aid, the developed world has been unable, over the past half century, to ameliorate poverty, particularly in Africa, to any demonstrable degree.

To make matters worse, demographic forces are not uniform. While populations in Africa are exploding, populations in the industrialized world are not only shrinking, but aging. Japan's population is aging faster than any other nation. The population of Russia is falling by almost three quarters of a million people per year as a result of tuberculosis, alcohol, AIDS, suicide, abortion, and other social ills. Similarly, the population of Western Europe is shrinking dramatically. The upshot of these powerful asymmetries is that enormous osmotic forces have developed, propelling people out of Saharan and sub-Saharan Africa into Europe, out of Mexico and Central America into the United States, and out of China to the developed world. For the most part, these migrants are illegals. One can only presume, deterministically, that as the population of the developing world (and of those states that seem to have almost no prospects of ever developing) continues to grow relentlessly, the movement of people worldwide will become even more intense and potentially violent.

How are we to feed and provide energy for this burgeoning planetary community? Forty years ago it was a near-heresy to suggest that the world was running out of oil. Now "peak

Some 80 percent of the world's ocean fish species have been over-exploited and are in rapid decline, such as these cod and other ground fish caught in a net in the Golf of Maine.

National Geographic

oil" is conventional wisdom. Bit by bit we are coming to terms with the fact that supplies of sweet crude are not inexhaustible. While there are variations in the outlook (for example a vast new oil field off Sao Paulo, Brazil), the underlying trend remains unchanged. There are fewer and fewer major discoveries. The appetite for energy on the part of the new oil-fired economies of Asia is insatiable. The price of a barrel of oil continues to rise through one psychological threshold after another. For all its appeal, ethanol appears to be the Piltdown Man of the energy world — half a hoax, half evolutionary dead end. While sugarcane biomass and algae hold out some promise, all the corn in the United States destined for conversion to ethanol (roughly 33 percent of the national crop) only produced five billion gallons in 2007, a figure equivalent to the production of one oil rig off the coast of West Africa. Furthermore, experience has revealed that it takes very nearly a barrel of oil to produce a barrel of ethanol. If those figures were not sobering enough, we have to face the likelihood that global automotive traffic will rise dramatically over the next 20 years — most of it in the developing world. Carlos Ghosn, the chief executive of Renault and Nissan, has calculated that the current number of passenger cars, 650 million, will rise to 2.9 billion by 2050. What does this mean in a world where there is relatively little elasticity in oil availability? What does greater energy consumption mean in terms of greenhouse gases and climate change? What impact will greater and greater oil scarcity mean on petroleum products like fertilizer, the cost of which doubled in 2007?

There are, of course, other considerations. If sweet crude supplies are becoming increasingly finite, what about the harder to extract stocks, the ones that come from tar sands or oil shale? The former entail a number of hard choices. The energy required to produce oil from tar sands contributes materially to global warming. And what is less well known is that it takes four barrels of water to produce one barrel of oil in this way.

Water is another of the resources coming under increasing strain. North Americans are monstrously profligate in their use of water: 350 litres per person per day in residential areas compared with 10 to 20 litres a day in sub-Saharan Africa. Water scarcity is becoming increasingly evident in the Middle East, in South Asia, and in Northern China. On many occasions in the past three decades, the Yellow River, one of the great rivers of China, has run dry before reaching its mouth. The Chinese have a saying, "When you drink the water, remember the spring," but as a planetary society we have forgotten this adage. Over one billion people on earth lack access to clean drinking water and breathtaking riverine pollution in Asia is certain to drive that figure upwards. What, we should ask, is the nexus between water scarcity and interstate conflict? The forecasts are dark. Global warming will exacerbate the water situation and shifts in the diet of peoples in the developing world (it takes 1,000 litres of water to produce a kilogram of wheat and 13 times as much to produce a kilogram of beef) hold out little hope that the situation will be ameliorated in the short to mid term.

Rising oil prices, the diversion of food stocks into alternative energy sources, the increased cost of fertilizers and herbicides, and the increasing scarcity of water are placing intolerable strains on global food production. In the developing and pre-developing world, individuals often spend the bulk of their income on two things — energy and food. Many have called for another Green Revolution, but the agricultural revolution of the 1960s and 1970s

Department of National Defence Combat Camera HS2008-L007-028

Scenes such as this of the Canadian Navy delivering humanitarian aid to Haiti in September 2008 are bound to become even more common in the decades ahead.

appears to have run its course. For the first time in human history there are more people living in cities than in the country-side. These people are at the mercy of local, national, or international food producers, but there are a host of structural impediments to the worldwide movement of inexpensive food. It is a tragic commonplace now to speak of farmers in western Europe being paid to destroy their crops while millions starve else-where. And our life-long expectation that somehow science will come to our rescue, as it has done so many times before, seems a fatally arrogant presumption. There is hubris in our belief that science is the silver bullet. We have pushed the planet to the brink, and even stereotypically inexhaustible sources like the fish in the sea have begun to run out. Indeed, we are told that 90 percent of all the top predators in the world's oceans are gone and that more than two-thirds of global fish stocks are at, or beyond, their sustainable limits. This is a matter of enormous consequence in view of the billions of people around the world who depend on the sea for their protein.

What is particularly daunting is the speed with which these phenomena are unfolding. Or perhaps, correspondingly, the lamentable slowness with which we have read the writing on the wall. Many of these existential developments were foreseeable, but, motivated by a deadly amalgam of greed and self-denial, we chose to ignore these realities. In no other arena is this more the case than with global warming. What is truly alarming is the speed and magnitude of this phenomenon. While there are those who can point to earlier periods in geological history when the earth's temperature rose, never in human history has it risen so quickly. Twelve of the last 15 years have seen the highest temperatures in recorded history. And what is even more frightening is that scientists from many walks of life are forecasting that climate change will trigger feedback loops within the next quarter century that will accelerate the rate of warming. Twenty-five years is the day after tomorrow in political terms and governments around the world seem content to tinker cosmetically at the margins. Disturbingly, a recent opinion poll in Great Britain revealed that 70 percent of voters were not willing to pay higher taxes in

Reuters

order to combat climate change. Thus, even the most ecologically assertive leaders are in retreat at the very moment when radical changes in energy consumption have become imperative.

What does this dismal recitation mean in the final analysis? We know with near mathematical certainty that the population of the earth will be about 8.3 billion by 2025. That is very nearly where our certainty runs out. Oil does seem to be a finite commodity, but how fast will we expend the global reserves? There is already evidence that increased fuel costs are having an impact on global shipping patterns and air travel. But are these merely variations on a theme? The upward trend in oil utilization and cost seems to be well established. Societal reactions seem unlikely to change those trends significantly. Even if they do, it appears to be a case of simply postponing the day of reckoning. And what is the interaction between demographic forces, energy availability, food, fresh water, and the environment?

All these phenomena are having a pronounced effect on world systems. Momentarily, oil prices are reinforcing authoritarian trends in countries like Russia, Venezuela, and Iran. Indeed, the corrupting influences of high energy revenues are well documented. While, in broad terms, democracy has been on the move globally over the past 40 years, that process may be slowing. There is widespread *schadenfreude* about the apparently diminished status of the United States (and its fiscal condition does warrant genuine concern), but the United

The Qingdao fleet review in April 2009, celebrating the 60th anniversary of the founding of the People's Liberation Army Navy, marked the first time China has displayed its nuclear-powered submarines, a sign of its aspirations to become a major sea power.

Cartels operating the Colombian cocaine trade are using homemade semi-submersible ships to transport up to 70 percent of the drugs leaving the country's Pacific coast.

Reuters

States remains an enormously important and powerful player on the world stage. There even appears to be some reason for optimism in Iraq. What makes the United States particularly influential is not just the extent of its hard and soft power, but the fact that it is able to advance a universal vision of freedom and democracy. No other emerging power has such an animating philosophy. China has none, nor does India, and Russia's message to the world is demonstrably bankrupt.

What is intriguing is the fact that while the developed world may account for 70 percent of global economic activity, the developing world is the driver of globalization. American power has been reduced in relative terms and after a fleeting moment of media-exaggerated unilateralism, Washington is increasingly open to multilateralism for pragmatic if not philosophical reasons. Balance of power politics has begun to reassert itself, and "coalitions of the willing" or "communities of democracies" are expressions of a jaded and beleaguered vision of the world emanating from Washington.

What does this mean for navies, and the Canadian Navy in particular? To begin with, as the historian Paul Kennedy and others have noted, the shift in the world centre of gravity from the Atlantic to the Pacific has been accompanied by a corresponding shift in naval power. The straitened circumstances in which the Royal Navy finds itself (who could imagine that what was once the greatest navy on earth would be abandoned to such a degree by its island people?) and the steady diminution in the number of vessels in the United States Navy (not to mention the malaise surrounding contemporary shipbuilding programs) lend credence to the Kennedy thesis.

The Europeans have moved into a post-modern age, where, weary of centuries of internal conflict, they have begun to forfeit Westphalian notions of national sovereignty voluntarily and to seek some larger sense of community. The European Union, with its rather effete and self-denying responses to international threats, stands in stark contrast to the robustly self-confident nationalism appearing in East Asia. East Asia is a complex arena — historically, geographically, and jurisdictionally. China and India have become unabashedly Mahanian in their pursuit of naval power to deal with these challenges, by adopting the "great battle fleet" concepts described by the nineteenth-century American sea power advocate, Admiral Alfred Thayer Mahan. In psychological terms, they are exhibiting the will to rule, something the Europeans have lost and the Americans are tiring of.

The upshot of all this is that Western navies are going to be increasingly hard-pressed to execute their traditional tasks. Demographic pressures are going to mount and this will place a premium on monitoring and/or interdicting greater and greater flows of illegal migrants seeking to make their way into the developed world. These flows will be both spontaneous and organized. One of the truly critical phenomena associated with the end of the Cold War (which "liberated" an array of criminal forces in the one-time Soviet Union; forces in league with intelligence agencies, the private sector, and politicians) and the continued progress of globalization, with its destruction of global barriers, has been the remarkable expansion of international organized crime. Autonomous criminal elements, dedicated to smuggling, counterfeiting, prostitution, and so forth, have proven to be far more nimble and adaptive than the hierarchically organized, anti-crime agencies that seek to combat them. The former have been able to act well inside the decision-making curve of counter-criminal

Sailing into the future: Her Majesty's Canadian Ships *Regina* (in the lead, gun firing) and *Algonquin*, with an American frigate during Exercise Trident Fury 2007.

Department of National Defence, Combat Camera, IS2007-0213

bureaucracies, which are constrained by legal inhibitions and inadequate budgets. As Moises Naim has noted, "despite massive efforts, governments are failing to stem the tide of illicit trade."[2] Navies and coast guards have long been engaged in trying to stem the flow of drugs, human trafficking, and other illegal activities at sea, and there seems every reason to believe that by 2025 they — the Canadian Navy included — will be even more committed to this constabulary role.

Successive Canadian governments have promised but almost invariably failed to live up to their commitments in areas such as overseas development and defence. With aging populations in North America (a condition ameliorated marginally by migration), will governments in 2025 be any different? Indeed, they will be even less likely to allocate the funds necessary to ensure an adequately equipped and manned (another ongoing demographic challenge)

Canadian Forces. Many years ago Norman Augustine forecasted presciently that the average unit cost of weapons would continue to mount sharply. As one wag has observed, the United States might end up spending its entire defence budget on a single aircraft by 2025. As John Christie notes, "it may be hard for most people to believe that our [American] defense establishment is in a serious decline at a time when we are spending more than $400 billion a year on defense … However, the facts bear out this alarming state of affairs. U.S. defense forces will continue to shrink and age and we rapidly will cease being a dominant military force in the world unless we make major changes soon."[3]

Presumably the CF and the navy will be subject to the same imperatives. Will successive governments forfeit Canada's international presence — as they have already done in a number of arenas — in the face of mounting defence acquisition costs? Will there be countervailing pressures brought to bear by Washington (and, no doubt other capitals in pursuit of the "community of democracies" construct or latter-day variants) to do more of what we have already been doing — supplementing U.S. Navy operations globally?

Clearly, our ability to do so will be determined largely by the number of ships that are built in the next 15 years. By then, we should have a new fleet; but what will it look like? To what extent will the Canadian Navy be the victim of a zero sum game in which ships destined for the Arctic have come at the expense of those traditional mid-sized, blue water combatants that are critical to the nation's global role? Or will a re-animated Canadian Coast Guard have assumed many of the maritime responsibilities in the Arctic — an arena that by 2025 should be open to fairly significant amounts of commercial traffic and offshore exploration and exploitation?

How would a new Canadian Navy function outside the Arctic? Terrorism of the sort that we have grown accustomed to since 9/11, if not before, will probably have run its course. The medieval, millenarian Al Qaeda movement, having failed to realize its goals to any considerable degree, will be largely discredited even in the eyes of the faithful. That is not to say that there will not be the occasional threats of terrorism. Afghanistan and Iraq will be behind us, but the nagging underdevelopment of the Arab world, coupled with the social ferment caused by a corrosive sense of envy, impotence, and marginalization (elevated and legitimated by recourse to a higher religious cause), will continue to fuel terrorist activity. But the Canadian Navy is likely to be far more engaged in combating organized crime, in all its many dimensions, than prosecuting a "War on Terror" at sea.

Climate change and the continued growth of urban coastal populations seem certain to dictate a continued humanitarian assistance and disaster relief role for the Navy. What is less certain is what are the interstate (and even intrastate) implications of mounting resource scarcity. Wood, water, and wheat will be the new currencies of 2025. Will states fight over diminished fish stocks? In view of the current rates of fish stock depletion and the continued presence of illegal fishers, there seems every likelihood that there will be clashes at sea, particularly in the geographically complex waters of the Indian and Pacific Oceans. Will the Western Pacific Naval Symposium, for example, act as a catalyst to bring navies and coastguards together in regional fisheries patrols? Probably so.

At the same time, more traditional demands are likely to impinge upon the Canadian Navy. Despite profound internal weakness, China will be the unquestioned hegemonic power

Government of Canada, courtesy of STX Canada Marine and BMT Fleet Technology

A new class of Arctic offshore patrol vessel will extend the navy's presence deeper into Canada's third ocean region for more of the year.

of East Asia by 2025. Canadian interests in the Pacific will be far more clearly recognized than they are now and there will be national and international (read the "Five Eyes,"[4] plus Japan, South Korea, India, and potentially others) pressure to maintain what amounts to a balance of naval power over and against China. Thus, a Standing Naval Force Pacific, ostensibly to provide peace and good order on the Ocean's commons, but designed to incorporate (and hedge against) the Chinese Navy will probably be a prominent feature of the maritime realm of 2025.

The fundamental changes that seem certain to occur by 2025 are existential in character, and will — individually or collectively — strain the global social fabric profoundly. The world in 2025 will be an increasingly problematic place, where threats to the established order will be commonplace, whether in the form of domestic instability, severe weather, transnational crime, mounting demographic pressures (destabilizing youth bulges, rapidly aging and diminishing populations, impoverished peoples, and legal and illegal migration), critical resource shortages, or progressive global warming. What is difficult to divine is just how all of these elements will interact and just how human intervention will shape that interaction.

Navies will be vitally important to ensuring good order in the face of these global phenomena. The Canadian Navy's role will be dictated in considerable part by the nature of the assets it acquires over the next decade and a half. The constant contraction of naval resources, on the specious grounds that each new generation of ships is more capable than the one that preceded it, must be prevented. More ships rather than less should be the order of the day. A "Little Canada" home game strategy must be resisted. The world of 2025 will require a global naval presence more than ever before, whether to combat illegal fishing, the illegal movement of people, disaster relief, or the more traditional "balance of power" naval role. The world will be increasingly Hobbesian, "political will" shall still be in short supply, despite incontrovertible signs of a planet under serious stress, and navies like the Canadian Navy will be needed to range the world's oceans ameliorating conditions of hardship and maintaining the peace.

Notes

1. Professor Danforth Middlemass, Dalhousie Centre for Foreign Policy Studies, Maritime Security Conference, 12 June 2008.
2. Moises Naim, *Illicit* (New York: Anchor Books, 2005), 217.
3. John D. Christie, "DoD on a Glide Path to Bankruptcy," U.S. Naval Institute *Proceedings* (June 2008), 25.
4. This term is derived from the long-established agreement on intelligence sharing ("eyes only") among the "AUSCANNZUKUS" allies: Australia, Canada, New Zealand, United Kingdom, and United States.

Contributors

James Boutilier is the Asia-Pacific adviser to the commander, Maritime Forces Pacific. He served as a navigating officer in the Royal Canadian and Royal Naval Reserves, and as a professor and dean at Royal Roads Military College. He lectures nationally and internationally, specializing on Asia-Pacific maritime security.

Isabel Campbell is an historian at the Directorate of History and Heritage contributing to the official history of the post-war RCN (1945–68). A former archivist and librarian, she has published in English and French on NATO, the influence of foreign policy on military decision-making, strategic matters, and archival issues.

W.A.B. (Alec) Douglas served in the RCN 1950–73 as a specialist in navigation and operations. He was the official historian of the Canadian Armed Forces, 1973–94, and is adjunct research professor of history, Carleton University, and a past president of the Canadian Nautical Research Society.

Richard H. Gimblett is command historian of the Canadian Navy and past president of the Canadian Nautical Research Society. A former serving officer, he is the author of studies on Canada's role in the Persian Gulf and a contributor to Volume One of the official history of the RCN (1867–1939).

Donald E. Graves is a member of the professional team writing the official history of the post-war RCN (1945–68). He is also the author, co-author, or editor of 15 books and many articles relating to Canadian military and naval history.

Peter T. Haydon is a senior research fellow with the Centre for Foreign Policy Studies at Dalhousie University in Halifax, specializing in Canadian defence policy and activities during the Cold War era. A former career officer in the Canadian Navy, he was the founding editor-in-chief of the *Canadian Naval Review*.

Pat Jessup is the community relations officer at Canadian Forces Base (CFB) Halifax. Her field of expertise is naval war art, specifically the images produced to document the Second World War. Her master's thesis, from Saint Mary's University, was a biography of Commander C. Anthony Law, naval war artist and MTB commander.

William Johnston is a historian with DND's Directorate of History and Heritage. He is a co-author of official histories of both the RCN and the RCAF, including the forthcoming *The Seabound Coast*, Volume One of the RCN official history, and is the author of *A War of Patrols: Canadian Army Operations in Korea*.

Richard Oliver Mayne is lead author for the military and security section of DND's Directorate of Future Security and Analysis's study on Future Conflict. A naval reserve officer, he is the author or co-author of two books and has also published numerous articles on Canadian naval history.

Harold M. Merklinger graduated from the Royal Military College in Kingston (1965), and the University of Birmingham (1971). His career as a defence scientist was spent primarily at the Defence Research Establishment Atlantic (later DRDC-A, Halifax), with a term at NDHQ. Prior to retirement in 2001 he was scientific adviser maritime and director-general/DRDC-A.

Marc Milner is best known for his books on the Canadian Navy and the Battle of the Atlantic. Since 1986 he has taught military history at the University of New Brunswick and is currently director of UNB's Gregg Centre for the Study of War and Society.

Bill Rawling is the author of *Victor Brodeur: officier de la marine canadienne, 1909–1946*, and of several articles on Canadian naval history. A contributor to Volume Two of the official history of RCN operations, 1939–45, he is currently a member of the team working on Volume One (1867–1939).

Roger Sarty was at the NDHQ Directorate of History 1981–98 as naval team leader and then senior historian. He was deputy director at the Canadian War Museum, in charge of exhibition development for the new museum building that opened in 2005, and became professor of history at Wilfrid Laurier University in 2004.

Index